HISTORY OF
United States Naval Operations
IN WORLD WAR II

★

VOLUME TWO

Operations in North African Waters
October 1942–June 1943

HISTORY OF UNITED STATES NAVAL OPERATIONS
IN WORLD WAR II

By *Samuel Eliot Morison*

Also
Strategy and Compromise

Vice Admiral Henry Kent Hewitt USN
Commander Task Force 34, 1942; Commander Eighth Fleet, 1943

HISTORY OF UNITED STATES NAVAL
OPERATIONS IN WORLD WAR II
VOLUME II

Operations in
North African Waters
October 1942–June 1943

BY SAMUEL ELIOT MORISON

With Illustrations

CASTLE BOOKS

HISTORY OF UNITED STATES NAVAL OPERATIONS IN WORLD WAR II

OPERATION *in* NORTH AFRICAN WATERS
October 1942 – June 1943
VOL. II

ISBN: 0-7858-1303-9

To
The Memory of
FRANK KNOX
1874–1944
Secretary of the Navy
1940–1944

Of the events of the war, I have not ventured to speak from any chance information, nor according to any notion of my own; I have described nothing but what I either saw myself, or learned from others of whom I made the most careful and particular inquiry. The task was a laborious one because eyewitnesses of the same occurrence gave different accounts of them as they remembered, or were interested in the actions of one side or the other. And very likely the strictly historical character of my narrative may be disappointing to the ear. But if he who desires to have before his eyes a true picture of the events which have happened, and of the like events which may be expected to happen hereafter in the order of human things, shall pronounce what I have written to be useful, then I shall be satisfied.

— THUCYDIDES, *Peloponnesian War*, i.22 (Jowett Trans.)

Preface

THE present volume covers the operations of the United States Navy in North African waters, both on the Atlantic coast and in the Mediterranean, from the beginning of World War II through the capture of Pantelleria in June 1943. More than half the volume is devoted to the capture of bases in French Morocco, which was an all-American operation and in many respects one of the most remarkable of the war.

I had the good fortune to take part in Operation "Torch" as a member of Captain Francis C. Denebrink's staff in U.S.S. *Brooklyn.* The writing of this volume began on board ship and was continued at Headquarters Amphibious Force Atlantic Fleet, where Admiral Hewitt and members of his staff afforded me every courtesy and facility. Official reports and my personal observations are not the only sources used; immediately after Morocco was secured I visited many ships that participated and obtained additional information from numerous officers and men.

Readers of the first edition (1947) and of the revised edition (1950) have been generous in sending me comments and corrections, most of which have been incorporated here. And in the summer of 1951 I visited headquarters of the Service Historique de la Marine in Paris and talked with the officers who were engaged in writing the history of these operations. At my request they made a rigorous examination of this volume and sent me many additional emendations. I am particularly indebted to Capitaine de Vaisseau Sizaire and Capitaine de Frégate Rostand, the successive chiefs of this section; to the eminent French naval historian Jacques Mordal, whose *La bataille de Casablanca* appeared in 1952; and to Captain John W. McElroy USNR, who took charge of corrections under the direction of Rear Admiral John B. Heffernan USN, Director of Naval History.

SAMUEL E. MORISON

HARVARD UNIVERSITY
March 1953

Contents

PART II

THE EXPEDITIONS AGAINST ALGERIA AND TUNISIA

Contents   xiii

List of Illustrations

(All photographs not otherwise described are Official United States Navy)

List of Charts

Drawn by L. O. Donovan, Sic USNR.
Following the sources listed under each title

PART I

The Expedition against French Morocco[1]

[1] The most important sources for the Expedition are Admiral Hewitt's Operation Plan 5–42 9 Oct. 1942; Preliminary Report of Torch Operation to Cinclant 28 Nov. 1942, and Comments and Recommendations on Torch Operation to Cominch 22 Dec. 1942; Capt. A. G. Shepard Report on Torch Operation to Cinclant 31 Dec. 1942; Gen. Patton's Final Report Western Task Force. In the Office of Naval Intelligence Combat Narratives, *The Landings in North Africa* (1944), written independently of this History, has proved useful in making the last revision, especially as the writer had access to Admiral Hewitt's annotated copy.

Officers' ranks and bluejackets' ratings are those contemporaneous with the event. Officers named will be presumed to be United States Navy (USN) unless otherwise stated; Naval Reservists are designated USNR. In the case of United States Army Officers, no distinction has been made between United States Army (USA) and Army of the United States.

Other service abbreviations, following an officer's name, are:—

RN, Royal Navy; RNVR, Royal Navy Volunteer Reserve.
USMC, United States Marine Corps; USMCR, Reserve of same.

In footnote references, only the titles of printed or multigraphed books, pamphlets and periodicals have been italicized. Other documents, including the Action Reports and War Diaries of ships and naval commands, are in Roman type. Some of these have been printed or multigraphed since I consulted them. Eventually, it is hoped, copies of all naval documents here mentioned will be found in the Office of Naval Records and Library at the Navy Department, Washington, but I consulted many of them at sea or in temporary naval files at shore commands, and cannot answer for their present locations.

Some of the common abbreviations used in this volume are as follows:—

AFAF — Amphibious Force Atlantic Fleet
BLT — Battalion Landing Team
Cinclant — Commander in Chief, Atlantic Fleet
Cincmed — Commander in Chief, Mediterranean
Cominch — Commander in Chief, United States Fleet
H.M.S. — His Majesty's Ship, of the Royal Navy
N.O.B. — Naval Operating Base
O.N.I. — Office of Naval Intelligence
O.S.S. — Office of Strategic Services
RCT — Regimental Combat Team
SOC — Scout Observation plane, the kind carried by battleships
        and cruisers
S.S. — Steamship, of Merchant Marine
U.S.S. — United States Ship, of the Navy

CHAPTER I

Preliminaries

July 1940 – October 1942

1. *The Diplomatic Contest over North Africa*

THE MOST ambitious and successful undertaking of the Atlantic Fleet of the United States Navy in 1942 was the amphibious operation which secured French Morocco in early November. Closely integrated with it was the combined Anglo-American operation that took possession of Algeria. D-day for both, 8 November, came two weeks after the British Eighth Army began its victorious advance from Egypt westward. The Moroccan enterprise was conducted independently of the Algerian; but they were essentially one in purpose, planning and overall command — the Atlantic and the Mediterranean sections of Operation "Torch."

To understand why Operation "Torch" was mounted we must go back two years.

One of the several unpleasant prospects unfolded before the United States by the fall of France in 1940 was that of Germany obtaining control of the French Empire in Africa, as well as the French Fleet. If she succeeded in the former, every transatlantic harbor from the North Cape to the Gulf of Guinea, except those of Great Britain, Spain and Portugal, would be in Axis hands. And if Hitler obtained control of the Toulon fleet, he would have a formidable surface navy to supplement the U-boats and defend his territorial gains. President Roosevelt initiated diplomatic action to prevent either event happening, almost a year before the United States entered the war.

General Maxime Weygand, Marshal Pétain's overall commander

of French North and West Africa, was known to be a steadfast French patriot, utterly opposed to a shameful collaboration with Germany. Hence the President, advised by the Department of State, decided in the summer of 1940 that North Africa was the place to halt the Axis encirclement of the Atlantic. A careful program was also worked out with the purpose of turning the eyes of Frenchmen again toward the Statue of Liberty. While the British government (with the full knowledge and consent of Washington) encouraged and supported General de Gaulle, and so kept the resistance movement going outside French territory, the United States government (with the knowledge and at times the reluctant consent of the British) continued to recognize and deal with the official French government at Vichy. We accepted the odium of appeasement for very good reasons: to keep a foothold in Africa, and exert a counterpressure on Marshal Pétain to that of Hitler and Laval, who wished to make France a complete ally of Germany. In spite of numerous snags, squabbles and unexpected turns of events, this dual diplomatic policy made possible the occupation of Algeria and French Morocco by the United Nations in 1942, with a minimum of bloodshed.[2]

That triumph was brought reasonably nearer on 23 November 1940, by the appointment of Admiral William D. Leahy as American ambassador to France. No better choice could have been made. Admiral Leahy's long and distinguished naval career, which began in U.S.S. *Oregon* during the Spanish-American War and culminated in the office of Chief of Naval Operations, had included a quasi-diplomatic command in Turkish waters and the governorship of Puerto Rico. He had been intimate with the President since the last war. As a sailor he could speak bluntly with Admiral Darlan,

---

[2] Demaree Bess, under the unpromising title of "The Backstage Story of Our African Adventure" *Sat. Eve. Post* 3, 10, 17 July 1943, has produced the most accurate and informing account of the diplomatic-military negotiations about North Africa that the writer has seen in print. Other facts were obtained from conversations with President Roosevelt, Fleet Admiral William D. Leahy, and from the study by Prof. William L. Langer, *Our Vichy Gamble* (1947), written from British, French and captured German sources for the Department of State.

commander in chief of the French Navy and one of Marshal Pétain's closest advisers. Admiral Leahy's instructions were to cultivate close relations with the Marshal, in order to prevent France from doing anything inimical to American interests. In particular, he was to prevent the French Fleet and naval bases from falling under German control, maintain the *status quo* in the West Indies, assist France to preserve her authority in North Africa, and support the economic status of that region.[3]

This economic improvement clause was the egg from which the regeneration of French North Africa was hatched. The population of Algeria and Morocco was beginning to suffer from the British blockade; not much in the matter of essential food, but for lack of cheap cottons, oil, tea, sugar and other articles that the natives consumed in large quantities.

Mr. Robert D. Murphy, Counselor of the American Embassy at Vichy, had already gone to Algiers on 18 December 1940, and thence proceeded to Dakar to report on conditions and command personalities in French Africa. General Weygand and Governor Boisson of French West Africa appeared to be determined to oppose any German effort to dominate that continent. They begged the United States to send food and supplies in order to help them to organize resistance if, as they feared, the Germans should attempt some sort of *coup* in the spring. The British government, on 7 February 1941, somewhat reluctantly expressed its willingness to grant navicerts to ships bringing American supplies to Morocco and Algeria, provided the United States sent an adequate number of control officers to ensure that the goods did not reach the Axis. Admiral Leahy then sent Mr. Murphy back to Algiers, where on 26 February 1941 he and General Weygand initialed an agreement. This was accepted both at Washington and at Vichy.

The Murphy-Weygand agreement[4] provided that the United States would supply North Africa with certain American products

[3] Admiral Leahy's instructions, dated 20 Dec. 1940, are printed in *Peace and War* (1943) p. 596.
[4] Department of State Memorandum *Trade with North Africa* ("North African Economic Memorandum" I No. 75) 28 Feb. 1941.

to be paid for out of blocked francs in the United States, and that we should send control officers to supervise the distribution of these supplies, and ensure that they were not directly or indirectly used by the Axis. Although the supplies actually sent from the United States were far from considerable, they were well appreciated. The thirteen control officers who went over in 1941, with the rank of vice consuls, acquired much useful information about the politics and personalities of French North Africa, collected military intelligence and made contacts that proved exceedingly valuable when the showdown came.[5] Mr. Murphy took up residence in Algiers as consul general, to supervise these officers and to exert a continuous American influence on the French authorities there.

General Weygand declared to our representatives his readiness to facilitate an American military occupation of French North Africa, provided it were mounted in sufficient force to have better than an even chance of success. He naturally did not wish to sacrifice his position for a Dakar fiasco or a hit-and-run raid.[6]

While these cautious contacts were being made in North Africa in 1941, Admiral Leahy afforded Marshal Pétain an anchor to resist the pressure of the east wind. Yet the Mediterranean situation was deteriorating fast. On 27–30 March, Admiral Sir Andrew Cunning-

---

[5] Although these officers were not in a position, by reason of their functions, to gather much information about the landing beaches, their political and economic action was highly important. Vice Consuls David W. King, W. Stafford Reid, C. D. Wilkes, Frederick P. Culbert and John C. Knox, the last-named a graduate of St. Cyr and both he and Mr. King former members of the Foreign Legion, were particularly useful because of their familiarity with military matters. Mr. Culbert (a graduate of the Naval Academy) and Mr. Knox returned to the U.S. and England respectively in Sept. 1942 to take part in the planning, and accompanied the Western and Eastern Task Forces respectively in the landings. Kenneth W. Pendar *Adventure in Diplomacy* (1945) is a colorful narrative by one of these control officers; Henry S. Villard "Action in North Africa" *American Foreign Service Journal* XIX 637ff. Dec. 1942 (by the Chief of the African Division Department of State) tells the principal facts; and there are others in Dept. of State Release No. 177, 13 Mar. 1946.

[6] Pendar points out that the attack on Dakar brought increased German pressure on North Africa, and "gave Frenchmen a horror of what they called commando raids." Weygand is reported to have said of the British in Sept. 1940: "If they come to North Africa with four divisions I'll fire on them; if they come with twenty divisions I'll embrace them." Louis Rougier *Les Accords Pétain-Churchill* (Montréal 1945) p. 111.

ham RN whipped the Italian Fleet off Cape Matapan, but next day Rommel launched the land drive that brought the African littoral from Tunisia almost to Alexandria under Axis control. In April, too, the Germans almost completed a conquest of the Balkans and Greece. With airfields on both sides of the Mediterranean in Axis hands, it became increasingly difficult for the Royal Navy to maintain communication with Egypt. There was much reason to fear lest the Germans follow up these successes by infiltrating French North Africa between Bizerta and Dakar, and that they could overcome the objections hitherto made by General Franco to a march through Spain to the Straits. "Too few of us realize, and still fewer acknowledge," said the Secretary of the Navy on 24 April 1941, "the disaster to American hemispheric safety if Germany, already the conqueror of France, should establish herself in Dakar. From there, with her surface ships, submarines and long-range bombers, a victorious Germany could substantially cut us off from all commerce with South America and make of the Monroe Doctrine a scrap of paper." [7]

Hitler had already demanded that Pétain permit German armies to cross unoccupied France and French North Africa; and although the Marshal categorically refused, he was in no position to resist if Hitler insisted.

Darlan conferred with Hitler at Berchtesgaden on 11–12 May and received flattering promises of German concessions in return for collaboration in the war against England. Knowing what generally happened after such visits, President Roosevelt issued a public statement on 15 May to the effect that it was "inconceivable" that France would voluntarily deliver the "French African colonies and their Atlantic coasts, with the menace that that involves to the peace and safety of the Western Hemisphere."

Both the American and British governments were very much alarmed lest Pétain do just that. It was reported that French army officers and colonial officials in North Africa "objectionable" to Germany were being weeded out. Admiral Darlan had in fact

---

[7] Speech of the Hon. Frank Knox in New York. *N.Y. Times* 25 April 1941.

agreed to have this done; and a purge of this sort in a neutral country was the normal prelude to a German invasion. In his radio address of 27 May the President pointed out that the Cape Verde Islands off Dakar are only seven hours' flying distance from Brazil. "The war is approaching the brink of the Western Hemisphere." The Germans had already captured Crete. And on 28 May 1941 Admiral Darlan signed a secret accord with the German ambassador at Paris, agreeing to support a rebellion in Iraq against the British — an obvious threat to the Suez Canal; to grant the Axis the use of the port of Bizerta in Tunisia and the railway thence to Gabès; and to concede Germany the right to base submarines, warships and planes at Dakar.[8]

Apparently the game for North Africa was over, and Germany had won. But the Vichy government was a strange organization; no member seemed to know what the other was doing, and things were seldom as bad as they seemed. Admiral Leahy, General Weygand, Admiral Esteva and Governor Boisson all used their influence on Marshal Pétain to prevent this agreement being accepted by him; an immediate break with the United States was threatened, and the proconsuls declared that if necessary they would resist a German landing at Bizerta or Dakar by force of arms.[9] The pressure worked. On 6 June the Marshal discarded the Darlan agreement, and another crisis passed.

The Germans accepted this diplomatic rebuff because Hitler, disregarding the advice of his naval strategists, had turned from the Mediterranean to Russia. Control of the classic sea, with all that that implied, was within the Fuehrer's grasp, but geopolitics won over sea power; on 21 June he declared war on Russia. For the time being German pressure on France was relieved. The British Army forced the Governor of Syria to turn that French protectorate over to De Gaulle, and held Rommel before he reached Egypt. Suez and the western reaches of the Mediterranean were saved,

[8] This document was produced at the Pétain trial. *Procès du Maréchal Pétain* (Paris 1946) p. 332.
[9] Admiral Leahy did not know the terms of this agreement, only its general nature.

at least temporarily, for the maritime nations. United States forces occupied Iceland in July and a "shooting war" began in the Atlantic.

Yet nothing stayed put in our relations with France. On the other side of the world Vichy yielded to Tokyo, and in July acquiesced in Japanese armed forces' taking possession of Indo-China. Although this could not be helped, since America would not and Britain could not furnish France with means to defend her eastern empire, it seemed unnecessary and despicable. One newspaper after another demanded a complete breach of relations with Vichy and the recognition of De Gaulle's government in exile as the government of France. It took uncommon resolution on the part of President Roosevelt to resist this pressure; but there is now no doubt that he was right in so doing.

Mr. Murphy and the American control officers in North Africa were building up a nucleus of French patriots prepared to receive us as an ally when the time came. In North Africa, for reasons that we need not enter into here, General de Gaulle was so unpopular that recognition of him would have ended this preparatory work. Admiral Leahy saw the issue very clearly, and he had his own means of influence on the Vichy government. He advised the President to bear with Pétain yet a little while. The connection afforded us much valuable intelligence; and if all channels of American influence at Vichy and in North Africa were blocked, there was every reason to expect that Germany would soon renew her demands for Bizerta and Dakar.

Although the Axis pressure on North Africa was somewhat relieved, it continued. Admiral Darlan was putting his henchmen in everywhere, and the Germans, observing the value of our control officers, urged Pétain to terminate the Murphy-Weygand food agreement. He resisted them there but yielded another important point. General Weygand, on whom we could probably rely in case of a landing in North Africa, was recalled on 18 November 1941, and his duties split up among four officers. General Alphonse Juin was placed in charge of military affairs in North Africa, and Ives

Chatel appointed Governor of Algeria. Both, fortunately, were strongly anti-German and friendly to the United States.

The recall of Weygand discouraged Admiral Leahy. He could no longer hope to "give some resemblance of backbone to a jelly-fish." [10] He admitted that the stoppage of economic aid to North Africa would be justified, but could not bring himself to recommend the break. Nor, for that matter, could Mr. Murphy or General Weygand. The General begged Mr. Murphy to continue this connection between America and France, "necessary for the near future of the world." [11] Pétain on 12 December gave fresh assurances respecting the French colonies and fleet, and of neutrality in the war, which we had now formally entered. Mr. Roosevelt decided to continue the policy of economic aid to North Africa.

That was the situation shortly after the United States found herself at war with Japan, Germany and Italy in December 1941. The President decided to play along with Vichy as long as that policy seemed to serve our interest. Only by so doing could we keep France even nominally neutral, continue the economic aid to North Africa under our control officers, keep in touch with the French and native authorities there who were friendly to us, and facilitate a future landing. We were fighting a delaying diplomatic action in the French Empire, parallel to General MacArthur's delaying military action in Bataan. "Every week gained in the campaign against French collaboration with Germany is as important as any action in the field." [12]

As the weeks slipped by, this policy became increasingly difficult to maintain; yet, as the dividends were accumulating, it would be unwise to lose our investment.

It was the more difficult to maintain because of one irritating incident after another, such as the capture of St. Pierre and Miquelon by De Gaullist forces on 24 December 1941. A fresh offensive by Rommel began in January of 1942 and Mr. Murphy discovered

[10] To the President 22 Nov. 1941.
[11] Murphy to Secretary of State 21 Nov. 1941.
[12] The shrewd conclusion of Anne O'Hare McCormick in *N.Y. Times* 7 Jan. 1942.

that Darlan had been furnishing him with food, trucks and gasoline from North Africa; but the Marshal stopped it on Admiral
Leahy's complaint. When Laval returned to power on 15 April
1942, the President ordered our ambassador to return home "for
consultation," but maintained a skeleton diplomatic staff at Vichy.[13]
The British, believing that our diplomatic action had failed, made
fresh difficulties about granting navicerts to American ships loading
supplies for North Africa. Even in Washington the execution of
the Murphy-Weygand accord was hampered by officials of the
Treasury Department and the Board of Economic Warfare, who
could not be told the purpose of it and had not the wit to guess. At
any moment the fortunes of war or caprice of Hitler might revive
German pressure to take over the Toulon fleet or French North
Africa or both; and the means of resisting such a move were no
better than they had been two years earlier. The prospect of the
Axis controlling this vast territory, with great reservoirs of min-
erals, foodstuffs, and with new bases for submarine warfare, was
profoundly disturbing to the United Nations. Even had there been
no positive advantage to be derived from occupying North Africa,
the probable consequences of doing nothing were so grave as to
demand military action.[14]

Nevertheless it was only in the second half of 1942, after protracted discussion and considerable vacillation, that a military
occupation of North Africa was decided on.

2. *The Decision, 25 July 1942*

a. Africa — Thank God!

The first step was taken at Christmas time, 1941, when Mr.
Churchill and President Roosevelt, conferring in Washington,

[13] On the Admiral's return in July 1942 he was appointed the Chief of Staff
to the President, and continued informally to exert a strong influence on our
diplomatic action.

[14] Alfred Vagts in *Landing Operations* (1946) p. 718 states that the government
learned from Frenchmen friendly to us in North Africa that the Germans were
preparing to invade North Africa via Sicily and Tunis about 1 Jan. 1943.

agreed that a major military operation against Germany must be attempted in 1942.[15] The problem of where, when and how was submitted to the Combined Chiefs of Staff (including Admirals Stark and King and Generals Marshall and Arnold, Field Marshal Sir John Dill and Admiral Sir Andrew Cunningham RN), whose first meeting was held at Washington on 23 January 1942. Every possible target for an amphibious operation along the Axis-held coast, from Norway to Biarritz, and along Africa from Tunis to Dakar, was then discussed.[16] Simultaneous landings in Morocco and Algeria were suggested and even urged by President Roosevelt, but the Combined Chiefs of Staff eliminated them on 3 March 1942. At this time the Joint (American) Chiefs of Staff favored an invasion of northern France; Mr. Churchill did not, but was willing to follow his own military advisers. General Marshall and Mr. Harry Hopkins visited London in April to discuss such an operation with the British, and the planning for a colossal cross-channel invasion of Normandy in April 1943 actively began.

Major General Dwight D. Eisenhower USA, appointed Commander United States Military Forces in Europe, arrived in London on 24 June to take charge of the military build-up and participate in the planning.

Thus, in the first half of 1942, an American or Allied occupation of French North Africa appeared to be sidetracked, much to the regret of President Roosevelt. But he had to admit that the direct approach to Germany was better than the indirect, and his military advisers did not see where we could find the men and the ships for both, even in 1943.

Events now took such shape that we were almost compelled to put North Africa back on the main line. In the first place, there was the Russian situation. In early June the Russian Minister of Foreign

---

[15] The account that follows is primarily derived from a conversation with the President 16 Dec. 1942, with additional details from Admiral King; from Lt. Col. H. L. Litzenberg Jr. USMC "Occupation of French North Africa — Outline History," prepared for Admiral King 28 Dec. 1942; and from Capt. Harry C. Butcher USNR *My Three Years with Eisenhower* (1946).

[16] Norway, Denmark, Netherlands, Belgium, Pas-de-Calais, the Cotentin, Brest, the Gironde and Dakar.

Affairs visited the President in Washington and painted the situation of his country as highly critical. Inaction by the Western Allies in Europe had permitted Germany to concentrate the bulk of her army on the eastern front. Sevastopol was firmly resisting, supplies were being sent in at great sacrifice to us,[17] but it was a question whether Russia could hold out unless something were done, and that soon, to divert German forces elsewhere. As a result of this conference Mr. Roosevelt promised M. Molotov to do his best to bring about a European or African operation in 1942; and a press communiqué was issued on 11 June stating that the President agreed on the "urgent task of creating a second front" that year.

Mr. Churchill with a number of British staff officers visited Washington from June 18 to 25, and during that week news came in of the fall of Tobruk and Rommel's advance into Egypt. Now we were threatened not only with the defeat of Russia, but with the cutting of the Suez "life line." "It was a very black hour," as General Marshall has said.[18] The whole question of a second front in 1942 was threshed out again between the President and the Prime Minister. Mr. Roosevelt was disturbed to find that Mr. Churchill, who had always favored an indirect or "underbelly" approach to the heart of the Axis, did not believe that a frontal, cross-channel invasion of Northern France was possible even in 1943. His military advisers doubted whether the United Nations would

[17] The story of the North Russia convoys will be found in Volume I.

[18] *General Marshall's Report* (1 Sept. 1945) p. 9. During the Prime Minister's visit General Marshall called a meeting of the Combined Chiefs of Staff to ascertain what the United States could do to help the British to hold the El Alamein line. What Montgomery needed most were tanks, as he had lost all his General Grants at Tobruk and the British light tanks were unable to cope with those of the Germans. Accordingly the U.S. Army supplied over 400 General Shermans with engines not yet installed. These were shipped out in special Convoy AS-4 escorted by the U.S. Navy in July, with the engines all in one ship. That very vessel was singled out by *U-161* and sunk on 17 July, 5th day out. The Army then "scraped the barrel" for more General Sherman tank engines, and these were sent forward in a fast ship, unescorted, which caught the convoy before it called at Recife. Consequently Montgomery had 400 Shermans at the Battle of El Alamein. They proved superior to anything the Germans then had, and a British tank expert has stated: "There is little doubt that the Sherman was one, probably the main deciding factor in our victory." Brigadier R.M.P. Carver "Tank and Anti-Tank" *Journal* Royal United Service Institution p. 45 Feb. 1946; information from a participant in the C.C.S. conference.

have sufficient trained soldiers to establish a beachhead or enough shipping and troops to exploit it, before 1944. The President turned to his Joint Chiefs of Staff; they advised him to accept a continuance of the defensive blockade of Europe until 1944, and to concentrate on the Pacific war, in which the Guadalcanal operation had just been ordered, until the British felt ready to undertake a big European offensive.

The President disagreed with this view; probably the Joint Chiefs of Staff only put it forward in order to needle the British into doing something. All our plans and military deployment had been made on the assumption that defeating Hitler first was the best strategy. Russia was engaged in so doing and must be supported, lest Germany beat her while we were engaged elsewhere. Our military build-up in the United Kingdom was well under way. We had neither the troops nor the transports to mount a large-scale offensive in the Pacific before 1943; little enough for Guadalcanal. Before the Prime Minister left Washington the President had brought him around to the view that something must be done in the European-African theater in 1942. The two statesmen put their decision in the form of an order; and the Combined Chiefs of Staff put "Second Front, 1942" back on their agenda.

For another month the American Joint Chiefs of Staff, the British Chiefs of Staff and the Combined Chiefs of Staff (which comprised both) intensively canvassed all possibilities in order to arrive at a sound military decision as to this 1942 front. The Americans favored a limited invasion of some point in Northern France such as the Cotentin Peninsula, where a beachhead could be retained and exploited during the winter in preparation for a big cross-channel movement the following spring. The British pointed out that any such beachhead would be subjected to the full fury of the Luftwaffe for months on end, and that it would not take many German troops away from the Russian front.[19]

---

[19] This proposed Operation "Sledgehammer" had no connection with the Anglo-Canadian commando raid on Dieppe in Aug. 1942, as that was never intended to be anything but a hit-and-run affair.

In mid-July the discussion was shifted to London, where Admiral King and General Marshall for the Joint Chiefs of Staff and Mr. Harry Hopkins for the President consulted with the British Chiefs of Staff [20] and the Prime Minister. The Americans had written instructions not to accept any substitute unless and until all means of obtaining the cross-channel operation were exhausted. But in the discussion, which extended over several days, King, Marshall and Hopkins found their British colleagues so set against a limited invasion of France in 1942 that they were forced to give way rather than go into it with an unwilling partner. Then, after canvassing all possible alternatives, North Africa was settled on. At the same time it was accepted – very reluctantly by Admiral King and General Marshall – that the military effort required for a successful occupation of North Africa would probably require the postponement of the big cross-channel movement from 1943 to 1944.

The important decision was made at London by the Combined Chiefs of Staff on 25 July 1942: A combined Anglo-American occupation of French Morocco, Algeria, and possibly Tunisia, to take place within four months; the supreme commander to be a United States Army officer; detailed planning to begin immediately. That night Harry Hopkins cabled to President Roosevelt in code the one word: AFRICA.

"Thank God!" was the President's reply to the Prime Minister.[21]

b. The Concept

The positive strategical concept of the North African operation, designated Operation "Torch," was thus stated by the Combined Chiefs of Staff: —

[20] Admiral of the Fleet Sir Dudley Pound RN, General Sir Alan F. Brooke, and Air Chief Marshal Sir Charles Portal. Vice Admiral Lord Louis Mountbatten sat in, but Mr. Hopkins only did so when Mr. Churchill was present.

[21] Shortly after, Mr. Churchill conveyed the news to Marshal Stalin at Moscow. Strictly speaking, the action of the C.C.S. 25 July was only tentative; it was President Roosevelt who made the definite decision the same day, announcing it to Secretary Stimson, Admiral Leahy and Generals Arnold and McNarney without prior consultation with the J.C.S. Matloff & Snell *Strategic Planning for Coalition Warfare 1941–42* p. 282.

1. "Establishment of firm and mutually supported lodgements" (*a*) between Oran and Tunisia on the Mediterranean, and (*b*) in French Morocco on the Atlantic, in order to secure bases "for continued and intensified air, ground, and sea operations."

2. "Vigorous and rapid exploitation" of these lodgements, "in order to acquire complete control" of French Morocco, Algeria, and Tunisia, and extend offensive operations against the rear of Axis forces to the eastward.

3. "Complete annihilation of Axis forces now opposing the British forces in the Western Desert, and intensification of air and sea operations against the Axis in the European continent." [22]

On the negative side, the purpose as we have seen was to deny the economic resources and potential bases in French North Africa to the enemy.

Overall planning began almost immediately at Combined Headquarters in Norfolk House, London; although General Eisenhower was not appointed Commander in Chief of the Allied Expeditionary Force, or Admiral Sir Andrew Cunningham RN the Allied Naval Commander, until 14 August. The plans shaped up with exasperating slowness. Neither navy involved liked Operation "Torch," nor did the United States Army, for that matter; General Marshall reported that important Army officers in Washington believed it had only a fifty-fifty chance of success. General Eisenhower at one time considered it an operation "of quite desperate nature," which depended more for success on political arrangements with the French in North Africa than on "the wisdom of military decisions"; he even compared it with Napoleon's return from Elba. [23] Admirals Stark, Kirk, Bieri, and Bennett were in on the planning from the start; Admiral King, Generals Marshall, Patton and Truscott, and members of Admiral Ingersoll's and Admiral Hewitt's staffs, flew over for conferences. What Captain Butcher calls a "transatlantic

[22] Litzenberg "Outline History," quoting Combined Chiefs of Staff Directive for Commander in Chief Allied Expeditionary Force.
[23] Butcher *Three Years with Eisenhower* p. 84. Pp. 49-150 of this book give a lively running account of the changing plans and the *va-et-vient* of planning personalities at London.

essay contest" in the choice of objectives went on for six weeks. Should the weight of the expeditionary force be thrown eastward, entirely inside the Mediterranean — or westward, beginning at Casablanca? There were not enough troops or ships for all; should we then assault Oran, Algiers, Bône and Philippeville, or Casablanca, Oran and Algiers, or only Casablanca and Oran? Not until 9 September, after making detailed arrangements with the Royal and Canadian Navies as to relieving our escorts on transatlantic convoy routes, could Admiral King specify exactly what ships of the United States Navy would be available.[24] In the meantime D-day, originally 30 October, was moved on to 8 November; and that was the very latest day in 1942 when a landing on the iron-bound coast of Morocco, because of winter weather conditions, could be risked.

By 9 September Operation "Torch" had almost assumed its final form. It was broken down into three principal parts: — [25]

1. *Task Force 34*, Rear Admiral H. Kent Hewitt, comprising *Western Naval Task Force* (Admiral Hewitt), with Western Task Force United States Army (Major General G. S. Patton Jr.). Initially about 35,000 troops to be embarked in the United States, to land on the Atlantic coast of French Morocco and capture Casablanca and Port Lyautey.

2. *Center Naval Task Force*, Commodore Thomas Troubridge RN, with Center Task Force United States Army (Major General L. R. Fredendall). Initially about 39,000 troops, embarked in the United Kingdom, to capture Oran.

3. *Eastern Naval Task Force*, Rear Admiral Sir H. M. Burrough RN, with Eastern Assault Force (Major General C. W. Ryder USA). Comprising about 23,000 British and 10,000 American troops, embarked in the United Kingdom, to capture Algiers.

[24] Butcher pp. 91–95 is not quite accurate on this point. Ralph Ingersoll *Top Secret* (1946) is wildly inaccurate as to the purposes of the operation and its conception and planning.
[25] Vice Admiral Horne Memorandum on "Occupation of French North Africa."

Thus, Task Force 34 was to be all American, and cross the Western Ocean from the United States to the Atlantic coast of Morocco. The Center Naval Task Force consisted of British ships escorting and transporting an American army from the United Kingdom to Oran. The Eastern Naval Task Force consisted of both British and American ships escorting and transporting British and American troops to Algiers. All the combat ships of the two Mediterranean-bound task forces were to be of the Royal Navy.

One of the most amazing things about this bold operation was the secrecy with which so great an expeditionary force was assembled and transported. The Germans knew from ship and troop movements that something was in the wind, but they never guessed what. Hitler, annoyed at the failure of his secret service to find out, showed his irritation by announcing in a broadcast on 30 September that he could not be expected to divine the plans of Germany's enemies, since they were such "military idiots"! Right up to D-day the German high command miscalculated, and thought that the Eastern and Center Task Forces were either relief expeditions to Malta, or intended to land on the shores of Tripoli in Rommel's rear.[26]

The United States Navy in setting sail for the Barbary Coast was picking up a thread in history that had been broken in 1816.

[26] *The Ciano Diaries 1939–1943* (1946) p. 540. This is borne out by the *Kriegstagebuch* (War Diary of German General Staff), captured at the end of the European war. On 5 November a report was received from Paris that an American landing was to be expected at Casablanca but apparently no reliance was placed on that. On the sixth the passage of warships through the Straits began to be noted, but "the goal and size of the menace has not been determined." On 7 November "the hourly situation reports did not give a clear picture of the movement of the enemy formation from the Straits of Gibraltar eastward," but the Italian naval high command believed that a landing would take place within forty-eight hours between Bougie and Cape Bon, with perhaps some of the ships reinforcing Malta. That evening the German ambassador at Madrid relayed a Spanish report that the landings were to be made in Italy. News of the Algerian landings began to come in at 0330 November 8, but the very first report of Task Force 34 received at German Headquarters was one from French sources at 0750 that day, to the effect that "Morocco fired upon two enemy torpedo boats in the harbor entrance of Safi." Ciano heard the news at Rome from Ribbentrop at 0330, and reported that the Germans at the embassy were "literally terrified by the blow, which is very severe and above all absolutely unexpected." It was not until 8 November that the German Admiralty ordered U-boats to concentrate against shipping off the Moroccan coast.

As far back as 1637 Captain William Rainsborough, an early settler of New England, and Sir George Carteret, later a proprietor of New Jersey, conducted for the English Admiralty an expedition to punish the "pyrattes of Sallee" (Salé opposite Rabat) and to release Englishmen whom the pirates had enslaved; before returning they dealt with those of "Saffee" (Safi) as well.[27] After independence, when the sultans and deys of North Africa failed to respect the American flag, the United States declared war on them in 1801, a war in which Hull, Preble, Decatur and Somers made their reputations. Brigadier General William Eaton USA even conducted a motley expeditionary force of Arabs, Greeks and "nine United States Marines" along the western desert, supported by U.S.S. *Argus*, *Nautilus* and *Hornet* under Commodore Barron, to capture Derna in 1804[28] The Dey of Algiers was forced in 1816 to give up piracy at our expense, and American commerce in the Mediterranean was secured until such time as the Axis adopted the bad maritime manners of the ancient Barbaresques.

3. *The Western Naval Task Force*

a. Amphibious Force Atlantic Fleet

At this point we shall cut loose from London, where the overall planning for the entire operation was conducted, and take up the planning and preparation of the all-American Task Force 34 which effected the western landings, on the Atlantic coast of Morocco.

Although this force included no Marines except the shipboard Marine guards and a few staff officers, it evolved from the United States Marine Corps by way of Amphibious Force Atlantic Fleet.

Amphibious warfare, the oldest form of naval warfare, had always been a specialty of the Marine Corps. Between the two world wars the Corps resumed practice and experimentation with amphib-

[27] W. R. Chaplin "William Rainsborough" *The Mariner's Mirror* XXXI 178, Oct. 1945.
[28] F. R. Rodd *General William Eaton* (1932). The General had a train of 200 camels, and covered 520 miles.

ious technique, in conjunction with the Navy. An important step was the creation on 7 December 1933 of the Fleet Marine Force, a "force of Marines maintained by the Major General Commandant in a state of readiness for operations with the Fleet" and "available to the Commander in Chief for operations with the Fleet or for exercises either afloat or ashore in connection with Fleet problems." [29] The first Fleet Marine Force consisted of the 1st Marine Brigade stationed on the Atlantic Coast, and the 2nd Marine Brigade stationed in San Diego.

In May and June 1934 there took place the first comprehensive Fleet Landing Problem at Culebra Island east of Puerto Rico. Admiral Joseph M. Reeves, Commander Battle Force, brought the entire Fleet through the Panama Canal to cover and participate. [30] Almost every year thereafter there was a similar exercise at Culebra. Significant experiments were made in landing technique, in naval gunfire support and in close support of troops after they had landed. As a result of these exercises, a manual on landing operations was issued to the Fleet and the Marine Corps in 1938. This laid down organization and doctrine of amphibious warfare on such sound lines that it could be followed, with amplification rather than alteration, throughout the entire course of World War II.

Admiral Ernest J. King, Commander in Chief Atlantic Fleet, was in charge of the exercises at Culebra in January 1941; Captain R. R. M. Emmet was one of the transport division commanders. A number of Higgins (Eureka) landing craft (the LCPs) were used instead of ships' boats to land the Marines. No special landing craft for tanks and vehicles had yet been constructed, but their prototype, a 100-ton steel fuel barge with an improvised ramp, propelled by four Navy launches secured one to each corner, transported to the beach tanks swung out from the ships' holds.

After the fall of France the 1st Marine Brigade was held in a state

[29] General Order No. 241, 7 Dec. 1933, signed by Claude H. Swanson, Secretary of the Navy. (In *Navy Department General Orders* this appears as General Order 56, 15 May 1935.)
[30] Admiral David F. Sellers, Commander in Chief of the Fleet, was in overall command; Admiral Reeves relieved him 15 June 1934.

of readiness at Guantanamo, and expanded to the 1st Division United States Marine Corps early in 1941. A part of this division was sent to Iceland. The rest of it on 13 June 1941 was combined with the 1st Infantry Division United States Army, which had already enjoyed some amphibious training as the Emergency Striking Force, commanded by Major General Holland M. Smith USMC. General Smith formed a staff of Army, Navy and Marine Corps officers and continued training. After sundry renamings and reorganizations, during which both the Marines and the 1st Division were released for other duties, this Emergency Striking Force emerged as the Amphibious Force Atlantic Fleet in March 1942.

Rear Admiral Henry Kent Hewitt succeeded to command the AFAF in April 1942. Admiral Hewitt, who had seen active service in the Navy for thirty-five years, was admirably adapted for this position by his seagoing experience, his organizing ability and his tact. He was the very person to solve the difficult administrative questions involved in an amphibious force.[31] A man of impressive port and massive character — never self-seeking but always generous in giving credit to others, firm but just to his subordinates, tactful and conciliatory with compeers in other armed services — Admiral Hewitt inspired loyalty, confidence, and affection.

The Admiral was imbued with the Navy tradition of doing one's best with the human and physical material available. He augmented the staff, not by an intensive combing of the Navy for great brains and organizing genius, but by accepting the men assigned to him by the Bureau of Naval Personnel. It is to his credit and theirs that they were welded into an expert and harmonious team. Very little change was made in the staff even after the Admiral became Commander Eighth Fleet and conducted the major Mediterranean operations of 1943–1944. Rear Admiral John L. Hall Jr., his acting chief of staff during the crossing, became Com-

[31] Henry Kent Hewitt of Hackensack, N. J., born 1887, Class of 1907 Naval Academy; Navy Cross 1919 for distinguished service as C.O. of U.S.S. *Cummings;* gunnery officer *Pennsylvania;* instructor at Naval Academy and member of Staff Naval War College; C.O. of *Indianapolis;* Commander Special Service Squadron operating in Canal Zone (1940); Commander Cruisers Atlantic Fleet 1941; Rear Admiral 1 Dec. 1940, Vice Admiral 17 Nov. 1942, Admiral 3 April 1945.

mander Sea Frontier Forces after Casablanca was secured; Captain
E. A. Mitchell (Operations) left him after "Torch" to become planning officer for Admiral Kirk in Sicily and Normandy; Colonel
Lewis B. Ely USA (Army Intelligence) and Colonel E. C. Burkhart
USA (Army Operations) were also detached for other important
duties. But Commander Robert A. J. English (War Plans), Commander Leo A. Bachman (Intelligence), Commander Donald S.
Evans (Communications), Commander Stephen R. Edson (Supply), Commander Harold R. Brookman USNR (Materiel), Lieutenant Commander Julian McC. Boit USNR (Flag Secretary) and Lieutenant Ben H. Griswold III USNR (Flag Lieutenant) stayed with
Admiral Hewitt throughout successive Mediterranean campaigns
against the Axis powers.

Around the first of June 1942, the organization of Amphibious
Force Atlantic Fleet was as follows: —

1. Admiral Hewitt and staff, housed in a small building at Naval
Operating Base, Norfolk, Virginia, and after 1 September in the
Nansemond Hotel, Ocean View, near Norfolk.

2. Transports Atlantic Fleet, in six divisions (one of which went
to Algiers via United Kingdom), including both troop transports
and cargo vessels, commanded by Captain R. R. M. Emmet at
Naval Operating Base, Norfolk.

3. Several thousand Navy and Coast Guard personnel, being
trained in the handling of landing craft at the Amphibious Force
training center at Little Creek, Virginia, and Solomons Island,
Maryland, under the immediate command of Captain W. P. O.
Clarke.

4. Outside the Amphibious Force Atlantic Fleet command, al-
though destined to be intimately associated with it, was the Western
Landing Force of the Army, consisting of the 9th Infantry Division
United States Army, commanded by Major General Manton S.
Eddy,[32] in cantonments at Fort Bragg, North Carolina, to which

[32] General Eddy did not take part in this operation. He went over later, arriving in Africa 25 Dec. 1942. Before departure the Western Task Force was called
Western Landing Force.

elements of the 2nd Armored Division (Major General Ernest N. Harmon) were added from time to time. Major General George S. Patton Jr. became commander of the Western Landing Force of the Army on 24 August 1942.

As this force shaped up, one regiment at a time was sent on board transports at Norfolk, and went through day and night landing exercises at the Solomons Island training area in Chesapeake Bay. The fire support ships conducted shore bombardment exercises at the near-by Bloodsworth Island.

Admiral Hewitt's staff, as soon as it was formed, began to study amphibious warfare in general. In June, very secretly, it commenced planning for operations overseas, including North Africa, anticipating a decision of the higher command to effect a landing there. As soon as that decision was made, a reinforced regiment of the 9th Infantry Division was sent to Great Britain, carried by Transport Division 11 of the Atlantic Fleet, to join the 1st Infantry Division and effect one of the landings near Algiers. The 3rd Infantry Division United States Army (Major General Jonathan W. Anderson, an Annapolis graduate), reinforced by one battalion of the 67th Armored Regiment, was then added to the Landing Force.[33] Both planning and training became more intensive shortly after 1 August.

b. Joint[34] Planning and Training

The Army and Navy are well used to coöperating in simple operations such as escort of troop convoy or seizing an objective that commands an enemy fleet (as in 1898). In such operations the sphere of each is so easily defined as to require no unity of command under the President. But a properly conducted amphibious operation requires an organic unity rather than a temporary part-

[33] Major Francis M. Rogers USMC "History of Amphibian Units under the Atlantic Fleet."

[34] Throughout this work "Joint" refers to coöperation between armed services of the same nation; "Combined" to coöperation between armed forces of two or more nations. The British use "Combined" for both.

nership, and neither the organization nor the traditions of our two armed services were then particularly receptive to a commingling of that nature — they have since learned better. The contingency had been provided for by a manual prepared by the Joint Board of the Army and Navy first issued in 1927 and revised in 1935.[35] In 1942 the will to coöperate, which (with a few important exceptions) was strong in both Army and Navy, overrode most but not all difficulties. But the success of Operation "Torch" can only be appreciated by knowing the difficulties in planning and preparation.

There was no unity of command until the expedition got under way. Until then, General Patton, commanding the Western Landing Force United States Army, was completely independent of Admiral Hewitt, although Army units were placed temporarily under the Admiral's command during their periods of amphibious training.

Joint planning, as prescribed in the 1935 manual, was rendered difficult by the isolation of Norfolk from Washington, where the intelligence material was centered and the United States Army command was located. Many visits were exchanged by section chiefs of each staff, the Admiral and the General had frequent personal conferences, and together observed joint training exercises; and Admiral Hewitt's war plans officer spent several weeks in General Patton's Washington office, advising on the naval aspects of their plans for the landing forces. The operation, as we shall see when it unrolls, was very intricate and meticulous to plan, with odd features such as troop-laden destroyers running into narrow harbors or up shallow rivers at night, fighting ships stationed twelve miles from the principal landing beaches to be neutralized, and probable U-boat concentrations to be avoided. Politics, diplomacy, and military action had to be coördinated: we must steer a course between antagonizing the French forces in North Africa if they were well disposed, and being too considerate of their feelings if

[35] This was the edition in use in 1942. During the war it was superseded by directives for the exercise of command in various localities.

they were determined to resist. Yet almost every contingency was anticipated. Captain Mitchell and his able collaborators, Commander English, Commander Bachman (Intelligence), Commander R. W. D. Woods (Staff Air Officer), Commander T. F. Wellings (Gunfire) and Commander Evans (Communications), produced, under Admiral Hewitt, one of the outstandingly intelligent and successful plans of the entire war.

Besides the usual difficulties of joint Army-Navy planning, there was little time; Admiral Hewitt was uncertain up to a few weeks before sailing as to the number of transports and the number and types of landing craft that would be available. Brigadier General Lucian K. Truscott Jr. USA, designated commander of the troops to land at Mehedia, arrived at Washington from London (where he had been a liaison officer on Admiral Lord Mountbatten's staff, and had taken part in the overall planning) only on 19 September 1942. The naval operation plan, by Captain Mitchell, was then ready.

For Intelligence, Admiral Hewitt's staff drew on Army, Navy and Army Air Force Intelligence Services, on Allied Forces Headquarters in London, the Office of Strategic Services, the Hydrographic Office, the various weather bureaus, and on the food control officers who had been working in Morocco.[36] But Military Intelligence should be a seamless fabric, designed to fit the operations for which it is intended, and not a patchwork of oddments from here and there. It was the duty of Admiral Hewitt's staff to weave this fabric for the Moroccan occupation, and anyone who took part in it will thankfully testify that the design well fitted the task. Even after combing all the usual sources, there were great gaps; for our armed and diplomatic services had only recently contemplated the possibility of an offensive landing in North Africa. Readers may remember the call on the public in 1942 for snapshots and movie pictures of foreign travel. That was done in the hope of filling some of these gaps. For instance, the Moroccan beaches and their immediate sea approaches, an exact knowledge of which

[36] Comdr. L. A. Bachman "Intelligence for Amphibious Operation" O.N.I. *Weekly* II 605–610, 3 Mar. 1943; lecture by Col. L. B. Ely USA on same subject.

was necessary for night landings, were a sort of no man's land (or water) that was neither depicted on charts nor described in coast pilots or other literature. Thousands of photographs taken by British reconnaissance planes over a period of a year provided a good body of hydrographic information and enabled the Amphibious Force staff to choose the most feasible beaches. But w⁻ dearly wanted, and never were able to obtain, photographs of the Barbary coastline taken from sea level just offshore, in order to enable our forces readily to identify beaches and other landmarks at night.

This operation was essentially different from a big commando raid, for we intended to hit and stay; but as night landings were an essential part of the plan, men with either commando or amphibious training were urgently wanted. Yet very few could be spared. The Marine Corps, deeply committed at Guadalcanal and elsewhere in the South Pacific, could not be drawn upon; the 3rd Infantry Division had had just enough amphibious training in California to create the illusion that it needed no more. Some units received draftee replacements at the last minute.[37] In amphibious operations, however, troops should be embarked as organized combat teams, trained and equipped to fight from the moment they hit the beach.

Nor was there sufficient time to train the transport personnel. Of the thirty transports and cargo vessels used in the operation, only fourteen were actually in commission and under Captain Emmet's command on 1 August. Only six of the transports[38] and four of the cargo vessels[39] had been in commission for a year or more; and the topheavy _Harry Lee_ (nicknamed "Leaning Lena" because of her list) broke down and did not sail. Some of the other sixteen were still under conversion from merchant marine service or en route from the Pacific. None "were received in a satisfactory

[37] The Report of Maj. James Adams (Army Observer with the Southern Attack Group) states that the 47th Regiment of that group received 450 recruits two days before leaving camp for Norfolk.
[38] _Wood, Dickman_ (Coast Guard-manned); _Rutledge, Penn, Biddle;_ and _Harry Lee_, for which _Calvert_ was substituted.
[39] _Algorab, Arcturus, Electra, Procyon._

operating condition," [40] and all previously used as transports had to be altered in their interior arrangements for combat loading.

In ordinary transport loading, as much cargo and as many troops as the ship will carry are placed on board in the expectation of disembarking on a friendly dock or shore where everything can be sorted out. Combat loading, to facilitate an immediate assault on a hostile shore, is a very different and highly complicated art. The principle of it is this: essential equipment, vehicles and supplies must be loaded in the same ship with the assault troops that are to use them, and stowed in such manner that all may be unloaded in the order that it is likely to be wanted to meet tactical situations immediately upon landing. Special davits have to be fitted for handling the landing craft, rope ladders or cargo nets for debarking troops, and the crew has to be trained to unload in complete darkness. The Navy had prescribed sound principles of combat loading in its amphibious manual referred to above, but the Army had slightly different principles in a field manual of its own. And the two did not agree. In planning every joint operation during this war there was difficulty in reconciling the Navy view — that assault troops, especially if landed at night, should be very lightly equipped and slenderly supplied, leaving the big stuff to follow later — and the Army desire to get as much as possible ashore in the assault boat waves. In this instance, the Navy difficulties were aggravated by the Army's fear lest the follow-up convoy be decimated by submarines, and by a last-minute decision of General Anderson to increase the initial troop landings at Fedhala by some 50 per cent, which necessitated a very complicated and difficult boat plan.

Several transports did not report to Captain Emmet [41] in time to

[40] CTF 34 (Rear Admiral Hewitt) Report on Material and Logistics Operation Torch 27 Nov. 1942.

[41] It may be noted here that the only important mistake in naval planning, one which was not repeated, was heaping too many commands on Capt. Emmet. He was not only Commander Center Attack Group, the largest and most complicated of the three, but Commander Transports Western Naval Task Force and Commander Center Group Transports. He was in poor health, yet in spite of the many and complicated burdens thrust upon him, did an outstanding job.

take part in the rehearsals of day and night landings held between August and October at Solomons Island. These rehearsals were unrealistic at best, because of smooth and protected waters; re-hearsals under surf conditions on ocean-facing beaches were con-sidered too risky with U-boats hovering about. Some ships had to be pulled out of the rehearsal to take their turn at being fueled, or to receive new radio installations.[42]

For manning the landing craft, over three thousand Navy and Coast Guard personnel were required. It would have been desirable to select young men who were used to lobstering, fishing, and other small-craft work, for boat handling is not an art that can be learned in a hurry. But there were not enough such men available.[43] So, as frequently in this war, the Navy had to do the best it could to make boat sailors out of raw recruits who had never seen salt water.

The training of landing craft crews, under the direction of Captain W. P. O. Clarke, began at the end of June 1942. As the objective at that time was the projected shore-to-shore amphibious operations from the United Kingdom to France in 1942–1943, which called for men to handle the seagoing infantry and tank landing ships,[44] the training was not well suited for a ship-to-shore movement; and Captain Clarke was told nothing about Operation "Torch" until late August. He then switched the entire training program from shore-to-shore to ship-to-shore. Boat crews were taken off the transports to practise surf landings on Virginia Beach; Navy Beach Parties were trained with hydrographic, maintenance, medical and communication sections, Army Shore Parties were

[42] Conversations with and letters from Capt. Emmet and Capt. English, and from Admiral Hewitt's Report on Material and Logistics.
[43] The Army Engineer Corps before Pearl Harbor made a recruiting drive along the New England coast for young men used to boat handling, and trained them in landing operations at Martha's Vineyard. These Engineer units later performed excellent service in the Mediterranean and the Southwest Pacific. If the Navy had anticipated the need, it might have recruited along the Atlantic Coast several thousand such men, who were later drafted into the Army, or enlisted in the Coastal Picket Patrol. The value of previous experience in small-boat handling was proved by the superior performance of the Coast Guard, who manned the landing craft of U.S.S. *Joseph T. Dickman* at Fedhala.
[44] The British equivalent of the U.S. Navy LCI and LST.

trained to unload landing craft.[45] Captain Clarke had less than two months, about one third of what had been considered the minimum, to train these men to conduct night ship-to-shore landings.[46] Considering the time limitations, his performance was remarkable. Some of the landing craft did not have engines installed until 15 October.[47]

The principal types of landing craft used in Operation "Torch" were (1) the original "Higgins boat," a 36-foot Landing Craft Personnel Large, designated LCP(L), built of plywood, with a low, square bow, some propelled by gasoline and others by diesel engines; (2) the 36-foot Landing Craft Personnel Ramped, designated LCP(R), differing from the above by the addition of a small bow ramp; (3) the 36-foot Landing Craft Vehicle, designated LCV, fitted with a larger bow ramp so that it could land a truck or other vehicle. Each of these types carried thirty-six troops and a crew of three, and was supposed to make nine knots loaded. The first, commonly known as the "Higgins boat," proved inadequate, and was little used after this operation. It was easily holed on rocks or wrecked on beaches; exposed the troops unnecessarily; and was very difficult for a heavily equipped infantryman to get out of. The other craft were capable of carrying one truck or armored vehicle. Experience in Morocco proved that ramped personnel landing craft were essential. When these hit the beach the ramp is lowered, and the men go ashore without having to scramble over the side. If the sea is calm and the beach is of the right gradient, they can even land dryshod from a ramped boat.

Finally, we used one of the earliest models of the Landing Craft Mechanized, designated LCM, built of steel, diesel-powered, 50 feet long, and capable of carrying one 30-ton tank.[48]

[45] Col. Nathan E. McCluer USA of AFAF Training Group took charge of this part of the training.
[46] Conversations with Capt. Clarke at Norfolk 2 Mar. 1943.
[47] Hewitt Report on Material p. 2.
[48] These were the LCM-3, speed loaded 8 knots. I believe we had none of the 45-foot LCM-2s in this operation. They were capable only of carrying a 13½-ton tank. Another useful type which was not intended to be beached was the Support

Communications was a particularly difficult and vulnerable aspect of this operation, since the Army and Navy then had independent systems. In order to coördinate them, an amphibious signal school for Army Signal Corps and Navy Communications personnel was set up at Little Creek under Lieutenant Colonel Haskell N. Cleaves USA. Shore parties for control of naval gunfire support, with naval liaison officers, and joint ship-to-shore communication teams, were organized and trained. These groups stayed together at the rehearsals, on the voyage, and in the landings. The most novel of these communication teams were the four naval air liaison parties attached to headquarters of the four regiments that took part in the attack. Each consisted of one naval aviator and one aviation radioman, and an SCR–193 radio set mounted on a jeep. These air liaison parties went ashore with the assault troops, joined the command posts ashore, and were used very effectively to obtain carrier-based air support for the ground forces. Much of the radio equipment provided proved unsuitable for amphibious warfare because it could not stand a ducking in the surf; there were the usual difficulties from inexperienced personnel; but on the whole shore-to-ship communications were "not too bad." [49]

The numerous and elaborate communication nets in an amphibious operation really require a special ship for the top command. A new type for this purpose, the AGC (Amphibious Force Flagship),[50] converted from a transport or Maritime Commission C–2 hull, was then being worked out by the Bureau of Ships with the aid of Admiral Hewitt's staff. The Royal Navy already had something similar; but none could be made ready in time for Task Force

---

Boat, designated LCS, which carried two machine guns and an armed crew to protect the landing boats. (Admiral Hewitt's comments and recommendations; see note at head of chapter.)

[49] Vice Chief of Naval Operations (Vice Admiral Horne) "Lessons Learned in Wartime Communications, Amphibious." *Navy Department Bulletin* II No. 5 Mar. 1943 has selected passages from Action Reports on this subject.

[50] The letters stand for "Auxiliary General Communications." Also called "Auxiliary Combined Operations and Communications Headquarters Ships." U.S.S. *Ancon*, flagship in the Sicilian operation, was the earliest to be ready. Eighteen of them, in addition to six converted Treasury class Coast Guard cutters, were in commission at the end of the war.

Air Group en route to Morocco
Rear Admiral E. D. McWhorter and Captain J. J. Ballantine, on flag bridge of
U.S.S. *Ranger*

Flight deck of U.S.S. *Ranger* spotted for launching; destroyer crosses wake

34. As the next best thing, the handsome eleven-year-old heavy cruiser *Augusta*, a former Atlantic Fleet flagship with comparatively ample space and communication facilities, was chosen for Admiral Hewitt's flagship.

Finally, the air problem in this operation was crucial.[51] The Western Task Force was to approach a coast where the French had an estimated 168 planes operational at airfields very handy to the shore. This coast might also be within striking range of the larger Axis bombers. The one small landing field at Gibraltar had to be used by the Royal Air Force to cover the Center and Eastern Task Forces, and remote Malta could hardly take care of herself. So the only possible means of applying air power to this amphibious operation was aircraft carriers. And we were very short of carriers in October 1942. The Japanese had sunk the *Lexington, Yorktown, Wasp* and *Hornet*, and damaged the *Saratoga* and *Enterprise;* none of the new *Essex* class were in commission. U.S.S. *Ranger*, the only large carrier in the Atlantic Fleet, became the flagship of Rear Admiral Ernest D. McWhorter, commander of the "Torch" air group. The new *Sangamon* class, of four escort carriers converted from tankers,[52] was thrown into the operation with less than one-half the normal shakedown training. Their inclusion with the air group also helped to solve the fuel problem, for even after conversion they retained an enormous oil capacity with plenty to spare for other ships. All together the *Ranger* and her four consorts carried to Morocco 28 Grumman Avenger torpedo bombers (TBF), 36 Douglas Dauntless dive-bombers (SBD) and 108 Wildcat fighter planes (F4F-4), in addition to ferrying over 76 United States Army P-40s for basing at the Casablanca airdrome as soon as it was captured. Most of the pilots were untried in combat. *Ranger's* Air Group 9, the best trained, only reported on board 3 October.

Without this air support to neutralize the French air force, cover the landings, and bomb hostile shipping and installations, the inva-

---

[51] Cinclant to Cominch, "Comment on Aircraft Operations during Operation Torch" 30 Mar. 1943, enclosing Rear Admiral E. D. McWhorter's Reports.
[52] See Vol. I for a description of the different classes of escort carriers.

sion of Morocco might have been a long-drawn-out and bitter struggle. The successful performance of Admiral McWhorter's air group, despite the inexperience of most of the pilots, assured carrier-based air an important place in every future amphibious operation that could not be covered from the land. Two of the commanding officers, Captain C. T. Durgin of *Ranger* and Captain J. J. Clark of *Suwannee*, became famous carrier admirals in the Pacific War; *Ranger's* Air Group 9 made history on board U.S.S. *Essex* in 1943–1944.[53]

The escort carriers in this unit were just out of the yards, and their pilots had had so little training in carrier landings that Admiral McWhorter did not dare to risk their lives making practice flights on the way over. Thus it was all along the line. Operation "Torch" was a colossal undertaking for the United Nations at that stage of the war, and the first of its kind. As Admiral Sir Andrew Cunningham wrote, when the chips were all in and the gripes all aired and the post-mortems examined: —

No officer commanding a unit will ever be satisfied that he has had adequate preparation and training until his unit is trained and equipped down to the last gaiter button. There are times in history when we can not afford to wait for the final polish. I suggest that it should be made widely known to all units that for "Torch" particularly we could not afford to wait, and that the risk of embarking on these large-scale operations with inadequate training was deliberately accepted, in order to strike while the time was ripe. We must now push forward our training so that such a situation can not again arise.[54]

Now, reader; even if you have read these words of wisdom once, please read them again. "Cincmed," Admiral Cunningham, has the truth of the matter. We could not afford to wait. So do not look for the perfection and polish in "Torch" that you find in the amphibious operations of 1944. Everyone was green at the game, and

---

[53] *U.S. Carrier Air Group 9, Record of First Two Years* (privately printed. 1945). Lts. M. T. Wordell usn and E. N. Seiler usnr *"Wildcats" Over Casablanca* (1943) is a good popular account.

[54] Admiral Cunningham "Lessons of Operation Torch" 7 Feb. 1943 p. 1.

there was no time for more training and rehearsals. If D-day, 8 November, could not have been met, winter conditions on the beaches would have forced postponement until next year. British and American high commanders remembered very well that the Dardanelles campaign, the principal amphibious operation in World War I, failed because General Sir Ian Hamilton insisted on a postponement of several months in order to gain time for training.

Thus, Task Force 34 resembled a football team forced to play a major game very early in the season, before holding adequate practice or obtaining proper equipment. But, after all, the enemy did not know where or when he must play ball.

c. The Plan

Final plans called for the Western Naval Task Force (Admiral Hewitt) to land approximately 35,000 troops and 250 tanks of the Western Task Force (General Patton) at three different points on the Atlantic coast of Morocco, beginning at 0400 November 8, 1942. The Center Attack Group (Captain Emmet) was to place the Center Landing Group (General Anderson) of about 19,000 soldiers on the beaches at Fedhala, a small fishing town and beach resort about 15 miles from Casablanca. The Northern Attack Group (Admiral Kelly) was to land the Northern Landing Group (General Truscott) with about 9000 soldiers near Mehedia at the mouth of the Wadi Sebou,[55] and take possession of Port Lyautey with its airport. The objective of the Southern Attack Group (Admiral Davidson) and Landing Group (General Harmon) was Safi, 140 miles south of Casablanca, where some 6500 troops and about half the tanks were to be placed ashore.

A glance at the map will show the strategic reasons for this plan. All three landings, if successful, would secure the narrow coastal plain at the foot of the Middle Atlas, through which all principal

---

[55] *Waddy* or *Wadi* is the usual English equivalent of the Arabic word for river; the French use *Oued.*

lines of communication run in French Morocco. Mehedia on the Wadi Sebou was the nearest practicable landing place to the modern city of Port Lyautey, near which was located the best and most accessible airfield in Morocco on which to base Navy planes; and possession of Port Lyautey would secure the railroad that runs parallel to the border of Spanish Morocco through the Taza Gap to Algeria, where the Center and Eastern Task Forces were to land. The Fedhala beaches were the nearest practicable landing place to Casablanca. That modern city of over 250,000 population had the only large harbor on the Atlantic coast of Morocco, and important installations which fitted it to be a future supply base and railhead for our North African army. Casablanca was so well defended that any attempt to seize the harbor by a surprise attack would have been suicidal, like the Anglo-French attack on Dakar in 1940; and there were no landing beaches more favorably located than those of Fedhala. Finally, Safi was selected because it covered the native metropolis of Marrakech, and its harbor offered the only opportunity of running medium tanks ashore, and bringing them up north for an assault on Casablanca. No Landing Ships Tank (LSTs) were completed in time for this operation.

Amphibious Force Atlantic Fleet was an assault force with training responsibilities. Only a skeleton of it remained at Ocean View in charge of training when the first great enterprise was under way. As soon as the Force was actually afloat it was known as "the Western Naval Task Force," or "Task Force 34."

The final composition of this force, arranged in task groups according to the place of attack, will now be given.

d. Composition

As this is the first Task Organization given in this History, a short explanation of the method of compilation is in order.[56]

Such lists are initially compiled from the basic Operation and

[56] The main work of compiling and checking these Task Organizations has been done by Donald R. Martin USNR, who came to the historical staff from Amphibious Force Atlantic Fleet in Feb. 1943, and is now Chief Yeoman.

Attack Plans.[57] They should include all ships that actually take part in a given operation up to the time when enemy resistance ends. In this instance the inclusive dates are 7–14 November 1942. Only vessels that steam in under their own power are included; landing craft, crash boats and the like carried on deck are not mentioned. An attempt is made to give the names of all commanding officers, and all division, squadron, group and force commanders. These names, if not in the Operation Plan, are obtained from the Fleet Organization of nearest date to the operation, checked from action reports, ships' rosters and, as a last resort, officers' individual files ("jackets") in the Bureau of Naval Personnel. The composition of air groups on carriers and the names of air group and squadron commanders are obtained from the weekly *Location of United States Naval Aircraft* issued by the Bureau of Aeronautics, and from the Fleet Organization. Names of Army units embarked in the transports, and of Army officers, are obtained from Army Reports.[58]

The ships are grouped, as far as possible, functionally. Thus Rear Admiral McWhorter's Air Group, a unit in the Operation Plan, is broken down into the carriers that operated with the Northern, with the Center and with the Southern Attack Groups. Destroyers are included, as far as possible, with the groups that they screened on the approach. It must be remembered that as soon as the assault begins, a large part of the Organization is broken into by the assignment of destroyers, minesweepers and other vessels to fire support or other duties.

The first ship mentioned after the name of the commander of each group is the flagship, unless otherwise stated. All officers mentioned will be understood to be of the United States Navy, unless otherwise designated.[59]

[57] In this instance, Amphibious FAF Operation Plan No. 5–42 as corrected in Admiral Hewitt's Landing Attack Plan No. 1–42.

[58] In this instance, a Report by Major Carl E. Bledsoe (Army Observer with the Northern Group), consulted at office of Historian Ground Forces, Lt. Col. K. R. Greenfield.

[59] Absolute accuracy is impossible to attain in lists of this sort; but every possible effort has been made to make them so, as a valuable record for future generations. The writer will be grateful for errors being called to his attention.

TASK FORCE 34
Rear Admiral H. Kent Hewitt, Commander, in *Augusta*

WESTERN NAVAL TASK FORCE,
Admiral Hewitt

Embarking Western Task Force United States Army,
Major General George S. Patton Jr. USA

TG 34.1 COVERING GROUP,
Rear Admiral Robert C. Giffen

BB 59	MASSACHUSETTS	Capt. F. E. M. Whiting
CA 45	WICHITA	Capt. F. S. Low
CA 37	TUSCALOOSA	Capt. N. C. Gillette

Screen, Captain D. P. Moon (Comdesron 8)

DD 419	WAINWRIGHT	Lt. Cdr. R. H. Gibbs
DD 402	MAYRANT	Lt. Cdr. E. K. Walker
DD 404	RHIND	Cdr. H. T. Read
DD 447	JENKINS	Lt. Cdr. H. F. Miller

Tanker

AO 30	CHEMUNG	Capt. J. J. Twomey

TG 34.8 NORTHERN ATTACK GROUP,
Rear Admiral Monroe Kelly

Embarking 60th Infantry Regiment (Reinforced) of 9th Division; [60] 1st Battalion 66th Armored Regiment 2nd Armored Division; 1st Battalion 540th Engineers; and special units. Brigadier General Lucian K. Truscott Jr. USA, Commander. 9099 officers and men, 65 light tanks.

Fire Support Group

BB 35	TEXAS	Capt. Roy Pfaff
CL 42	SAVANNAH	Capt. L. S. Fiske

Northern Attack Group Transports, Captain Augustine H. Gray (Comtransdiv 5)

AP 30	HENRY T. ALLEN	Capt. P. A. Stevens
AP 51	JOHN PENN (ex-*Excambion*)	Cdr. Charles Allen
AP 57	GEORGE CLYMER (ex-*African Planet*)	Capt. A. T. Moen
AP 72	SUSAN B. ANTHONY (ex-*Santa Clara*)	Capt. Henry Hartley
AK 21	ELECTRA (ex-*Meteor*)	Cdr. J. J. Hughes
AK 25	ALGORAB (ex-*Mormacwren*)	Cdr. J. R. Lannom
AP 70	FLORENCE NIGHTINGALE (ex-*Mormacsun*)	Capt. E. D. Graves Jr.
AP 76	ANNE ARUNDEL (ex-*Mormacyork*)	Capt. L. Y. Mason Jr.

[60] Also called "60th Regimental Combat Team," divided into three Battalion Landing Teams. An RCT is a regiment reinforced by special units; a BLT is a battalion similarly reinforced.

NORTHERN ATTACK GROUP (*Continued*)

Screen, Commander D. L. Madeira (Comdesron 11)

DD 418	ROE (also *fire support*)	Lt. Cdr. R. L. Nolan Jr.
DD 429	LIVERMORE	Cdr. Vernon Huber
DD 432	KEARNY (also *fire support*)	Cdr. A. H. Oswald
DD 440	ERICSSON (also *fire support*)	Lt. Cdr. C. M. Jensen
DD 604	PARKER	Lt. Cdr. J. W. Bays

Beacon Submarine

SS 235	SHAD	Lt. Cdr. E. J. MacGregor

Air Group

ACV [61] 26	SANGAMON (ex-*Esso Trenton*)	Capt. C. W. Wieber

VGS-26: 9 TBF-1 (Avenger), 9 SBD-3 (Dauntless), Lt. Cdr. J. S. Tracy
VGF-26: 12 F4F-4 (Wildcat), Lt. Cdr. W. E. Ellis

ACV 28	CHENANGO (ex-*Esso New Orleans*)	Capt. Ben H. Wyatt

Carrying 76 Army P-40Fs (Curtiss) for future basing at Casablanca

Air Group Screen, Captain Charles Wellborn Jr. (Comdesdiv 19)

DD 455	HAMBLETON	Cdr. Forrest Close
DD 458	MACOMB	Cdr. W. H. Duvall

Special Units

DD 199	DALLAS	Lt. Cdr. R. Brodie Jr.
DD 430	EBERLE	Lt. Cdr. K. F. Poehlmann
AO 36	KENNEBEC (ex-*Corsicana*)	Cdr. S. S. Reynolds
AM 55	RAVEN [62]	Lt. Cdr. C. G. Rucker
AM 56	OSPREY	Lt. Cdr. C. L. Blackwell
S.S. (Honduran)	*Contessa,* William H. John (Br.)	Lieut. A. V. Leslie USNR [63]
AVP 10	BARNEGAT [64]	Cdr. J. A. Briggs

TG 34.9 CENTER ATTACK GROUP,
Captain Robert R. M. Emmet in *Leonard Wood*

Embarking 3rd Infantry Division (7th, 15th, 30th Regiments reinforced), 1st Battalion 67th Armored Regiment 2nd Armored Division, and special units. Major General J. W. Anderson USA, Commander. 18,783 officers and men, 79 light tanks.

Fire Support Group

CA 31	AUGUSTA	Capt. Gordon Hutchins
CL 40	BROOKLYN	Capt. F. C. Denebrink

---

[61] "Auxiliary Aircraft Carrier" — designation later changed to CVE, "Escort Carrier."
[62] The minesweepers in each group formed part of the Anti-Submarine Screen when not engaged in their special duties.
[63] Naval Liaison Officer on board. Mr. John was the Master.
[64] This seaplane tender joined the formation at sea from Iceland 6 Nov. and served as additional screen to the Northern Attack Force.

CENTER ATTACK GROUP (*Continued*)

Control and Fire Support Destroyers, Commander E. R. Durgin (Comdesdiv 26)

DD 441	WILKES	Lt. Cdr. J. B. McLean
DD 443	SWANSON	Cdr. L. M. Markham Jr.
DD 428	LUDLOW	Lt. Cdr. L. W. Creighton
DD 603	MURPHY	Lt. Cdr. L. W. Bailey

Center Attack Group Transports, Captain Emmet

AP 25	LEONARD WOOD (ex-*Western World*)	Cdr. Merlin O'Neill USCG
AP 60	THOMAS JEFFERSON (ex-*President Garfield*)	Capt. C. Gulbranson Cdr. C. R. Crutcher

Transdiv 3, Captain R. G. Coman

AP 58	CHARLES CARROLL (ex-*Del Uruguay*)	Cdr. H. Biesemeier
AP 26	JOSEPH T. DICKMAN	Cdr. C. W. Harwood USCG
AP 15	WILLIAM P. BIDDLE (ex-*City of San Francisco*)	Cdr. P. R. Glutting
AP 50	* JOSEPH HEWES (ex-*Excalibur*)	Capt. R. McL. Smith
AP 42	* TASKER H. BLISS (ex-*President Cleveland*)	Capt. G. C. Schetky
AP 52	* EDWARD RUTLEDGE (ex-*Exeter*)	Capt. M. W. Hutchinson Jr.
AP 43	* HUGH L. SCOTT (ex-*President Pierce*)	Capt. H. J. Wright

Transdiv 9, Captain W. M. Quigley

AP 66	ANCON	Capt. P. L. Mather
AP 69	ELIZABETH C. STANTON (ex-*Mormacstar*)	Capt. Ross A. Dierdorff
AP 77	THURSTON (ex-*Del Santos*)	Capt. Jack E. Hurff
AK 19	PROCYON (ex-*Sweepstakes*)	Cdr. L. P. Padgett Jr.
AK 56	OBERON (ex-*Del Alba*)	Cdr. Ion Pursell
AK 18	ARCTURUS (ex-*Mormachawk*)	Cdr. J. R. McKinney

Screen, Captain John B. Heffernan (Comdesron 13)

DD 453	BRISTOL	Cdr. J. A. Glick
DD 437	WOOLSEY	Cdr. B. L. Austin
DD 439	EDISON	Lt. Cdr. W. R. Headden
DD 641	TILLMAN	Cdr. F. D. McCorkle
DD 600	BOYLE	Lt. Cdr. E. S. Karpe
DD 405	ROWAN	Lt. Cdr. R. S. Ford

* Sunk by enemy action.

CENTER ATTACK GROUP (*Continued*)

Minecraft, Commander A. G. Cook Jr. (Cominron 7)

DMS 5	PALMER	Lt. Cdr. J. W. Cooper
DMS 6	HOGAN	Lt. Cdr. U. S. G. Sharp Jr.
DMS 8	STANSBURY	Lt. Cdr. J. B. Maher
CM 10	MIANTONOMAH (ex-*Quaker*)	Lt. Cdr. R. D. Edwards
AM 57	AUK	Lt. Cdr. W. D. Ryan USNR
CM 5	TERROR [65]	Cdr. H. W. Fitch

TG 34.2 *Air Group*, Rear Admiral Ernest D. McWhorter

CV 4	RANGER	Capt. C. T. Durgin

Air Group 9, Commander D. B. Overfield, 1 TBF

VF–9: 27 F4F–4, Lt. Cdr. John Raby
VF–41: 27 F4F–4, Lt. Cdr. C. T. Booth II
VS–41: 18 SBD–3, Lt. Cdr. L. P. Carver

ACV 27	SUWANNEE (ex-*Markay*)	Capt. J. J. Clark

VGF–27: 11 F4F–4, Lt. Cdr. T. K. Wright
VGS–27: 9 TBF, Lt. Cdr. M. A. Nation
VGF–28: 12 F4F–4, Lt. Cdr. J. I. Bandy
VGS–30: 6 F4F–4, Lt. Cdr. M. P. Bagdanovitch

Air Group Screen

CL 55	CLEVELAND	Capt. E. W. Burrough

Desron 10, Captain J. L. Holloway Jr.

DD 454	ELLYSON	Cdr. J. B. Rooney

Desdiv 20, Captain T. L. Wattles

DD 461	FORREST	Lt. Cdr. M. Van Metre
DD 462	FITCH	Lt. Cdr. Henry Crommelin
DD 463	CORRY	Lt. Cdr. E. C. Burchett
DD 464	HOBSON	Lt. Cdr. R. N. McFarlane

Beacon Submarines

SS 253	GUNNEL	Lt. Cdr. J. S. McCain
SS 233	HERRING	Lt. Cdr. R. W. Johnson

Tanker

AO 38	WINOOSKI (ex-*Calusa*)	Cdr. J. E. Murphy

TG 34.10 SOUTHERN ATTACK GROUP,
Rear Admiral Lyal A. Davidson in *Philadelphia*

Embarking 47th Regimental Combat Team, 9th Infantry Division; 3rd and elements of 2nd Battalion 67th Armored Regiment 2nd Armored Division, and special units; Major General E. N. Harmon USA, Commander. 6,423 officers and men, 54 light and 54 medium tanks.

BB 34	NEW YORK	Capt. Scott Umsted
CL 41	PHILADELPHIA	Capt. Paul Hendren

[65] Detached from D+5 convoy and reported 14 November.

SOUTHERN ATTACK GROUP *(Continued)*

Control and Fire Support Destroyers, Captain C. C. Hartman (Comdesron 15)

DD 489	MERVINE	Lt. Cdr. S. D. Willingham
DD 633	KNIGHT	Lt. Cdr. R. B. Levin
DD 640	BEATTY	Lt. Cdr. F. C. Stelter Jr.

Southern Attack Group Transports, Captain Wallace B. Phillips

AP 8	HARRIS (ex-*President Grant*)	Capt. O. M. Forster
AP 65	CALVERT (ex-*Delorleans*)	Capt. J. W. Whitfield
AK 55	TITANIA (ex-*Harry Culbreath*)	Cdr. V. C. Barringer Jr.
AP 67	DOROTHEA L. DIX (ex-*Exemplar*)	Cdr. L. B. Schulten
AP 71	LYON (ex-*Mormactide*)	Capt. M. J. Gillan Jr.
AP 49	LAKEHURST (ex-*Seatrain New Jersey*)	Cdr. H. J. McNulty

Screen, Commander H. C. Robison (Comdesdiv 30)

DD 632	COWIE	Lt. Cdr. C. J. Whiting
DD 490	QUICK	Lt. Cdr. R. B. Nickerson
DD 634	DORAN	Lt. Cdr. H. W. Gordon Jr.

Assault Destroyers

DD 155	COLE	Lt. Cdr. G. G. Palmer
DD 153	BERNADOU	Lt. Cdr. R. E. Braddy Jr.

Minecraft

CM 9	MONADNOCK (ex-*Cavalier*)	Cdr. F. O. Goldsmith
DMS 7	HOWARD	Lt. Cdr. C. J. Zondorak
DMS 18	HAMILTON	Lt. Cdr. R. R. Sampson

Tankers [66]

AO 35	HOUSATONIC (ex-*Esso Albany*)	Cdr. A. R. Boileau
AO 37	MERRIMACK (ex-*Caddo*)	Capt. W. E. Hilbert

Beacon Submarine

SS 220	BARB	Lt. Cdr. J. R. Waterman

Air Group

ACV 29	SANTEE (ex-*SeaKay*)	Capt. W. D. Sample

VGF–29: 14 F4F–4, Lt. Cdr. J. T. Blackburn
VGS–29: 8 TBF, 9 SBD (Douglas), Lt. Cdr. J. A. Ruddy Jr.

Air Group Screen

DD 456	RODMAN	Cdr. W. G. Michelet
DD 457	EMMONS	Lt. Cdr. H. M. Heming

Ocean Tug

AT 66	CHEROKEE	Lieut. J. H. Lawson

[66] These were joined by *Kennebec, Winooski* and *Chemung* as soon as they had discharged their "Crash Boats," and operated between long. 12° and 16° W and lat. 33° and 34° N in order to be accessible to all.

Admiral Royal E. Ingersoll, Commander in Chief Atlantic Fleet, to which all these vessels belonged, kept his flag flying on the American side of the Atlantic, but his careful and intelligent oversight of training the combat ships and crews contributed vastly to the success of the operation. Admiral Ernest J. King, Commander in Chief United States Fleet and Chief of Naval Operations, played a vital rôle in the overall planning, and, in spite of his world-wide responsibilities and current anxieties over the Guadalcanal campaign, kept a finger on the pulse of Operation "Torch." The same applies to President Roosevelt. An early advocate of winning French North Africa, he had acquiesced in postponement as a military necessity; but from the moment he received the word AFRICA his heart was in this operation.

On the day before sailing, 23 October 1942, a conference of about 150 naval and military officers concerned in the expedition was called at Norfolk by Admiral Hewitt, in order to elucidate the main features of the attack plan. So well had secrecy been maintained that, for most of those present, this was the first indication of the objective; and the great majority of officers on board the Naval Task Force never knew where they were bound until after they had cleared the Virginia Capes.

At this shore conference, Admiral Hewitt gave a calm and reasoned statement of Operation "Torch" and its purpose. Captain Emmet, Commander Transports, stressed the difficulties and struck the keynote: "The Navy's mission in this operation is to serve the troops — to die for them if necessary." Commander R. W. D. Woods, air officer on Admiral Hewitt's staff, described what the carrier-based planes intended to do.

General Patton, commanding the embarked Army troops, delivered a typical "blood and guts" oration. He exhorted the Navy to remember Farragut, but predicted that all our elaborate landing plans would break down in the first five minutes, after which the Army would take over and win through. "Never in history," said he, "has the Navy landed an army at the planned time and place. If you land us anywhere within fifty miles of Fedhala and within one week of D-day, I'll go ahead and win. . . . We shall attack for sixty days, and then, if we have to, for sixty more. If we go forward with desperation, if we go forward with utmost speed and fight, these people cannot stand against us." [67]

With these fighting words ringing in their ears, the officers of the Western Naval Task Force went on board and prepared to get under way.

[67] A short time before Task Force 34 sailed, President Roosevelt called General Patton and Admiral Hewitt to the White House. To avoid notice and comment by the press the Army and Navy leaders were admitted at different entrances and brought together by devious routes in the anteroom of the President's office. They discussed the forthcoming operation and the President wished them both "God Speed."

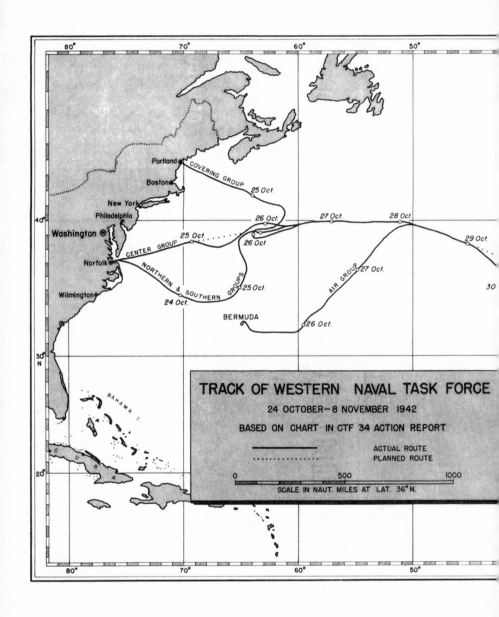

80° 70° 60° 50°

Portland
COVERING GROUP
Boston
25 Oct.
New York
26 Oct.   27 Oct.   28 Oct.
40° Philadelphia
Washington ⊛   25 Oct. ....   29 Oct.
CENTER GROUP   26 Oct
Norfolk   30
NORTHERN & SOUTHERN GROUPS   27 Oct.
25 Oct.   AIR GROUP
Wilmington
24 Oct.
BERMUDA
26 Oct.

30°
N

BAHAMA I.

TRACK OF WESTERN NAVAL TASK FORCE

24 OCTOBER – 8 NOVEMBER 1942

C U B A

20°   BASED ON CHART IN CTF 34 ACTION REPORT

—————————   ACTUAL ROUTE
....   PLANNED ROUTE

0   500   1000

SCALE IN NAUT. MILES AT LAT. 36° N.

80° 70° 60° 50°

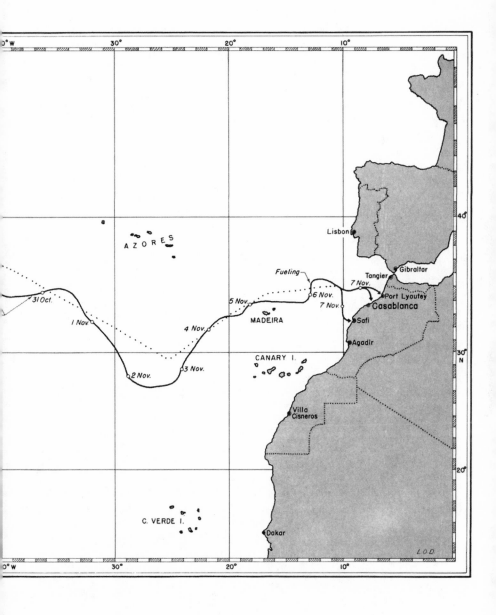

30° W   30°   20°   10°

40° N

A Z O R E S

Lisbon

Fueling

7 Nov.

Tangier

Gibraltar

6 Nov.

Port Lyautey

7 Nov.

Casablanca

31 Oct.

5 Nov.

Safi

1 Nov.

4 Nov.

MADEIRA

Agadir

30° N

2 Nov.

3 Nov.

CANARY I.

Villa
Cisneros

20°

C. VERDE I.

Dakar

L.O.D.

30° W   30°   20°   10°

CHAPTER II

The Crossing[1]

20 October – 7 November 1942

A LTHOUGH small in comparison with later invasion forces in the Pacific, this armada of 102 sail was considered too large and conspicuous to be concentrated in a single port, or depart as one group. The five beacon submarines,[2] whose mission was to reconnoiter the Moroccan landing beaches and Dakar, and help guide the transports to their unloading areas, rendezvoused at New London and took their departure from Montauk Point on 19 and 20 October. The Covering Group, consisting of the new battleship *Massachusetts*, heavy cruisers *Tuscaloosa* and *Wichita* and four destroyers, had been shifted to Casco Bay; the Air Group, together with one light cruiser, one oiler and nine destroyers, was sent to Bermuda for training between 3 and 11 October. Most of the Northern and Southern Attack Groups sortied from Hampton Roads on 23 October and took an initial southeasterly course, as if they intended to pick up the carriers at Bermuda and continue to the West Indies. False rumors had been circulated to the effect that these ships were bound for the Gulf of Léogane, Haiti, for maneuvers. The remainder of the Task Force sortied from Hampton Roads on 24 October, escorted by two stately silver blimps, and steered northeasterly as if headed for Britain. Two days later they were joined by the Covering Group from Casco and by the

---

[1] Data for this chapter are taken principally from Admiral Hewitt's Preliminary Report of Torch Operation to Cinclant 28 Nov. 1942; Capt. A. G. Shepard's Report on Operation Torch 31 Dec. 1942; war diaries of U.S.S. *Brooklyn* and *Leonard Wood*.

[2] Organized as TG 34.11. In addition to the four mentioned in the Task Organization, U.S.S. *Blackfish* (Lt. Cdr. J. J. Davidson) operated off Dakar. Captain Norman S. Ives, the group commander, was embarked in *Augusta*.

ships that had feinted to the southward. On 25 October Admiral McWhorter's Air Group sortied from Bermuda, and took a course resembling "the track of a reeling drunk in the snow";[3] but the course must have been well calculated, since rendezvous was made 28 October exactly on schedule, at a point about 450 miles SSE of Cape Race.

Task Force 34 was now complete,[4] and a brave sight it was, from air or sea; a tempting sight from under the sea. In the van, as flagship of Rear Admiral Giffen's Covering Group, steamed the mighty *Massachusetts*. The O.T.C. of the fleet was in heavy cruiser *Augusta*, flying the two-starred flag of Rear Admiral Hewitt, and screened by a semicircle of destroyers. *Brooklyn* acted as liaison vessel between the flagship and the main body of the convoy: thirty-five big transports, cargo vessels and tankers steaming one thousand yards apart, in nine columns and five lines, with the veteran battleships *Texas* and *New York* on the two flanks of the front line.[5] Twelve miles astern of the main convoy steamed the Air Group, *Ranger* and four escort carriers, accompanied by cruiser *Cleveland* and nine destroyers. In all, more than forty destroyers were patrolling assigned stations in the outer and inner anti-submarine screens. The air patrol of cruiser-based and carrier-based planes swooped about overhead, keeping watch for U-boats and intrusive neutral merchantmen. When complete, Task Force 34, including the outer screen, covered a space of ocean roughly twenty by thirty miles. Yet, so expert had the signalmen become, that a flag hoist made on Admiral Hewitt's flagship *Augusta* could reach the entire Fleet in ten minutes.

Equally impressive were the men. They were not scarred veterans of "the battle and the breeze," but men of the Atlantic Fleet

---

[3] Admiral McWhorter's Report 3 Dec. 1942.

[4] Except transport *Calvert*, substituted for *Harry Lee* two days before sailing, sortied 25 Oct. with two destroyers and joined on the twenty-ninth; S.S. *Contessa*, sailed unescorted 26 Oct. and joined off the beaches; seaplane tender *Barnegat*, joined from Iceland 6 Nov.

[5] CTF 34 Cruising Order 6-42. The fifth line included the two minelayers and two assault destroyers. *Cole*, the third assault destroyer, and tug *Cherokee* were in the fourth line.

"Ships, Fraught with the Ministers and Instruments of Cruel War"
Sections of Task Force 34 en route to Morocco

Flagship *Augusta* fueling at sea from U.S.S. *Merrimack*

"Right down to bare steel" — scraping paint in living quarters

Incidents of the Crossing

whose only encounters so far had been with submarines. The great majority of them had been civilians in 1940, and thousands had never been to sea before. So great had been the expansion of the Navy, that the entire Task Force was diluted with reserve officers and new recruits. In the cruiser *Brooklyn*, half of the sixty-five officers were reservists, only nine had been in the Navy more than three years; of the one thousand and fifty bluejackets and Marines, over half were at sea for the first time, and not one man on board had ever been in a naval engagement. Half the ship's company of the escort carrier *Sangamon* had been in the Navy but a few months, and had never gone to sea. An appreciable number of the bluejackets on every ship were eighteen years old or under. These boys were eager, competent and alert. They volunteered for work far beyond their assigned duties; and three days' fighting was to prove, if it needed proof, that young Americans of this generation, brought up to hate war, are the best potential fighters in the world.

Magnificent autumn weather was enjoyed for the first ten days; no breakdowns, no straggling and no submarine attacks as Task Force 34, the greatest war fleet yet sent forth by the United States, forged ahead at fourteen knots, zigzagging by day and steaming direct courses at night. Yet the responsible officers were far from overconfident, or puffed up with that *hubris* which brings down the wrath of the gods. The Navy is always ready for action against a hostile fleet, no matter what the odds; but when almost defenseless transports and troops are in its charge, the weight of responsibility is oppressive. Those senior officers who had studied the operation knew that they were taking tremendous risks. No amphibious operation so far from base had ever been undertaken. To steam four thousand miles and attempt a night landing on a hostile coast flew in the face of accepted theories of naval warfare. Yet, assuming (as we must assume) that the French forces in Morocco under Vichy control would resist, a night landing was considered essential to give us the advantage of tactical surprise; for the only practicable landing beaches were subject to heavy fire from numerous shore batteries, fixed and mobile. In 1944 the armed forces accepted the doctrine and worked out a technique of intensive, prolonged bombardment by ships' gunfire and aircraft before landing, in order to destroy or neutralize shore defenses. But this was 1942. The French surface and submarine forces based on Casablanca were known to be powerful, and the principal debarkation, at Fedhala, would take place only twelve nautical miles from that enemy base; while a few days would suffice to bring up more formidable fighting ships from Dakar. In the last war the British expedition against the Dardanelles had the use of advanced bases in the Aegean and at Alexandria, yet failed. Famous and successful amphibious operations, such as Port Arthur in 1904, and our own Santiago campaign in 1898, and those of the Japanese in the Pacific early in 1942, had been close to bases already secured. For anything comparable to this, one had to go back to the Athenian expedition against Syracuse in 413 B.C.; and the Thucydides account of that was not encouraging. One recalled the speech of Nicias to the Athenian assembly on the eve of departure: —

You ought to consider that we are like men going to found a city in a land of strangers and enemies, who *on the very day of their disembarkation must have command of the country;* for if they meet with a disaster they will have no friends. . . . Wherefore I must trust myself and the expedition as little as possible to accident, and would not sail until I had taken such precautions as will be likely to ensure our safety.[6]

Athens had taken every precaution and failed. We had taken every precaution. . . .

Yet, as Pericles had said before the Syracuse expedition, we feared our own mistakes rather than our enemies' designs; and we feared foul weather more than either. Surf on the Moroccan beaches often ran fifteen feet high in winter, and only a few calm days could be expected in November. If weather made it impossible to land on the appointed day, the Task Force would be in a sad

[6] Thucydides *Peloponnesian War* (Jowett trans.) vi. 23.

pickle, with U-boats ganging up and the French completing preparations ashore. Surprise was the essential element of success; we *must* land as planned, or shoulder the responsibility for one of the greatest military disasters in history. One of the leading generals of the Army had called the plan "fantastic," and still thought it was so. If things went wrong, we could well imagine what Congress and the newspapers and the public would say of those who planned and conducted this expedition.

The route followed by the Northern, Southern and Center Groups between 25 and 28 October was laid out to give the impression to any hostile observer through a periscope, or on board a neutral merchantman,[7] that it was a troop convoy bound to the United Kingdom. That day the course was changed to the southeastward in order to suggest that the force was headed for Dakar. Reports of French naval forces being concentrated at Dakar, while women and children were shipped away, suggested that this ruse was successful. On the thirtieth and thirty-first, in a section of the ocean that we hoped was free of submarines, fueling operations were carried out at a speed of eight knots, with complete success. Advantage was taken of the reduced speed to distribute mail by destroyers, and General Truscott made visits to his regimental commanders on board other transports.

In the meantime every ship was a floating school of amphibious operations. On the capital ships and destroyers, officers and chief petty officers studied the parts they had to play, and on board the transports and carriers there were endless lectures, discussions and rehearsals for all hands. Large silhouettes of the Moroccan coast were constructed from contour maps and from data furnished by the Amphibious Force staff; pictures and models of enemy ships and aircraft were studied; the air pilots were so well indoctrinated in Moroccan geography that by the time they arrived they could

[7] The routes of neutral merchantmen (Spanish and Portuguese) known to be at sea were carefully plotted by Cominch, and whenever any was contacted by the screen, before the final approach, the Task Force made an emergency turn to avoid it. Several Portuguese and Spanish vessels were encountered 7 Nov., and one or two had prize crews placed on board to prevent their broadcasting our position.

fly straight to their designated targets. All enlisted personnel not performing other duties were constantly engaged in scraping paint from interior bulkheads and overheads down to bare metal, in order to reduce fire hazard during combat.[8] In this crossing, as was aptly said by one of the Army officers, there were no longer two services, only one group of fighting men planning the attainment of a great objective. The transports' officers went out of their way to cater to the comfort and convenience of the troops, and one military commander even turned his men to, and "policed" the transport from stem to stern, and truck to keelson.

The crossing was not without humor. During the sortie from Hampton Roads some of the commanding officers fell into the bad habit of talking to each other over the TBS — the ship-to-ship radio telephone — as a short way to make inquiries and give orders. Rear Admiral Robert C. ("Ike") Giffen, on joining the Task Force, was so outraged by this breach of radio silence that he sent out the following characteristic message to his Covering Group: —

"The amount of useless chatter over the TBS at night is disgraceful, and sounds more like a Chinese laundry at New Year's than a fleet going to the wars. We are not training broadcasters."

To which the commanding officer of *Wichita* replied by flag signal: —

"Congratulations and good morning, sir. In my opinion the Chinese laundry signal is the best I have seen so far."

After fueling was completed 31 October, the force turned southeasterly again, heading toward Dakar until the evening of 2 November. Then, near lat. 27° N, long. 27° W, about 700 miles west by south of Ferro, the course was altered to the northeastward, in order to give any snooper the impression that the ships were bound for the Straits.

Admiral Hewitt directed his force so intelligently, with refer-

---

[8] Following a directive issued by Commander Cruisers Pacific Fleet 26 Sept. and reissued by Cinclant, occasioned by the loss of the *Quincy*, *Astoria* and *Vincennes* at the Battle of Savo Island.

ence to the probable submarine positions,[9] that not a single attack developed.

As this was the 450th anniversary of the discovery of America by Columbus, there was a sentimental significance in the fact that on 31 October, and again on 3 November, Task Force 34 crossed the track made by the *Santa Maria*, *Pinta* and *Niña* on their westward voyage in 1492. It seemed that America was at last repaying her debt to the first Admiral of the Ocean Sea, and in a sense fulfilling his ambition to deliver Jerusalem; for these seventy thousand young men from the New World of his discovery were returning to rescue the Old World of his affections from the most iniquitous bondage to which she had been subjected in a thousand years. Even in Columbus's native city of Genoa, now in enemy territory, and in his adopted country Spain, which officially regarded us with a disdainful neutrality, thousands of people were praying for our success, and for the speedy victory of the forces of light, of which we were the flaming spearhead.

On 4 November, when the Task Force was steaming on a northeasterly course between latitudes 31° and 32° N, the sea made up fast with a rising northwest wind, and landing prospects for the immediate future seemed very dark. One of the minelayers had to drop out of formation after she began rolling 42 degrees; one of the battleships feared losing her boats and the 20-mm guns mounted on her forecastle. By 6 November "heavy seas reported off Moroccan coast gave rise to considerable doubt as to the possibility of success in executing landing attack plan." [10] Admiral Hewitt would then have to break out alternate plans for landing inside the Mediterranean, or await favorable weather under way.

Both Washington and the Admiralty sent out the gloomiest of weather forecasts for D-day, 8 November, on the Moroccan coast — surf fifteen feet high, landings impossible. On the other hand, the Task Force aërologist, Lieutenant Commander R. C. Steere, predicted that the storm which then threatened to cast high waves

[9] See Volume I of this History for the methods of determining these positions.
[10] Commander Transports (Capt. Emmet) War Diary.

on the African coast was moving too rapidly to have a dangerous effect, and forecast locally moderating weather, which would make for good landing conditions on the eighth.

Admiral Hewitt had a difficult decision to make, and it had to be made quickly, because next morning the Task Force would begin to divide. If he discounted the predictions from Washington and London, and pushed through the planned landings, the result might be disastrous. If he played safe, he must stay at sea or use an attack plan which would take his force, possibly past a heavy submarine concentration and through the Straits, to land on the short stretch of French Moroccan coast east of the Spanish border. The beaches there had been insufficiently studied to be approached with confidence; and even if the landing were successful our troops would have to fight their way through the Taza Gap, and for hundreds of miles further, to secure Casablanca.[11] Seldom has so much depended on the decision of one officer.

The Admiral chose the bolder alternative. At midnight 6–7 November he decided to risk the weather and stick to the preferred plan. Fortune as usual favored the brave. That night the sea moderated sensibly. Task Force 34 was then completing a wide sweep to the northward of Madeira and Porto Santo. Next, it zigged northeasterly almost to the latitude of Gibraltar, and after dark zagged southeasterly toward Casablanca.

November 7 opened overcast, with a light wind from the northeastward, calm sea, moderate ground swell and temperature 68°. My sextant brought down the last of the old moon, a pale ghost gondola skimming the southern horizon. At daybreak the Southern Attack Group, destined for Safi, broke off; Admiral Davidson sending a parting message: "Keep your eyes to the sky and your

[11] In the Alternate Plan the Northern Group would land at Beni Saf to capture near-by airfields; the Center Group would assault the beach northwest of Port Say, capture Oujda and two airfields; the Southern Group would capture Nemours and Marina; after which armored elements of the two last groups would move southwest on Guercif and seize the Taza Gap. If this plan had been executed it is very unlikely that Admiral Darlan would have ordered cease-firing as early as he did, since it would have left the majority of French armed forces in North Africa, and practically all the French Navy, initially unopposed.

ears to the sea." The rest of the Task Force feinted towards the Straits for the last time. At their appointed hours the Covering Group, and the carrier *Ranger* with cruiser *Cleveland* and destroyer screen, faded out of the picture, intent on their several missions; and at 1600 the Northern and Center Attack Groups parted company. Three distinct groups, each led by two or three minesweepers, were now approaching three different points on the Moroccan coast, while the Covering and Air Groups moved to their assigned operating areas.

This final approach had been very carefully planned in order that the force might profit by cover of darkness as far away from the coast as was compatible with reaching the unloading areas by midnight. Four hours would then be available to load the landing boats and start the initial assault waves inshore by 0400 on 8 November, well before daybreak. So closely was the timetable executed that the Northern Attack Group arrived at its planned position off Mehedia at 2400, the Southern Group made Safi at 2345, and the Center Group was in Fedhala Roads at 2353. For precision planning and faultless execution, this on-the-minute arrival of a large, complicated task force after a voyage of about 4500 miles [12] merits the highest praise.

Some difficulty, however, was experienced in reaching the exact areas assigned to the transports, six to eight miles off their respective beaches. An unexpected northeasterly set of current moved each group a few miles off the dead-reckoning position based on its evening star fix. The SG radar, that marvelous new invention which projected all surface objects on a luminous screen, revealed this error when six to ten miles offshore. Two of the three groups were then brought to their unloading positions by emergency turns, which were unexpected and therefore confusing on a night so dark that even "fog buoys" (towing spars) could not be followed. Consequently, the Northern Attack Group, in two col-

[12] The sum of days' distances made good adds up to less than that; but, what with zigzagging and evasive courses, the larger ships steamed about 4500 miles from Hampton Roads, and the destroyers considerably more. *Brooklyn's* pitometer log registered 4450 miles from Hampton Roads to Fedhala.

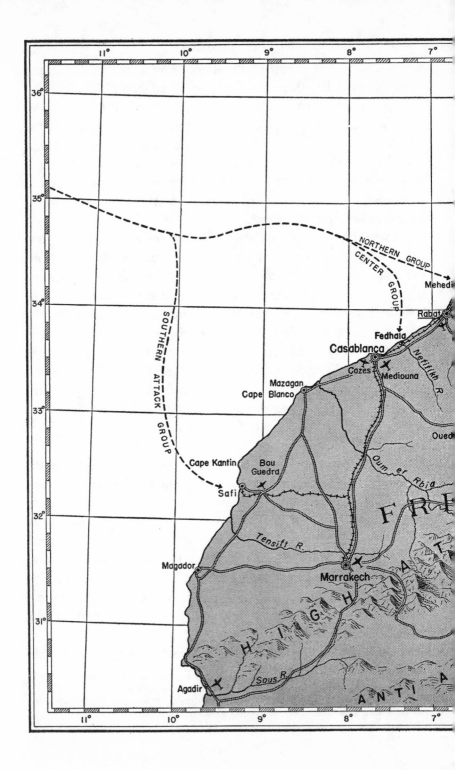

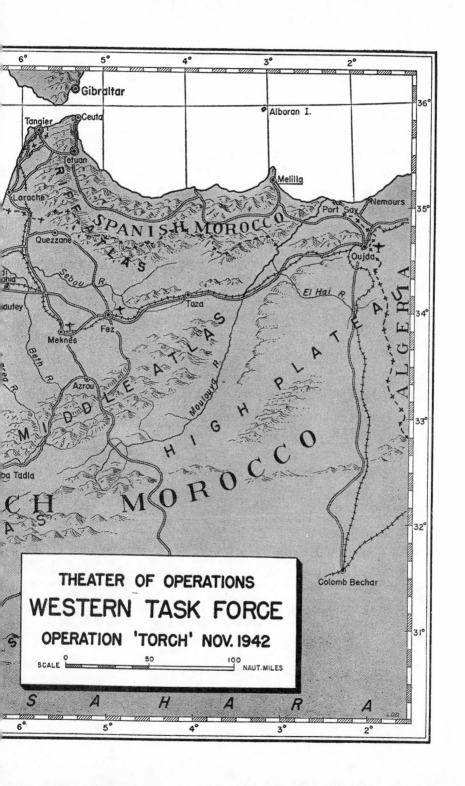

THEATER OF OPERATIONS
WESTERN TASK FORCE
OPERATION 'TORCH' NOV. 1942

SCALE 0 50 100 NAUT.MILES

umns, and the Center, in four columns, were somewhat scrambled during the last half hour of the approach, and debarkation was correspondingly delayed.[13]

It was a curious sensation for those who had labored so long and painstakingly over the plans of this operation to know at midnight that they were now off the coast of the "High Barbaree"; that beyond lay the mighty Atlas and the Sahara Desert. Off Mehedia and Safi a few dim lights suggested human habitation to Admiral Kelly's and Admiral Davidson's Attack Groups; and the loom of city lights at Casablanca was seen by some of the Covering Group. From off Fedhala, however, not a light showed; only a pungent smell of charcoal smoke floated out with the offshore breeze to suggest that land lay within striking distance. Africa was never so dark and mysterious to ancient sea rovers as she seemed that night to these seventy thousand young men who had retraced the path of Columbus. Most of them, from midnight on, were far too busy loading and lowering boats, standing to their guns, or performing innumerable shipboard tasks, to bother about anything but the task at hand. But all hands — admirals and generals with the weight of responsibility, much-traveled colonels and four-stripers, grim top sergeants and imperturbable chief petty officers, the eager young second lieutenants and ensigns just out of officer training school, soldiers, bluejackets and coastguardsmen completing their first ocean passage, and mess attendants approaching their mother country — felt a new and strange thrill at the thought of carrying their flag into battle in the coastal waters and on the soil of Africa.

[13] The beacon submarine, U.S.S. *Gunnel*, who had patrolled the area for two or three days in advance, lay to in the transport area to coach the Center Attack Group in. Destroyer *Boyle* was sent ahead of the Force to locate *Gunnel*, did so at 2230 and reported to *Augusta*; but Capt. Emmet, not Admiral Hewitt, was then in tactical command and the submarine was not seen from *Leonard Wood*.

CHAPTER III

Landing at Fedhala

8 November 1942

All times are Greenwich. The French were using
Central European time (Z+1), one hour later.

1. *Initial Landings*[1]

THE EIGHTH of November, D-day, broke fair but hazy;
sea calm with a moderate ground swell, light offshore wind.
Morning twilight began about 0600, and the sun rose at 0655.
Everything had been planned with the object of placing at least
6000 troops ashore before daybreak, in order that they might seize
the town, neutralize (with the aid of naval gunfire) the shore batteries, and establish a beachhead for an assault on Casablanca. Accordingly, the Fedhala landing had been carefully thought out, to
the last detail, like a game planned by a chess expert; but it was
well understood that, given variables such as sea, weather, enemy
action, accident and inexperienced men, all plans were subject to
dislocation — as indeed General Patton had cheerfully predicted.
The Center Attack Group was the most important of the three.
The twelve transports and three cargo vessels carried 19,870 officers and men, of the Army, 1701 vehicles and about 15,000 long
tons of supplies, to be discharged in four days.[2] The total naval
personnel in this Center Group, including those in the destroyers

[1] Action Reports of commanders of the four leading transports, *Leonard Wood,
Thomas Jefferson, Charles Carroll* and *Joseph T. Dickman;* War Diary, Narrative
of Events and Action Report of Capt. R. R. M. Emmet, Commander Transports
and CTG 34.9; Report of Beachmaster (Comdr. J. W. Jamison) to Capt. Emmet
27 Nov. 1942. The Army criticisms are in Reports of Lt. Col. Harry M. Roper
(Army Observer) and of Major James R. Weaver to Admiral Hewitt 7 Dec. 1942.
[2] Capt. Emmet's Action Report, Enclosure D.

and the carriers assigned to serve it offshore, was 17,723. Both the Northern and Southern Attacks might have failed without greatly affecting the major objectives; but if the Center Group failed the whole expedition was a disaster.

With reference to the chart, suppose we describe briefly the landing plan worked out at Amphibious Force headquarters, and then relate the story of how it was carried out.

The approximate two-and-one-half miles of coastline between Cape Fedhala and the Sherki headland [3] is one continuous beach, with a gradient of about one in forty, and an average width between high and low water of four to five hundred feet. Reefs and other obstructions to the approach divide the shore into five beaches practicable for troop landings; these were designated as Red, Red 2, Red 3, Blue and Blue 2. One mile west of the neck of the Cape is a beach designated Yellow; and three miles east of Sherki is another, called Blue 3. Eliminating Beach Red as too close to enemy artillery, and the two outlying ones, this left four beaches for the initial landings: Red 2, Red 3, Blue and Blue 2.[4]

These beaches, and the waters for ten or twelve miles offshore, were covered by the following enemy artillery: (1) the Batterie du Port, three 100-mm coast defense guns, facing northwesterly on the shore just west of the neck of the Cape, but capable of enfilading the two central beaches; (2) a battery of two fixed 75-mm guns, near the eastern tip of the Cape, which commanded at least three beaches; (3) the Batterie Pont Blondin, of four modern 138.6-mm coast defense guns in sunken emplacements on the Sherki headland, with range of 18,000 yards; [5] (4) several machine-

---

[3] On available maps called Sidi Mohammed ben Sherki (also spelled Shorki, Cherqui and Chergui), after the tomb of a Moslem marabout or saint, which was the one conspicuous building on it. The name of the coast defense battery on it was Batterie Pont Blondin, but we generally referred to it as "the Sherki," or even "the Turkey."

[4] The blacked-out raider unit from *Scott*, which was supposed to land on Beach Yellow before daylight and seize the bridges over Wadi el Mella, arrived after sunrise and, feeling that commando stuff was then out of place, returned on board to wash their faces. Those directed to Beach Blue 3 were unable to locate it.

[5] Inspection Report of Col. E. C. Burkhart and Col. Louis B. Ely on 14–15 Nov. 1942. Divide by 25 to reduce millimeters to inches.

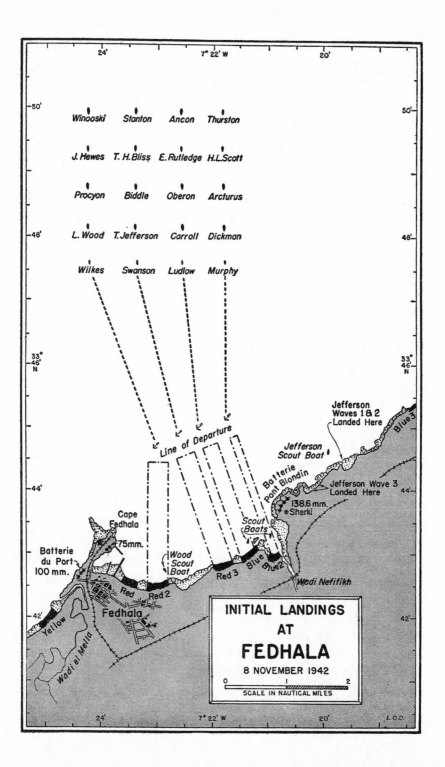

INITIAL LANDINGS
AT
FEDHALA
8 NOVEMBER 1942

SCALE IN NAUTICAL MILES

gun installations on the Cape and at Sherki; and (5) a mobile battery of 75s at an unknown location in the town.

The transport area, where the twelve transports and three cargo vessels were supposed to anchor or lay-to at midnight, was a two-mile square, six to eight miles north of the beaches. All initial assault troops were embarked on the inshore line of transports, U.S.S. *Leonard Wood, Thomas Jefferson, Charles Carroll* and *Joseph T. Dickman.* Four hours were allowed to place men in the boats and conduct the first boat waves to the line of departure. H-hour, the time of first landing, was set for 0400. Many of the boats for these initial assault waves were carried on the same transports as the men they were to take ashore, but an appreciable number had to be borrowed from vessels in the second, third, or fourth line.

First to be hoisted out from the transports and to get away were to be the four scout or beach-marking boats, each in command of a Chief Specialist and manned by four enlisted men. These had been intensively trained at Little Creek, Virginia, by First Lieutenant Lloyd E. Peddicord USA and Ensign John J. Bell USN. Each boat was fitted with an engine silencer and a compensated compass. It carried strong flashlights and a small radio set; the men were armed with tommy guns and automatics. The mission of these scout boats was to locate and mark the four important beaches. Having done so, they were to anchor at designated positions just outside the surf line, to commence using their infra-red flashlights at 25 minutes before H-hour, and at H minus 10 to show signal flares corresponding to the color and number of the beach that they marked — for instance, two red lights for Red 2.

The four control destroyers, U.S.S. *Wilkes, Swanson, Ludlow* and *Murphy,* were to take position one thousand yards due south of the four leading transports at 0200. These positions, to which each landing boat would proceed as soon as loaded, were known as "the rendezvous area." When the signal was given by Captain Emmet, each control destroyer must conduct her waves of landing boats, at about eight knots' speed, from the rendezvous area to the line of departure, four thousand yards off the beaches. On that line she must drop anchor at a designated position which, it was expected, she could pick up by radar bearings on the land and infra-red bearings on the beacon submarine. Finally at H-hour, 0400, the boat waves bearing assault troops must start for the beach, guided in by the scout boats' lights, and accompanied by armed support boats in case protection were necessary. Before morning twilight exposed their positions, the control destroyers must get under way, leaving large buoys with colored streamers to guide later boat waves, and take designated gunfire support positions to the north and northwest of Cape Fedhala.[6] It was expected that the first assault troops would be able to leap ashore by 0415, after which the boats were to be retracted by their naval crews and proceed to their transports for another load. All this in pitch-darkness and on a falling tide.[7]

Now let us see what happened. The first line of transports, *Wood, Jefferson, Carroll* and *Dickman*, arrived on schedule, began hoisting out boats shortly after midnight and loading troops into them before 0100. But the rest of the formation, with few exceptions, had straggled badly when making the emergency turns. That was to be expected, since some of them had been hastily converted and their deck officers and quartermasters were inexperienced in such maneuvers.[8] Unfortunately, as we have seen, General Anderson wished to land a very large proportion of his troops before daylight. Hence all small landing craft and forty-three out of forty-four of the tank lighters brought over by this

[6] Operation Plan 5–42, Annexes I and K; Report of Major Weaver, who was in *Wood's* scout boat.

[7] High water at Fedhala was at 0140 and low water at 0744 Nov. 8, range 9.7 feet. Admiral Hewitt asked to have D-day postponed a week, so that the landings could be effected on a rising tide; but tide did not bother the Mediterranean landings. The overall command believed that the danger in postponement more than outweighed the inconvenience of an ebb-tide landing, and anticipated a large expenditure of landing craft.

[8] Capt. Emmet's Action Report to CTF 34. The *Carroll* and *Jefferson* had been well converted, but their officers and men were also inexperienced — they had not even been on a good shakedown cruise before this expedition.

Center Group had to be employed in the initial landings, which was much too complicated an assignment for even experienced coxswains at night. Each front-line transport which carried assault troops had to obtain boats from other ships, even from some in the rear line two or three miles away. *Wood, Jefferson, Carroll* and *Dickman* were expected to load over fifty boats each and have them at the line of departure by 0400. It could not be done, even in the perfect weather conditions that morning.[9] What with vessels straggling, and with boats from a transport whose relative position was unknown even to her own officers trying to find a front-line transport in the darkness, the four assault ships had an average of only thirty-two boats available for the first group that went ashore. "Failure of ships to arrive in the transport area as scheduled completely upset the timing of the boat employment plan." [10]

Once the boats were in the water, and had found the ship they were to serve, they formed circles handy to their proper embarkation net on the transport's topside, in order to embark the troops. Here there were more delays. *Leonard Wood* had all her boats in the water by 0130, allowing two hours for the troops to get into them; but that was not enough. Better trained in debarking ashore than in embarking off a transport, they were somewhat cautious going down the nets with their heavy equipment.[11] So, as a result of inevitable delays, H-hour was postponed from 0400 to 0445, and actually came off at 0500. If the enemy had not been surprised, this delay might have been costly.[12]

[9] *Carroll's* experience is illuminating. Her debarkation plan depended on 25 boats arriving from four different ships by about 0200. Those from *Oberon* reported at 0345, those from *Scott* at 0645, those from *Thurston* and *Arcturus* never did report.

[10] Report of Commanding General 3rd Infantry Division, enclosed in Gen. Patton's Final Report.

[11] Most assault troops carried 60 pounds of equipment, which was too much; the first wave, however, carried only rifle and ammunition.

[12] This delay in landing was the subject of a good-natured Army–Navy controversy. The most frequent Army allegations are (1) some transports were not ready to lower boats when they reached the area, and (2) coxswains of landing boats wanted sense of direction as well as common sense. The Navy rejoinders are (1) a primary cause of delay was what the skipper of *Thomas Jefferson* called

Each boat as soon as loaded proceeded to the control destroyer in the rendezvous area one thousand yards to the southward, forming, with five to seven other boats, a "wave" adjacent to the destroyer. Boat discipline on this phase of the operations off Fedhala was excellent.

Scout boats from *Wood, Dickman* and *Carroll,* which were to mark the beach approaches for the landing boats, rendezvoused alongside the *Wood* shortly after 0100.[13] At 0145, they shoved off under the leadership of the *Wood's* scout boat, on board which was the scout boat commander, Major Weaver. Proceeding to a point where the opening to Fedhala Harbor could be discerned in the darkness, they separated to spy out their respective beaches. Well before 0400 each one of the three had selected her position, and either anchored or lay-to, awaiting the time to turn on signal lights. These men in the scout boats had a peculiarly difficult and important mission, and conducted themselves with exemplary courage and intelligence.[14] Nobody informed them that H-hour was postponed, so their blinking must have informed a few people at Fedhala that something unusual was going on.

At 0355 Commander E. R. Durgin in U.S.S. *Wilkes,* westernmost of the control destroyers, signaled jubilantly: "The Yanks are coming!" Within ten minutes she and her three consorts (*Swanson, Ludlow, Murphy*) had left their rendezvous areas south of their respective transports (*Wood, Jefferson, Carroll, Dickman*),

---

"overall sluggishness of Army personnel," both in loading equipment in boats, and in embarking themselves; (2) the Army imposed on Commander Transports an unnecessarily complicated boat employment plan, because it wanted to get an unreasonably large number of troops ashore at Fedhala before daylight. It was pointed out that when Admiral King was Cinclant and supervising amphibious practice, he never permitted boats of one transport to be sent to another during darkness. To the writer it is clear that (1) the United States Navy then had much to learn about celerity in landing troops, and that more accuracy as to the boat navigation was wanted; (2) the Army had not yet learned to fit landing plans to the exigencies and limitations of water-borne transportation.

[13] *Jefferson's* scout boat had engine trouble and never showed up.
[14] Maj. James R. Weaver's Report to Admiral Hewitt 7 December 1942, Lt. R. H. Ballinger's Report on the beach-marking system to Capt. E. A. Mitchell at AFAF headquarters 15 Jan. 1943, Maj. Weaver's rejoinder to same Jan. 21, are my sources for the operations of the beach-marking boats.

conducting the first waves of landing boats to the line of departure. But the transports were unable to furnish them with more than about half of the waves scheduled. *Wilkes* had four out of ten; *Swanson,* five out of eight; *Ludlow,* five and a half out of fourteen; and *Murphy,* four out of ten waves.[15] Using radar bearings on the oil tanks of Cape Fedhala, the destroyers reached the line of departure between 0445 and 0457, and anchored. Every scout boat was observed to be blinking violently. After a sufficient pause to check up, the first assault waves left the line in a rush at 0500, and hit the beaches between 0515 and 0525; the second and third waves followed them five to ten minutes later. Surf was negligible; it was, in fact, the calmest early morning along that coast in the month of November.

These initial landings went off fairly well, considering they were made in darkness on a strange shore. The best job was done by boats of the Coast Guard-manned *Dickman* on Beach Blue 2, in the estuary of the Wadi Nefifikh, although this was the most difficult beach of all.[16] It is partially protected from the sea by the Sherki headland, but there are dangerous rocks adjoining it on one side, and the Pont Blondin battery threatened the boats on the other. Two boats missed the control destroyer, were set to the eastward and smashed up when attempting an unplanned landing; but the other twenty-five landed troops on Beach Blue 2 in close order without drawing enemy fire. And although they were then well up a tidal estuary on an ebb tide, these boats retracted before daylight, and returned to their ship by 0630.

The experience on *Carroll's* Beach Blue, next to the westward, was very different. This beach had a narrow entrance between rocky ledges, and the surf was high enough to give trouble. The

[15] Cdr. Durgin's and Capt. Emmet's Action Reports. There are supposed to be 8 personnel landing boats to a wave, and approximately 36 troops in each boat. But there may be only 5 or 6 boats to a wave that includes vehicle lighters, and, of course, any boat that carries vehicles has comparatively few personnel.

[16] Owing to an erroneous civilian report of mud on this beach (it looks muddy from the bridge, but is not), and the narrow entrance, it was originally planned not to retract the boats until after the fifth wave had landed. Fortunately this decision was changed en route. Cdr. Jamison's report as Beachmaster confirms the good job done by *Dickman's* boats.

boat coxswains had been well trained in recognizing points ashore, and in steering by Sirius, which at that early morning hour bore almost due south; but they lacked the seamanship to handle their boats properly. Out of twenty-five boats of the initial attack waves, eighteen were wrecked on the first landing — two by collision, two by flooded engines, three holed on rocks, and ten broached on the beach. That left seven to return to the ship and take part in the second landing, in which five more were wrecked. The scout boat for this beach grounded on Beach Red 3 and became a total loss.[17]

U.S.S. *Jefferson* had the worst luck of all. Unloading was very slow; a debarkation net carried away, flinging men into the water; the scout boat developed engine trouble, missed rendezvous with other scout boats off the *Wood* (where courses for the beaches were given out), and proceeded alone. She mistook a small rocky beach east of Sherki for her own Beach Red 3 (a miss of about two miles), and blinked her lights near a section of coast where surf was breaking high. Fortunately Ensign A. C. Taylor, who led the first boat wave, sized up the situation in time to avert a calamity, prevented his little fleet from cracking up on the rocks, and turned back to the scout boat, which then led the flotilla westward along the coast. The boats lost their leader in the darkness, turned back, and landed on the rocks at 0540 almost three miles east of where they should have been, losing four boats out of six. The second wave, landing at the same place five minutes later, lost three boats out of six; the third wave, composed of LCVs and LCP(R)s, did a good job at another unplanned landing place. In the meantime *Jefferson's* scout boat had found Beach Red 3, and *Swanson*, the control destroyer for that beach (who also had taken a wrong position by following the scout's blinkers) had found her correct station; so that the fourth wave hit the right beach and lost only two out of six LCVs.[18] Wave 5 collected various stragglers and

---

[17] *Charles Carroll* Action Report; Report of scout boat commander (John Weldon Johnson CSP) appended to Maj. Weaver's Report.

[18] Two boats of Waves 1 and 2, and four from Wave 4 that returned from the initial landing, were wrecked later, on 8 and 9 Nov.

landed with a loss of but one boat on the wrong beach at 0605. Then the "big noise" began, and no more were landed until after it was over. Only 17 out of 33 boats from *Jefferson* survived the initial landings, and of these six had to be repaired before they could be used again.[19]

The boats of *Leonard Wood*, the other Coast Guard-manned transport, had a run of bad luck, because both control destroyer *Wilkes* and scout boat were out of position. The latter had been instructed to take station off the east end of Beach Red 2, where a rocky reef begins, so that the landing boats would leave her to port, as if she were a black buoy at a harbor entrance. Before the first waves came in she was approached by a mysterious boat, which she believed to be hostile, and so cut her cable and drifted to a position off the rocks. At the same time the *Wilkes* was out of position to the westward. Consequently the first four boat waves, taking their course from the scout boat's blinker, approached the beach obliquely; and after passing the scout boat ran "full gun" on the rocks. This happened between 0520 and 0540. Some were retracted and made their way to the beach, others went hard and fast aground, the soldiers scrambling ashore over the rocks and losing much of their equipment. Thus, 21 out of 32 boats from the *Wood* making the initial landing were wrecked, and 8 more were lost during the day.[20]

All in all it is surprising that this night landing, the most ambitious yet undertaken by armed forces of the United States, was so successful. Many mistakes were made, but all shore objectives were promptly attained, with sufficient troops to hold them, and with few casualties. Control of the operation was never at any time lost. The Center Attack Group landing craft placed about 3500

[19] *Thomas Jefferson* Action Report with chart; Report of the scout boat commander (John G. Donnell), appended to Maj. Weaver's Report. He did not think that he was ever east of Sherki; but Capt. Crutcher of *Jefferson*, after analyzing reports of the boat-wave commanders, is positive that he was. The position shown on our chart represents Capt. Crutcher's considered opinion.

[20] Report of boat group commander (Lt. A. Keidel USCG), appended to Capt. Merlin O'Neill's Action Report of *Leonard Wood*. Maj. Weaver stoutly denies that his scout boat was off station, but Lt. Keidel's Report is supported by that of the Beachmaster to Capt. Emmet.

troops ashore on the beaches of Fedhala during the one hour of darkness and faint morning twilight that elapsed between 0515 and the beginning of enemy resistance. The combat teams went straight to their objectives, and had secured most if not all the initial beachhead before sunrise. If the French had been alert the story might have been very different, as at Omaha Beach in Normandy two and a half years later.

General von Wulish, the head of the German Armistice Commission at Fedhala, called on General Noguès at Rabat shortly after sunrise on 8 November, to say a long-wished-for farewell. "This is the greatest setback to German arms since 1918," he told the Resident General. "The Americans will take Rommel in the rear, and we shall be expelled from Africa." As he said it, tears rolled down his cheeks.[21]

2. *The French Side of the Fence*[22]

At this point we may pick up the story of our efforts, through diplomatic and other channels, to convince the French in North Africa that we came not to conquer but to free their country from Axis domination. On the success of these endeavors depended the ultimate success of the operation. We might fight our way ashore against French opposition, but could hardly hope to win Tunisia without their active coöperation.

Mr. Robert D. Murphy, Counselor of the American Embassy at Vichy, who had begun cultivating patriotic Frenchmen in Africa in 1940, by the spring of 1942 had, with the aid of Lieutenant Colonel William A. Eddy usmc, the American observer at Tangier, organized a resistance group. His key men were a prominent civilian financier, and two general officers of the French Colonial Army — Charles Mast,[23] chief of staff to General Juin, and Émile Béthouart,

---

[21] Told to the writer on 13 Feb. 1943 by Gen. Béthouart of the French Army.

[22] Many of the data in this section were told to the writer by Gen. Béthouart. See also references in second footnote to Chapter I.

[23] On D-day he commanded the Algiers division, and he succeeded Admiral Esteva as Resident General in Tunisia.

who had a military command in Morocco. A band of young men was organized to go into action when we passed the word. It was also planned and tentatively arranged, through the Office of Strategic Services and Mr. Murphy's office, with the knowledge of General Eisenhower, that General Henri Giraud, who in April 1942 had escaped from a German prison, would enter Algiers shortly after the assault, take over the government of North Africa, and organize his countrymen to assist in their own liberation. Giraud was acceptable to the French patriots in North Africa, which De Gaulle decidedly was not.[24] Giraud remained in France until just before the invasion. He was given only the vaguest information about the Allied plans and both hoped and expected that they would take the form of a simultaneous invasion of Southern France and North Africa early in 1943.

As D-day drew near the French leaders in North Africa favorable to us wanted reassurance as to our intentions, and knowledge of our plans, from some high officer of our Army or Navy. That was the purpose of Major General Mark W. Clark's secret landing from a British submarine for a conference with Mr. Murphy, General Mast, and others, on the Barbary Coast near Cherchel (about seventy-five miles west of Algiers), on 23 October 1942.[25] Even then, so closely was the secret guarded, General Clark did not feel free to disclose the exact date or place of our landings.[26] That was probably a mistake, for it left insufficient time or information as a basis to prepare elements of the

[24] This was the principal and deciding reason why De Gaulle was not placed at the head of the invasion by the Anglo-American forces. Our numerous consuls, control officers, and O.S.S. representatives, after two years' intensive sounding of French opinion in North Africa, had no doubt whatever that any attempt on our part to foist De Gaulle on Algeria or Morocco would precipitate a civil war. And there were other reasons as well. The General, in addition to his many admirable qualities, was notoriously touchy and uncoöperative; the British attempt to collaborate with him in Syria had been unsuccessful.

[25] Lt. N. L. A. Jewell *Secret Mission Submarine* (1945); Ridgeway B. Knight "General Clark's Secret Mission" *American Foreign Service Journal* XX 122, Mar. 1943; Capt. G. B. Courtney's article in *Life* 28 Dec. 1942.

[26] He empowered Mr. Murphy to inform Gen. Mast at the eleventh hour, but only the date, and there was no time to pass the word to Morocco.

French Army to coöperate. In Morocco, where Laval had been particularly assiduous in weeding out officers unsympathetic to him from the armed services, and where Admiral Darlan had made an inspection tour and endeavored to stir up fighting spirit while the Western Task Force was at sea,[27] the only two men who knew anything about our plans were General Béthouart, in command of the Casablanca area, and General Henry-Martin at Marrakech. They knew nothing except the approximate date. Mr. David King, the American Vice Consul at Casablanca, acting for the Office of Strategic Services, was in charge of "fifth column" activities there; but even he did not know exactly where his compatriots were about to land. And, to complete this triangle of uncertainty, nobody in the Western Task Force knew anything about General Béthouart's adhesion to the common cause, or what sort of coöperation to expect from the French. On board ship we anticipated a 100 per cent solution; either everyone would receive us with open arms, or everyone would fight.

It was not expected that anything could be done about the French Navy. The senior officers of that force, with ancient and honorable traditions, had been in a curious psychological state since the fall of France. With no part in the treachery and corruption that undermined French resistance, they had every intention of sticking fast to what was left of their country; and for them, Marshal Pétain was France.[28] In addition, the Oran and Dakar affairs, which they regarded as dastardly attacks on a defeated ally, left them hating the British as much as the Germans, and wanting to fight somebody just to show they could fight. The Navy through Admiral Darlan was closely tied up to the Vichy government, and the Navy manned the coast defenses of North

[27] The Admiral afterwards claimed that he did this to keep the Germans quiet and convince them that France was able to defend North Africa without Axis assistance.

[28] Moreover, French naval officers were largely recruited from the *haute bourgeoisie*, which welcomed the "discipline and order" that Marshal Pétain talked about so much.

Africa. So its attitude was most important for us; but the combined efforts of Mr. Murphy and his friends were unable to make the slightest dent on the French Navy's loyalty to Pétain.

General Béthouart did everything he could to prepare a bloodless landing and a favorable reception for the Americans, but he was not sufficiently informed to influence events. He did not even know the date of D-day until the evening before, when a young man laid on his desk a paper stating *"Débarquement à 0200 demain."* So, at 2200 November 7, the General ordered certain detachments of his troops to arrest the German Armistice Commissions at Casablanca and Fedhala, assuming that they would be the first to give the alarm. Vice Admiral F. C. Michelier, the naval commander at Casablanca, who controlled coast defense, heard of this order through an accidental leak, countermanded it, and sent the troops to their barracks. Béthouart then proceeded to the Rabat headquarters of General Noguès, Resident General of French Morocco, got the General out of bed at 0100 November 8, told him of the impending landings, and urged him to coöperate with the Americans. Béthouart timed this visit in order to give Noguès opportunity to countermand resistance, but too late for him to organize resistance.

General Béthouart had orders from General Giraud to take the place of General Lascroux as commander of French military forces in Morocco. Lascroux, who did not relish this change, was kidnaped by a Béthouart staff car and taken to Meknès. Béthouart then stationed some of his own subordinates along the waterfront of Rabat, in order to welcome the Americans when they landed; for he naturally assumed we would land there. It was the capital of Morocco, and it had no coast defense batteries manned by naval personnel to contest an assault. The capture of Rabat, had, in fact, been part of our operation plan until well into September, when Mehedia was substituted; but the news of this substitution never reached our agents and supporters in Morocco.

General Noguès, a shifty character at best, who naturally doubted the accuracy of General Béthouart's story, called Admiral Michelier by telephone [29] to confirm or deny the presence of an American amphibious force. Michelier replied that he had seen nothing, his aërial reconnaissance had reported no ships off the coast the night before, and he doubted both the accuracy of General Béthouart's information, and its significance if correct; for with the French forces at his disposal he believed that he could repel anything that the United States was likely to send. General Noguès found it difficult to make up his mind. He had been deeply impressed both by German power and by the propensity of the United Nations to muff every operation, like Norway, Crete and Dieppe, that they attempted overseas. If the American landing was only a commando affair, and he failed to resist it, the Germans would have an excuse to take over North Africa; and that was the last thing he wanted. An American landing in force at Rabat would probably have decided the question for Noguès. Béthouart was waiting there listening for the hum of American landing craft engines. Shortly after 0500 the first news of the landings at Safi and Fedhala reached Noguès in such form that he believed them to be mere commando raids. He then ordered all French armed forces to resist, and arrested Béthouart.

Thus, by a curious paradox, the efforts of the Allied armed forces to maintain secrecy probably lost whatever chance there was of an unopposed landing in Morocco. Secrecy about the place prevented General Béthouart from being of any assistance. Secrecy in the approach succeeded so well that the French doubted the existence of Task Force 34 when it was already debarking troops. It is interesting to conjecture what would have happened if the

[29] At 0130 Greenwich (0230 French) time, half an hour after Michelier had telephoned to him about the leak. In this conversation, according to my French informants, the General, being under duress, ordered the Admiral to take over the Morocco theater command. Michelier had already received an informal warning from Vichy at 0050, and at 0250 (both Greenwich time) he received official notice of the landings at Oran, from Admiral Rioult at that place, in plain language.

three powerful attack groups had approached the African coast
during daylight; those who know General Noguès think that in
the face of *force majeure* he would have joined the Allies promptly
and decisively. Admiral Michelier, who was dependent upon
Noguès in the French chain of command, would perhaps have
fired a few salvos for the honor of the French Navy. But it is most
amusing to learn that at the very moment when Michelier was
giving the comforting assurance to Noguès over the telephone
that the United States invasion force *"n'existait pas,"* U.S.S. *Massachusetts*, steaming about twenty-one miles off shore, made a 90-
degree turn out to sea lest she be observed by the French Navy!

The hue and cry raised by certain sections of American and
British opinion against the "appeasement of" or "collaboration
with" Vichy was misplaced. No successful landing of our forces
in North Africa could have been effected without keeping up relations with Marshal Pétain's government. On the contrary, an
unopposed landing might have been arranged if General Eisenhower had imparted his plans in advance to certain French officers
in North Africa. But that was a risk which could not possibly be
accepted in an operation where absolute secrecy was vital. And
the same consideration prevented a close coördination between
the preliminary activities of Military and Naval Intelligence,
Office of Strategic Services and Department of State.

Were the French in Morocco tipped off by President Roosevelt's broadcast, announcing the landings and begging the French
to facilitate them? All evidence at hand indicates that they were
not. This broadcast was timed for the landings in Algeria at 0100
November 8. General Patton, when he heard the plan, pointed
out in no uncertain terms that his troops were scheduled to land
in Morocco at least three hours later, and that if the French intended to resist, the President's announcement would give them
a headstart; either the Moroccan landings should take place at
0100 or the broadcast be postponed. The first could not be done,
because the Western Attack Force needed at least five hours of
darkness to make an unobserved approach. So General Eisenhower

decided to accept the risk. He cabled from London to the Adjutant General of the Army 14 October 1942: "I do not believe that any loss of surprise for your attack will result if the broadcast precedes your H-hour. Word of the action by the Center and Eastern Task Forces will certainly be transmitted to the Casablanca authorities, broadcast or no broadcast."

Actually, French intelligence was so incomplete that no word of the landings in Algeria shortly after 0100 reached the Casablanca authorities until almost 0300. And, strange as it may seem, nobody of any importance in Morocco, except the German Armistice Commission, heard President Roosevelt's broadcast.[30] His proclamation, followed by a French translation, was sent out from a disk by the B.B.C. in London, beamed for North Africa, every half hour from 0130 on. The writer heard it on board *Brooklyn* at 0200. The ship's officers were very much disturbed; thought someone had blundered. But almost everyone in Morocco seems to have been asleep, and the French armed forces apparently kept no radio watch. General Béthouart never heard the presidential broadcast, and he is certain General Noguès did not. None of the officers of the French ships in Casablanca heard the broadcast. When they sortied around 0815 and opened fire they had no idea whose ships they were shooting at; and only when they observed the big battle ensigns [31] on the cruisers did it dawn on them that they were engaging the Navy of their country's traditional friend.[32] They did not like it — and neither did we; [33] but if the French

[30] The French guarded their own military communication frequencies and did not normally cover other channels or listen to Allied broadcasts.

[31] The battle ensign, since sailing days, has been a national flag of extra large size. The original purpose was partly defiance, partly to ensure identification by friendly forces.

[32] Told Maj. Rogers by Capt. Sticca (formerly of *Fougueux*) and other French naval officers at Casablanca 18 Mar. 1943. Rear Admiral Gervais de Lafond, in command of this force, who afterwards became a good friend to Admiral Hewitt, told him the same thing; he did not know, nor did Admiral Michelier know, when the sortie was ordered around 0800, "whose those ships were." There is no evidence that the Safi people heard the broadcast either; they were alerted from Casablanca.

[33] A gunner's mate was heard to say to his crew at the start of the action, "Come on, boys, let's pretend they're Japs!"

Navy chose to give battle, and oppose the landing, there was nothing to be done but shoot it out with them.

3. *The Battle for the Beaches*

a. Silencing Shore Batteries

Although Admiral Michelier at Casablanca disbelieved the presence of our American force off shore, he caused a preliminary *alerte* to be issued at 0130 November 8, and an *urgente* at 0227.[34] These messages apparently never reached Fedhala. Effective French resistance there did not begin until fifty minutes after our first boat waves had landed on the beaches.[35] For some time after the action began the naval garrison of the Batterie Pont Blondin knew not whether they were firing on Germans, British, or Americans.[36]

For those waiting on board the two cruisers and the screening destroyers while the transports unloaded, the period between midnight and 0500 was rather tense. "A spirit of restlessness and subdued eagerness was in evidence. All expressed their desire for action. None had any doubt as to our success in overcoming any opposition. It was a good sign." [37]

A few minutes after 0500 *Brooklyn* observed searchlights ashore, and almost simultaneously a spray of tracer bullets was seen in the midst of the transport area, followed by the crackle of machine-gun fire. A little French steamer, escorted by a 600-ton

[34] This appears in the radio log at Front de Mer, Safi, which we captured 8 Nov., and from the report by Capt. Deuve, commandant of the Safi garrison, to the Commanding General of the Marrakech Division, a copy of which was obtained after the surrender.

[35] Reports of two scout boat commanders and of the *Wood's* boat group commander state that the firing by our support boats on the searchlights was returned in the shape of heavy machine-gun fire, at times variously given between 0525 and 0540. This fire was ineffective. It appears to have bothered nobody but the *Carroll's* scout boat; and either it was not heard by the control destroyers or was considered to be of insufficient importance to warrant a "Batter Up!"

[36] The writer was told this 16 Nov. by one of the American Army officers who received the surrender of this French garrison; and so Col. E. C. Burkhart was told by the French themselves on 14 Nov.

[37] Report of Executive Officer of *Wilkes*, Lt. Comdr. F. Wolsietler.

chalutier called *Victoria*, both showing their running lights, had blundered in among the transports. Minesweeper *Hogan* was sent to investigate. She placed herself across the Frenchman's bows and ordered him to reverse engines. Instead of so doing, the little scrapper tried to ram *Hogan*, and answered the warning shot with a whiff of machine-gun fire. The sweeper then gave her a burst of point-blank 20-mm bullets that killed the gunnery officer and stopped *Victoria* dead. *Auk* put a prize crew on board, and that incident was closed.[38]

At about 0520, just after the first boat waves hit the beach, two searchlights, one from Cape Fedhala and the other from Sherki, shot up in the air.[39] General Eisenhower, in his broadcast following the President's message, had urged the French to turn their searchlights vertically as a token of welcome. So this portent raised a momentary expectation that there would be no resistance.[40] But not for long. What had happened was this: French sentries at the two shore batteries heard motors humming as the boat waves came in, and took them to belong to planes which the searchlights were trying to spot. Almost immediately the searchlights dropped, and moved nervously about pricking holes in the darkness, pausing a split second to illuminate a landing boat, and then passing to another object. After the lights had been on about five minutes, one of the armed support boats that was accompanying the waves to Beaches Red 2 and Blue 2 opened up on them with machine-gun fire, and out they went.[41] Again silence; but plenty of noise to follow.

A hazy day began to break faintly at six o'clock, dimly outlining the foothills of the Atlas and prominent objects ashore, such

[38] *Hogan* and *Tillman* Action Reports.
[39] The exact time is uncertain. *Ludlow* Action Report says the Cape light was seen "about 0500," and the Sherki one at 0515. Cdr. Durgin in *Wilkes* says one at 0520 and the other at 0530. On board *Brooklyn* we observed the Sherki searchlight illuminating a landing boat at 0522.
[40] There were some mutterings of "Hell, they ain't gonna fight!" But the general feeling was one of relief, because we had come across to fight Germans and Italians, not French.
[41] Sound clocked at 0525 on board *Leonard Wood* and *Brooklyn*; Action Report of Capt. McLean of *Wilkes* says 0530.

as the oil tanks on Cape Fedhala. First a machine-gun battery on the Cape, a few minutes later one of the main batteries there, and next the Sherki (Pont Blondin) battery [42] opened fire on our scout boats, landing craft, and troops ashore, and then on the control destroyers, which were still on the line of departure, dangerously near. Captain Emmet had remarked at the shore conference, before leaving, that it would be "worth two destroyers to knock out those guns on Sherki." *Murphy* and *Ludlow* gathered that this meant them — especially as *Murphy's* code name was "Dissolve"; but they had no intention of dissolving before they had done plenty of damage. No boat waves at that moment required their attention; so Commander Durgin in *Wilkes*, after giving *Ludlow* the order to open fire, directed all four destroyers under his command to proceed to their fire support stations. He then signaled by voice radio to Admiral Hewitt, "Firing from Fedhala and Sherki, BATTER UP!" [43]

That was the code word for local resistance to our forces having begun. By 0610 *Murphy* and *Ludlow* were returning the fire of Sherki, while *Wilkes* and *Swanson* took on Cape Fedhala.

Almost simultaneously at about 0620 every ship's bridge in the Center Attack Group heard Captain Emmet's familiar voice over radio telephone giving the long-anticipated command that put the attack plan into effect: "PLAY BALL!" [44]

Morning twilight was still very faint. The sky had clouded up and haze lay over the land. *Brooklyn* came in fast from her patrol area outside the transports to her fire support area, catapulted a spotting plane, shot off a spread of star shell that failed to pene-

[42] *Murphy* Action Report; *Ludlow* says both opened at 0608; Cdr. Durgin and Capt. Emmet clocked them at 0604. Sherki first opened with a 13.2-mm anti-aircraft gun on a support boat off Beach Red 3, so the French told Col. E. C. Burkhart at his inspection 14 Nov.
[43] *Brooklyn* intercepted this message at 0607.
[44] The "N3G3 Journal" of Admiral Hewitt's staff states that the "Play Ball!" was given by the Admiral to Capt. Emmet at 0613. I believe that this marks merely a suggestion that Capt. Emmet should give it, since the Captain, not the Admiral, was in tactical command of the Center Group. According to Capt. Shepard on board *Augusta*, CTF 34 inquired at 0615 as to why CTG 34.9 had not given "Play Ball," and at 0617 Capt. Emmet gave it. That was the way we understood it on board *Brooklyn*, with slightly different timing.

AA GUNS REPORTED
oil Storage
Tower
100 m.m. Gun Battery
& AA MG.
MG. or Light AA
oil Storage
CHURCH
CASINO.
HOTEL
MIRAMAR
POST AND
TELEGRAPH
OFFICE
Breakwaters
TOWN HALL
SENEGALESE
ENCAMPMENT

Royal Air Force Photos

Fedhala from the Air

Vertical photos taken by R.A.F. reconnaissance planes 14 September 1942, with legends added by photo interpreters. These, fitted together, were furnished to the fire support ships and spotter planes, in order to help target identification and prevent firing on churches and other civilian buildings. A part of Cape Fedhala, with its oil tanks, is seen at lower part of photo. The beaches shown are Red and Red 2. Hotel Miramar, headquarters of the German Armistice Commission, was an objective of the assault troops

Photos by Author

(LEFT) A burst of star shell over Sherki in dawn's early light
(RIGHT) U.S.S. *Brooklyn* fires a salvo at Sherki

Photo by Author

(LEFT) The Wadi Nefifikh and Beach Blue 2
(RIGHT) An undamaged gun of the Battery, 16 November

The Reduction of Batterie Pont Blondin (Sherki), 8 November 1942

trate the haze over Sherki, and at 0622 fired the first salvo from her main battery. This little corner of the world, so hushed and dark and silent for five hours, was now split with blinding gun flashes, shattered with machine-gun fire, shaken by the crash of heavy ordnance.

For some time the Sherki battery concentrated on *Murphy*, who was heard signaling, "This damn Turkey is getting our range . . . Someone help me polish him off . . . I've got to get to hell out!" No wonder, as the range was then around 5000 yards, practically point-blank for coast defense guns. As she retired, this brave new fighting ship (she had just been commissioned in June) received a hit in her starboard engine room which knocked that engine out and killed three men. She withdrew to make emergency repairs; but in the early afternoon her skipper, Lieutenant Commander Leonard W. Bailey, reported she was "ready for any mission at any speed."

Brooklyn was now making east-and-west runs of about three miles, at a range of 10,000 to 12,500 yards, firing furiously at the Sherki battery, the fall of shot being well spotted by her plane. At the western end of each run, she steamed right into the waves of landing boats that were collecting south of the *Joseph T. Dickman*, firing over their heads; one could lean over her bridge and see the faces of troops in the boats lighted up by gun flashes. This bombardment sufficed to perform a feat then unusual, the silencing[45] of a shore coast defense battery by naval gunfire. A direct hit was scored on one of the four guns, disabling it[46] and killing several members of the crew; after about forty-five minutes of firing, another shell hit the fire control station, destroying its stereoscopic range finder. In a bombardment lasting eighty-five minutes

[45] Not "knocking out," which is a different matter; three of the Sherki guns were intact at the end of the bombardment, and if their gunners had not been disheartened by the loss of their fire control building, and both burned and demoralized by bursts all around them, they might have continued serving the three guns by hand.

[46] Col. E. C. Burkhart of Admiral Hewitt's staff, who visited the battery 14 Nov., reported that this gun had its recoil cylinder perforated in two places by shell fragments, and the U.S. Army officer in charge when the writer inspected the site 16 Nov. reported it to be unusable.

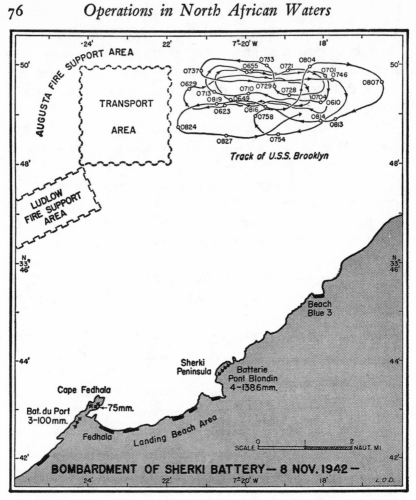

Track of U.S.S. *Brooklyn*

BOMBARDMENT OF SHERKI BATTERY— 8 NOV. 1942 —

Brooklyn fired 757 rounds of 6-inch, culminating at 0742 in two furious minutes of continuous rapid fire. Units of the 30th Infantry and 41st Field Artillery promptly moved in and received the surrender of the garrison, which had taken refuge in the one concrete building that was still intact — the lavatory.[47]

[47] It subsequently appeared that this bombardment was probably unnecessary. Batterie Pont Blondin was temporarily commanded by a French petty officer who had no stomach for bombardment, and he was negotiating for surrender with an officer of the 30th Infantry. He was, to be sure, firing at the destroyers while he dickered. When the *Brooklyn* opened up, shore-to-ship communication had not been established, so there was no way to inform her that a parley was going on.

With the batteries at the other end of the beaches, on Cape Fedhala, we were less fortunate. The Cape was the principal oil storage place in Morocco, containing about twenty cylindrical storage tanks for fuel oil and gasoline. Most of them were long since drained dry; but that we did not know, and wished to conserve the oil for our own use. Both the Batterie du Port of 100-mm guns and the two 75-mm near the northeastern end were emplaced very close to these tanks; hence the fire support ships assigned to Cape Fedhala could not afford to deliver a shower of shellfire such as that with which *Brooklyn* overwhelmed the Sherki. In addition to the main batteries, there were two groups of twin 13.2-mm (.50-caliber) anti-aircraft guns, one on the end of the harbor jetty and the other on the neck of the Cape. All four batteries gave our troops considerable trouble on the beaches, especially on Red 3 and Blue; and the 75s sank one of the *Jefferson's* support boats that rashly attempted to silence it with machine-gun fire.

Destroyers *Wilkes* and *Swanson* were the first to take Cape Fedhala under bombardment, around 0615–0625, after they had left their control stations. One of them hit a tank, said to be the only one on the Cape containing any oil, and it burned with a heavy black smoke. *Augusta* with her 8-inch guns came into the picture at 0710, expended 72 rounds at an opening range of 12,000 yards, and silenced the Batterie du Port at 0723, but made no direct hits. About an hour later the battery resumed fire on the beaches, and checked after a few rounds from the destroyers. Silence again until 1005, when the same battery opened a harassing fire on the beaches. U.S.S. *Swanson* and then *Edison* replied, but broke off on orders from Captain Emmet, owing to a report (subsequently ascertained to be false) that they had fired into our troops and killed townspeople. Captain Heffernan, of Destroyer Squadron 13, protested over voice radio that the Batterie du Port was still firing. "I see the shells landing among our men on the beaches. May I fire?"

(Capt. Shepard's Report to Cinclant p. 11.) The Report of the Commanding General 3rd Division states that the surrender was effected at 0730, twelve minutes before the bombardment ceased.

The answer was "Yes!" Heffernan passed on the privilege to *Wilkes*, who was ahead of his flagship *Bristol* and on a more favorable bearing to commence fire. *Wilkes* seemed slow to comply. Consequently Captain Heffernan again used voice radio to ascertain whether she had received and understood the squadron commander's previous order. But *Wilkes's* apparent hesitation was due only to her anxiety to get a good "solution." She opened up with a terrific volume of precise fire, and silenced the battery with four salvos. Yet at 1035 it reopened; *Bristol* then took it under fire at a range of 7200 yards. About an hour later, when the Army was ready to move in, it asked the destroyers to lay off; the platoon that took possession of the Batterie du Port found the fire control shot away, but the guns serviceable with plenty of ammunition remaining.[48]

The two fixed 75s on the point of Cape Fedhala gave as much trouble as the larger battery, and were even harder to find, as they were cleverly concealed in a gun pit among the oil tanks and rocks. At 1005 they obtained two hits on *Palmer*, who replied and knocked them out. A fragment of shell entered the muzzle of one 75, and the recoil cylinder of the other was shattered.[49]

That ended enemy ground resistance at Fedhala. Only about two hundred French troops, mostly Senegalese, were stationed there, and they surrendered gladly. But there was a strafing attack by nine enemy fighters on Beach Blue at 1055, again at noon, and several times in the afternoon.

b. The Landings Analyzed

Captain Emmet, when satisfied that the shore batteries were being well taken care of, began about 1000 to bring his transports closer inshore to facilitate debarkation. At 1200 *Miantonomah* commenced laying a mine field to the eastward, as protection. "The

---

[48] Action Reports of *Augusta*, and of Desron 13, with which individual destroyers' Action Reports are included; Report of Col. E. C. Burkhart, who visited the site 14 Nov. 1942; conversations with members of the party.
[49] Capt. Shepard's Report; Col. Burkhart's Report.

boys sure were glad to get those mines over the side!" said her skipper, Commander "Speed" Edwards. "We laid 'em steaming twelve knots — never did it at more than six knots before." [50] The transports moved in still closer at 1542, to an anchorage covering the old line of departure, and there remained until after the torpedoings on 12 November. There four of them still lie, on the bottom.

By 1700 on D-day 8 November, 7,750 officers and men, almost 40 per cent of the 19,870 embarked on the twelve transports and three cargo vessels of this Center Attack Group, had been landed. Percentages do not, however, tell the story. The four assault transports of the front line, and *Joseph Hewes*, had 90 per cent of their troops ashore, while eight other vessels had hardly landed a man; and the total score was far behind schedule. Expenditure of landing craft explains most of the difference between plan and performance. Inexperience, darkness and the necessity of landing on a falling tide were the principal causes of the loss of boats; but even after the tide turned, at 0744, many boats were abandoned temporarily by their crews when strafed by enemy planes or shot at by the guns on Cape Fedhala. Salvage facilities were inadequate, and if help was not forthcoming when the tide came in and a stranded boat floated, it broached-to and rolled over in the surf. Even more damage was done by boats crowding together on the beaches, so that waves banged them one against the other. Stranded boats became targets for enemy gunners, and a number were lost on rocky ledges.

Altogether, between 137 and 160 out of 347 landing boats in the Center Attack Group, 40 to 46 per cent of the total, were expended, [51] the great majority of them on D-day; and this loss

[50] *Auk* and *Tillman*, while screening *Miantonomah* during this maneuver, engaged a French armed corvette *W–43* which was conducting a convoy of small French fishermen and merchantmen along the coast. The *W–43* and three others beached themselves east of Sherki; three more were made prize of. (*Tillman* Action Report.)

[51] The larger computation is by Lt. Col. G. I. Cummings USMC. (Conversation 1 Dec. 1942.) This includes a few lost on 9 and 10 Nov. Ens. J. J. Martin counted 114 total wrecks on the beaches, and 25 or 30 that could have been saved, on the morning of 9 Nov., but this did not include those stranded east of Sherki or west

slowed up all landing operations subsequent to the initial assault waves. Only two or three of these were destroyed by direct hits from enemy batteries.

In some respects, the daylight landings were not so well done, relatively, as the initial ones in darkness. Boat crews who had been up all the previous night, with only catch-as-catch-can meals, began to feel the effects of fatigue. While the blinker lights in the darkness made excellent guides to the beaches, it was not so easy in daylight to tell one from the other, and landing boat compasses developed a new deviation every trip. One battalion landing team was deposited on three different beaches, greatly to the annoyance of its commanding officer.

Admiral Hewitt's operation plan called for opening the small harbor at Fedhala as soon as resistance ceased, which occurred about noon on 8 November. There was no sense in continuing to land troops and supplies on all four beaches, in a rising sea. Accordingly, the beachmaster, Commander J. W. Jamison, ordered all boats to land either in the harbor or on Beach Red, where the surf was least. Lateral beach communication was so slow and difficult that this order did not reach all officers concerned before daylight next day. Commander Jamison's vigorous efforts to direct boat traffic were not greatly appreciated at the time, and there were mutterings of "what we'd do to that fellow if we had him in the Army." Later, General Patton acknowledged that "Red" Jamison had "saved the whole goddam operation."

Naturally, the Army commented unfavorably on the manner in which the Navy put it ashore. Much of this criticism was justified,

---

of Cape Fedhala. (*Thomas Jefferson* Action Report, Enclosure O.) Capt. Shepard's Report p. 28 says that 172 stranded craft were counted on the Fedhala beaches about noon 9 Nov., but some of these were operational and others were salvaged. Capt. Mullinnix reported to Capt. Emmett at 0900 Nov. 10 that 162 (including 18 tank lighters) had been counted on the beaches, and 23 more were said to be stranded east of Sherki. (Capt. Emmet's Narrative of Events.) A computation made in a War Dept. Services of Supply Report ("Lessons Learned from Recent Amphibious Operations in North Africa" 12 Feb. 1943, Annex G) states that 137 boats out of 347 used (40 per cent) were "damaged or destroyed" at Fedhala, and 216 out of 629 (34 per cent) for the entire landing operations of the Western Task Force.

but some of it was based on lack of appreciation of the difficulties. Criticism at once severe and authoritative came from within the Navy. "The dire need of better training of boat crews was everywhere apparent," was the considered opinion of Admiral Hewitt's staff;[52] but everyone knew that before they sailed. The report of one transport officer, Commander H. Biesemeier of the *Carroll*, shows wherein the training was most lacking: —

It was noted from the time that landing boats and their crews reported for duty that instead of trained crews we had only a figurative crew. They were unskilled in handling their boats, they were unlearned in even the simplest elements of seamanship such as the rules of the road. . . . Some attention had been paid to the art of landing through surf and retracting again, [but] the supreme test of their training was made under conditions *where only experts could hope to succeed part of the time.* . . . Boats that had been broached were abandoned at the critical time when a little judgment might have saved them. And having been abandoned to the mercy of the surf, soon were hopelessly battered to pieces, the crews seeking safety in flight away from the beach, in some instances encouraged by the soldiers that had come ashore in the same boat, in other instances because there were no hopes, in their own minds at least, of salvaging the boat.[53]

The same officer pointed out that the early loss of landing craft resulted in emergency demands on the transports for supplies and equipment that broke the orderly sequence of unloading a combat-loaded ship, and caused time-consuming shifting of cargo and rummaging in holds.

Statements to the effect that there was "no doctrine of boat salvage" in the Amphibious Force Atlantic Fleet, and that no salvage efforts were made, are unfounded.[54] Admiral Hewitt's staff had a doctrine and devoted much thought to boat salvage, and a few of the larger LCMs were fitted up as boat salvage craft with specially

[52] CTF 34 staff notes, compiled by Capt. E. A. Mitchell and others on board *Augusta* on way home.

[53] *Charles Carroll* Action Report, endorsed by Capt. A. G. Coman, Comtransdiv 3.

[54] This refers especially to the O.N.I. Combat Narrative *Landings in North Africa* p. 13, and note 14, quoted (without mentioning the source) from a letter of Gen. Patton to Gen. McNair.

trained crews. The real want was lack of facilities to repair or assist landing craft when damaged or stranded.[55] That duty had been left to Admiral Hall's Sea Frontier forces, but by the time his organization got into action, after 11 November, the natives had picked clean every stranded boat. Even so, the proportion of boats lost in the Western Task Force compares very favorably with those of the Center and Eastern Task Forces where the crews did not have to contend with a nine-foot tide. In later amphibious operations a Landing Ship Dock or specially rigged Landing Craft Repair Ship was assigned to the task of keeping boats operating, and special repair and salvage units were set up ashore. Other recommendations of Admiral Hewitt, such as powering all landing craft with diesel engines, were carried out before the next amphibious operation.

Most of the senior naval officers present thought that the bluejackets and coastguardsmen who composed the landing boats' crews, considering their lack of combat experience and very brief training, deserved high praise for courage, persistence and intelligence. There were unsung heroes among them. When one wave of landing craft came under heavy fire from Cape Fedhala, and a boat was hit, the others hesitated, wondering whether they should not turn back. At this juncture the coxswain of one landing craft had his bow man break out a large American ensign and hold it aloft, while he stood up defiantly at the wheel, and led the wave in to the beach.[56]

The Army afforded little help in unloading. In the training exercises in Chesapeake Bay, Army shore parties had been provided to unload the boats, according to the standard procedure of the Amphibious Force. Landing craft crews were used to having soldiers rush down as soon as they hit the beach, and hustle ashore supplies and equipment. In the excitement and bustle of

[55] Admiral Hewitt's Report on Material and Logistics 27 Nov. 1942.
[56] Told by Cdr. Jamison, who observed the incident. The writer encountered some veterans of these landing craft crews at Saipan in 1944. They said that the Fedhala landings were much the toughest they had experienced, because of darkness and the surf.

Landing craft headed for Fedhala Beach. LCP(R) on left; LCM with the high ramp

Transport debarking troops with boat waves circling near by

Landing Operations, Moroccan Coast

Looking east on Beach Red 3 at 1100 November 8

Wrecked Higgins boats on Beach Red, 9 November

Views on the Fedhala Beaches

landing at Fedhala, this indispensable aid to orderly landing and prompt retraction was largely forgotten.[57]

The writer, after reading dozens of reports, hearing scores of individual stories, seeing the boats in action, and taking part in several subsequent amphibious operations in the Pacific, concludes that the difference in performance between boat crews of different transports is so glaring that no generalization is possible. A just conclusion is not to be reached by compiling a list of accidents and incidents, but by considering what was accomplished, within the framework of what was possible. By that token, the landing at Fedhala was to the credit of the Amphibious Force Atlantic Fleet.

The Army, too, learned a great deal about amphibious warfare on the beaches of Fedhala. Perhaps the "most definite and conclusive lesson" was the danger of overloading troops who have to go over the side of a transport into a tossing landing craft, and debark on a surf-swept beach. "The individual officer and soldier was woefully overloaded," says one Army report. "Men were so burdened by weapons, ammunition and equipment as to be virtually immobilized." Several soldiers were drowned in the landings simply because they were unable to regain their feet after being rolled over by a wave. The beaches were strewn with heavy water-soaked equipment discarded by the troops so that they could march and fight.[58] Here again the relatively slight enemy opposition on the beaches was a godsend to the Western Task Force.

General Patton, pleasantly surprised to have his prediction dis-

[57] "Unloading operations at Fedhala and at Casablanca were unsatisfactory in that the Army personnel, excepting the Army QM detail attached to the ship, which was industrious, efficient and capable, evidenced a marked indifference to their responsibilities in the matter. Assault gear hand loaded into the initial assault wave boats, at the sacrifice of valuable time, was abandoned in the boats when they landed and the gear was unloaded by boat's crews. Boat crews received no assistance in unloading supplies landed later at the beaches and additional men had to be sent into the beach with each loaded boat to assist in unloading them." Capt. Chauncey R. Crutcher's Action Report of *Thomas Jefferson* p. 16. This point was emphasized in conversation by Capt. W. P. O. Clarke, who trained the boat crews.

[58] War Dept. HQ Services of Supply "Lessons Learned from Recent Amphibious Operations in North Africa" 12 Feb. 1943, Annex C-2.

proved by a landing at the target and on time, and not altogether displeased with his grandstand view of a naval battle, was disposed to be generous in praising the Navy's service to his troops. "I have personally read all reports," he stated after the operation, and "practically all of the defects mentioned by Sub-Task Force Commanders resulted not from lack of forethought . . . but on account of lack of time. It will be noted that every branch except the combat troops considered itself slighted either in numbers or in vehicles. This will invariably be the case, because in a landing operation, fighting men must take precedence over everything else." [59]

c. Varied Adventures

Some of the landing teams that missed the right beach had strange adventures. Four landing craft carrying 113 officers and men of a Headquarters Military Police company took off from transport *William P. Biddle* after nightfall and missed Beach Yellow, where they were supposed to land. Two of the boats entered the roadstead of Casablanca and hailed a French patrol vessel, thinking she was one of ours, to ask their way. She opened up with machine guns, killed the M.P. company commander, sank both boats, and took the survivors prisoner. [60]

The most fantastic adventure befell Ensign Harry A. Storts and a crew of coastguardsmen from the transport *Joseph T. Dickman*. With a support boat borrowed from another transport they were trying, shortly after 0400, to escort three amphtracs to Beach Blue 2. These were experimental versions of the LVT, improved models of which in 1943–1945 served many an amphibious operation in the Pacific. The LVTs were supposed to get themselves and

[59] U.S. Army "Compilation of Reports on Lessons of Operation Torch" 16 Jan. 1943 p. 31.
[60] Details on this episode, which is not related in any of the Action Reports and was greatly enlarged by "scuttlebutt," were given the writer by Capt. P. R. Glutting of U.S.S. *William P. Biddle*, in a letter of 25 Sept. 1943. The *Biddle* was in her correct position at the time the boats left her side, and gave the coxswains the correct course. The other two boats also got lost, but returned to the ship.

their crews ashore under their own power. But they frequently broke down, and had drifted so far away from their destination by daylight that Ensign Storts was ordered to conduct them back along the coast and to land at the nearest available beach. He joined forces with two landing craft carrying anti-aircraft half-track batteries. They picked out a beach some ten or twelve miles east of Sherki and landed there at 0945, being strafed by an enemy plane during the process. Behind this beach were stationed French troops, who made their presence felt at once. Ensign Storts's landing force, which amounted to thirty-two Army and nine Navy and Coast Guard personnel, dug in, set up their "Buck Rogers" guns, and stood siege. French strafing planes appeared every half hour until dark, and killed five men, but the survivors used their guns to such good purpose that several French armored cars were driven off. After dark, two men put off in a rubber boat to intercept a destroyer, while Ensign Storts and four others set out on foot for Fedhala, hoping to make contact with the American landing forces. The twenty-nine men left behind shifted their position from the beach to a near-by concrete pigpen. "That pen sure looked good," said one of the coastguardsmen; "we crowded right in with the pigs and didn't mind the company at all." And there they held out for two days, until their ammunition was spent.

The rubber boat boys never caught their destroyer, but eventually returned to the Fleet. Ensign Storts and his party, what with losing their way and taking cover from French planes, took Sunday night and all day Monday to reach an Army command post near Fedhala. After resting they were provided by the 30th Infantry with a half-track, a 75-mm gun and a rescue squad. Off they rolled Tuesday morning 10 November guided by Ensign Storts. On the way they captured ten French soldiers and took them along, only to find that those they were seeking to rescue on the beach had themselves been captured. So back they turned toward Fedhala, everyone on board the half-track. On the way they were neatly ambushed by some 150 native troops led by French officers, who wounded or killed everyone in the party, including most of the French prisoners. The captors conducted surviving Americans to a French first-aid station at Bouznika, where their wounds were dressed. A French officer then loaded them on a farm truck, with the red cross painted on the hood, in order to take them to Rabat for questioning. One mile from Bouznika the truck was strafed and disabled by an American plane, which did not see the red cross in time, and three more of the French were killed. The survivors walked back to Bouznika, carrying their wounded, and were then shipped by truck to Boulhaut, fourteen miles inland. Next day — Armistice Day — a man came in saying that the fighting was over. A priest conducted Ensign Storts and one other survivor of the original amphibian party to Fedhala, where they reported on board ship. Such are the hazards of amphibious warfare.[61]

Of the numerous adventures enjoyed by Army landing teams, two will suffice. One, whose objective was the railroad bridge over the Wadi Nefifikh, halted an early morning train and pulled off it seventy-five very surprised French soldiers going on leave to Casablanca. A unit of the 30th Infantry that landed before daylight made straight for the Hotel Miramar, headquarters of the German Armistice Commission. According to one story, the Germans were about to make a getaway in cars, and all but one of the four officers, as well as six enlisted men, were captured in the hotel courtyard. According to another story the Germans were captured while running across the golf course in order to hop a plane.[62] They were sent on board the transport *Ancon* and brought to the United States: the first German prisoners to be taken by United States forces on land.

One of the German cars came in handy for a plan that Colonel Wilbur of General Patton's staff had very much at heart. The French General Béthouart had been a fellow student of his at the famous École de Guerre. Assuming that Béthouart had the military

[61] Ens. Storts's narrative is enclosed in Action Report of *Joseph T. Dickman*. Another version, told by the survivor James J. Berardi, is in *Christian Science Monitor* 18 Dec. 1942.

[62] The first version was told by General Patton next day; the second appears in Capt. Shepard's Report. The head of the commission, General von Wulish, escaped.

command at Casablanca (which was incorrect), Wilbur thought that if he could only contact his *ancien camarade* and explain matters, the French would join us instead of resisting. Accordingly he went ashore with the assault troops, commandeered a captured German car and, with a soldier as chauffeur and an impressed guide, dashed through the lines to the French military headquarters at Casablanca. There he was coldly informed that the Navy was in command. This gallant escapade seems mildly ridiculous in view of the fact that Béthouart had been working on our side for weeks — a good example of the faulty coöperation between American civilian agencies and the armed forces.

Despite all difficulties, in which inexperience was the major factor, 7,750 troops and a good deal of equipment were landed at Fedhala on D-day, 8 November; and by nightfall Major General Anderson's 3rd Division had attained all objectives set down in the attack plan. American troops had control of the town, the harbor, bridges over the rivers at each end of the area and the high ridges that commanded the town and beaches. Yet the story of this debarkation is only part of the picture, even at Fedhala. Twice on 8 November while the landings were going on, the French Navy at Casablanca tried to break up the operation, and this they could easily have done but for the quick and effective work of the United States Navy.

NOTE ON THE FRENCH CHAIN OF COMMAND

The Service Historique de la Marine have clarified this. General Juin was C. in C. of all French forces in North Africa. Under him were three theater commanders: General Noguès for Morocco, Atlantic side; General Koeltz for the rest of Morocco and Algeria, and General Barre for Tunisia. Under General Noguès were four sector commanders, of which General Henry-Martin commanded the Safi-Mogador, Vice Admiral Michelier the Casablanca, and General Dody the North Morocco sectors. The principle of unity of command over all arms pertained in each sector and in each area; but Michelier was dependent directly on the Admiralty at Vichy in respect of his command over naval vessels.

CHAPTER IV

The Naval Battle of Casablanca

8 November 1942

1. *The Carrier-based Planes*[1]

FROM the moment when it was light enough to launch planes, until all enemy resistance ceased, the carrier-based aircraft of the Navy showed the utmost fight and aggressiveness. U.S.S. *Ranger*, the one big carrier in Task Force 34, took station some thirty miles northwest of Casablanca and began shoving 'em off at 0615 when it was still quite dark. Nine Wildcats of her Fighter Squadron 9 (Lieutenant Commander John Raby) received their "Batter Up!" from anti-aircraft fire when over the Rabat and Rabat-Salé airdromes, headquarters of the French air forces in Morocco. Without loss to themselves, they destroyed seven grounded planes on the one field, and fourteen bombers on the other. Four planes in their second flight, which took off at 0845, shot down an enemy plane. In their third flight that day they destroyed seven enemy Dewoitine 520s fueling on the Port Lyautey field, but lost one plane with Ensign T. M. Wilhoite. The fourth flight, taking off at 1145, found no enemy to the eastward. The fifth, departing at 1300, strafed shore batteries; on the sixth, which began at 1515, four planes strafed four French destroyers while five planes strafed and bombed an anti-aircraft battery near Casablanca.

Fighter Squadron 41, taking off from *Ranger* at 0700, made straight for Les Cazes airfield near Casablanca, which it found to be patrolled by ten Dewoitine 520s and six Curtis 75-As.[2] In the ensuing dogfight three of the former and five of the latter were shot down, and fourteen planes were destroyed on the ground. Four Wildcats failed to return. Later in the day the same squadron made several more flights, destroyed grounded planes on airdromes, and strafed the French destroyers (effectively their officers admitted) when they first sortied from Casablanca.

Ranger's SBD squadron, consisting of eighteen Dauntless dive-bombers, was orbiting 10,000 feet in the air over Casablanca by 0700, waiting for the "Play Ball!" With the *Jean Bart* and anti-aircraft batteries on the harbor jetties throwing up everything they had, these planes bombed the submarine basin in the inner harbor, as well as various installations.[3] They were recovered in time for a brief rest before being sent out again to stop the cruiser *Primauguet* when she sortied at 1000.

Suwannee, in the meantime, commanded by that famous Cherokee Indian Captain "Jock" Clark, maintained combat and anti-submarine air patrol for the Center Group. Her only trouble was the prevalent light wind on D-day. Frequently she had to seek areas where ruffled water indicated a better breeze.[4] Most of her planes were recovered with only a 22-knot wind over the deck, which would have precluded flight operations in time of peace. Her Avengers joined those of *Ranger* in bombing missions.

These are typical examples of the unremitting activity of the Navy carrier-based planes. There were probably 168 French planes available in Morocco on the date of our arrival; 172 of ours were brought in by the four carriers.[5] These shot down about 20 enemy planes in the air, and destroyed a considerable number on the ground. Prompt and effective aggressiveness of the Naval air arm,

[2] Elsewhere these French fighter planes are designated P-36, or H-75.

[3] Wordell and Seiler *"Wildcats" Over Casablanca* pp. 42–46 contains an excellent account of the adventures and feelings of individual *Ranger* pilots.

[4] Presumably *Suwannee's* maximum speed through the water was the same as *Santee's*, 17.8 knots.

[5] Operation Plan 5–42, Annex A. The 76 Army planes on the *Chenango* are not included, as they, being land-based planes to operate from an airfield, took no part in the fighting.

combined with the fact that a considerable part of the French air force welcomed the landing, made this aspect of the Battle of Casablanca rather one-sided.

Air protection to the landing forces was far from complete; it never can be. At least five times on 8 November French fighter planes flew over the Fedhala beaches and strafed our troops; and, on the ninth, high-level bombers made fruitless passes at ships and beaches.[6] Yet, on the whole, the air opposition was very well taken care of. No enemy aircraft interfered with spotting planes from battleships and cruisers, and no air bombs hit the transports. The value of aircraft to protect amphibious operations was conclusively demonstrated; and it was immensely heartening to the Army to see our own planes overhead instead of those with enemy markings. Moreover, in addition to destroying and driving off enemy planes, the naval aviators delivered effective strafing and bombing attacks on French warships and shore batteries in the naval combats of 8 and 10 November.

Admiral McWhorter compiled this table[7] of the air operations under his command from 8 to 11 November inclusive: —

		RANGER	SANTEE	SUWANNEE	SANGAMON
Number of combat sorties ...		496	144	255	183
Number of bombs expended ..		952	96	66	237
Thousands of rounds of .30 and					
.50-cal. ammunition expended		120.9	75.3	8.8	27.2
Planes lost or missing, combat and operational	F4F–4	12	10	3	0
	SBD–3	3	4	0	2
	TBF–1	0	7	2	1
Planes on hand 12 November	F4F–4	42	4	26	12
	SBD–3	15	5	0	7
	TBF–1	1	1	7	8

[6] Several of the Action and other Reports state that this, and other bomber squadrons that attacked us, were German. This was not correct. The Axis air forces were too heavily engaged in Algeria to bother us in Morocco, and there is no evidence of German or Italian planes taking part in the operations on that coast, although a few Heinkel bombers and Junkers transport planes were observed grounded at Les Cazes. *"Wildcats" Over Casablanca* p. 61.

[7] Summary of 23 Nov. 1942. Operational losses before the eighth or after 11 Nov. not included.

Thus, 44 out of 172 Navy planes brought in by the carriers were expended in four days. Most of the pilots and crewmen were recovered alive.

2. *The Opening Bombardment*[8]

The Naval Battle of Casablanca was an old-fashioned fire-away-Flannagan between warships, with a few torpedo attacks by the enemy, and air attacks by us, thrown in. Lasting from dawn almost until late afternoon 8 November, it developed out of an action that commenced before sunrise between French batteries in Casablanca Harbor and airplanes of Rear Admiral "Ike" Giffen's Covering Group.

This group consisted of battleship *Massachusetts* on her shakedown cruise, heavy cruisers *Tuscaloosa* and *Wichita*, screened by destroyers of Captain Don P. Moon's Squadron 8, *Wainwright*, *Mayrant*, *Rhind* and *Jenkins*. Their mission, besides covering the entire Task Force against a possible sortie by the formidable French ships in Dakar, was to contain the enemy vessels in Casablanca Harbor, destroy them if and when they showed fight, and neutralize shore batteries in or near Casablanca.

During the approach on 7 November the Covering Group steamed on a course about ten miles southwest of the Center Attack Group, in the general direction of Casablanca. Naval tradition, since time immemorial, requires the "skipper" to make a speech to his men before going into battle; nowadays it is done over the ship's loudspeaker system instead of by straight voice or speaking trumpet. Accordingly at 1415 November 7 this message from Admiral Giffen was repeated by the commanding officer of each ship: —

[8] Principal sources: (1) Admiral Giffen's Action Report incorporating those of other ships of the Covering Group, 19 Nov. 1942; (2) information obtained between 12 and 20 Nov. from French naval officers and from an inspection of such French naval vessels as were still afloat, by Maj. Francis M. Rogers USMCR, assistant Intelligence Officer on Admiral Hewitt's staff, incorporated in a report headed "Naval Engagements"; (3) *Bulletin of Ordnance Information* No. 2–43, 30 June 1943.

The time has now come to prove ourselves worthy of the trust placed in us by our Nation. If circumstances force us to fire upon the French, once our victorious ally, let it be done with the firm conviction that we are striking not at the French people, but at the men who prefer Hitler's slavery to freedom. If we fight, hit hard and break clean. There is glory enough for us all. Good luck. Go with God.

To which Captain Whiting of the *Massachusetts* added: —

We commissioned the *Massachusetts* only six months ago; never have I seen a more responsive and hard-working ship's company than this one. You have met every demand I have made. We have the finest ship's spirit possible. We are *ready*. If it becomes our duty to open fire tomorrow, never forget the motto of the Commonwealth of Massachusetts whose name we proudly bear. That motto is: *Ense Petit Placidam Sub Libertate Quietem*, With the Sword She Seeks Peace under Liberty.[9] If we wield the sword, do so with all the strength in this mighty ship to destroy quickly and completely.

At 2215 November 7 Admiral Giffen's group turned away to the southwestward, and during the night steamed over a trapezoidal course whose base ran parallel to the coastline, about twenty-one miles off shore. After completing the last corner of the trapezoid at 0515 November 8, the big ships continued on a 168° course to the eighteen-fathom shoal bearing 14 miles NW by N from El Hank Light, turned westerly and at 0610 proceeded to catapult nine planes for spotting and anti-submarine patrol. The shore batteries at Fedhala were already opening fire, but Admiral Giffen was too far away to hear the report. He caught Admiral Hewitt's "Play Ball in Center" over the wireless telephone at 0626, but this did not apply to the Covering Group.[10]

[9] This motto, part of one composed by the English republican Algernon Sidney in the seventeenth century, was adopted by the Commonwealth of Massachusetts during the American Revolution.

[10] A spotter plane reported gunfire along Fedhala beaches at 0629. "Play Ball, all stations" was received on board *Massachusetts* from Admiral Hewitt at 0641, but this was modified to "Play Ball, Center Group only" at 0647. Following orders, Admiral Hewitt did not wish to force resistance in any area that was still quiet. Admiral Giffen's Report of 19 Nov., Enclosure E; *Tuscaloosa* Action Report, Enclosure I.

Battleship *Massachusetts*

Heavy Cruiser *Tuscaloosa*

(BELOW) Light Cruiser *Brooklyn* and Escort Carrier *Suwannee*

Victor Ships in the Battle of Casablanca

Admiral Hewitt and General Patton watching the battle from flag bridge,
U.S.S. *Augusta*

General Patton and Rear Admiral Hall go ashore in a crash boat

Gaudium Certaminis

Catapulting planes from a cruiser or battleship in early morning twilight is one of the finest sights in the modern Navy. The plane, poised on the catapult, snorts blue fire from its twin exhausts. The ship maneuvers so that the plane will shoot into the wind. Flag signals are made from the bridge and rhythmic arm signals from the plane dispatcher on the fantail. A nod from the pilot, and the plane rushes headlong down the catapult like some hagridden diver going overboard. Just as it leaves the skids, a loud crack of the explosive charge is heard. The plane falls a few yards towards the water, then straightens out and flies off and away.

Immediately after launching their planes the *Massachusetts*, *Wichita* and *Tuscaloosa* ran up battle ensigns, bent on twenty-five knots, and assumed battle formation. The four destroyers steamed in a half-moon about 3000 yards ahead of the flagship, which was followed in column by the two cruisers at 1000-yard intervals, their "long, slim 8-inch guns projecting in threes from the turrets, like rigid fingers of death pointing to the object of their wrath with inexorable certainty." [11] At 0640, when the formation had reached a position bearing about west northwest from Casablanca, distant 18,000 yards from Batterie El Hank and 20,000 yards from battleship *Jean Bart's* berth in the harbor, it began an easterly run, holding the same range. Ten minutes later, one of the flagship's spotting planes reported two submarines standing out of Casablanca Harbor, and at 0651 radioed: "There's an anti-aircraft battery opening up on me from beach. One burst came within twelve feet. Batter up!" Another spotting plane encountered "bandits" at 0652 and signaled: "Am coming in on starboard bow with couple hostile aircraft on my tail. Pick 'em off — I am the one in front!" [12] The big ships opened up on these planes with their 5-inch batteries at 0701, and shot one down. [13] The other retired; and almost simultaneously battleship *Jean Bart* and El Hank commenced firing. The coast defense guns straddled *Massachusetts* with their first salvo, and five or

[11] Quoted from the highly literary War Diary of Crudiv 7 compiled by Lt. Cdr. F. A. Storm USNR.
[12] *Massachusetts* Action Report, Enclosure A.
[13] Same and *Wichita* War Diary.

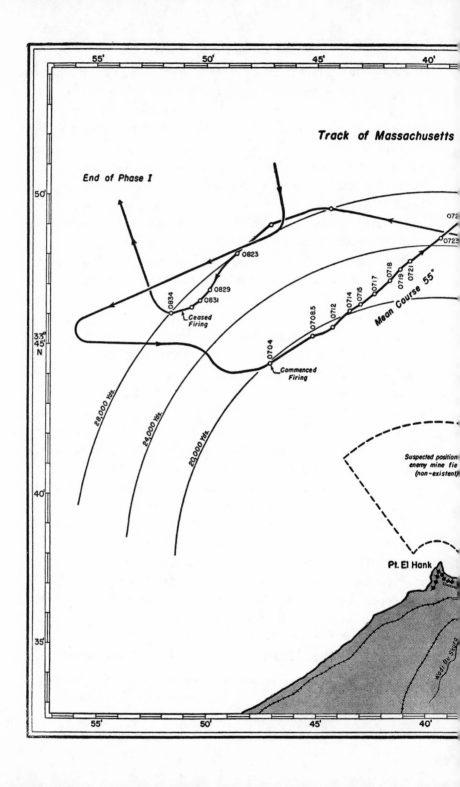

Track of Massachusetts

End of Phase I

50'

0823

0829
0831
0834
Ceased
Firing

0704
Commenced
Firing

0708.5
0712
0714
0715
0717
0718
0719
0721
0723

Mean Course 55°

072

33°
45'
N

28,000 Yds.

24,000 Yds.

20,000 Yds.

40'

Suspected position
enemy mine fie
(non-existent)

Pt. El Hank

35'

Wadi Bu Sheba

55'   50'   45'   40'

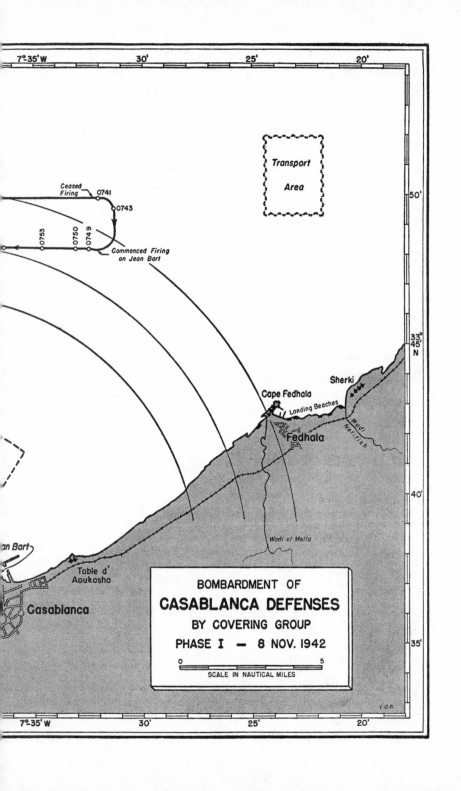

7°35'W   30'   25'   20'

Transport Area

Ceased Firing   0741
0743
0753   0750   0749
Commenced Firing on Jean Bart

50'

33°45'N

Sherki

Cape Fedhala
Landing Beaches
Fedhala
Wadi Nefifikh

40'

Wadi el Mella

Jean Bart
Table d' Aoukasha
Casablanca

BOMBARDMENT OF
CASABLANCA DEFENSES
BY COVERING GROUP
PHASE I — 8 NOV. 1942

0   5
SCALE IN NAUTICAL MILES

35'

7°35'W   30'   25'   20'

six splashes from *Jean Bart* fell about 600 yards ahead of her star-board bow. Admiral Giffen lost no time in giving his group the "Play Ball!" *Massachusetts* let go her first 16-inch salvo at 0704. Actually *Jean Bart* was shooting at the cruisers astern; she never saw, or at least never recognized, *Massachusetts* during the action; so our mighty battlewagon making her fighting début was reported to the Germans via Vichy as a "pocket battleship."

Jean Bart, the newest battleship of the French Navy, almost 800 feet long and of about the same tonnage as *Massachusetts*, had never been completed. Although unable to move from her berth along-side the Môle du Commerce in Casablanca, her four 15-inch guns in the forward turret and her modern range-finding equipment [14] made her a formidable shore battery. On El Hank promontory, just west of the harbor, was a battery of four 194-mm (approxi-mately 8-inch) coast defense guns and another of four 138-mm guns facing easterly. On the other side of the harbor toward Fed-hala, at a place called Table d'Aoukasha, was a somewhat antiquated coast defense battery. We had assumed that the approaches would be mined, but no mines had been laid. The sea approaches to Casa-blanca were, however, nicely covered by gunfire.

For several minutes *Massachusetts* and *Tuscaloosa* concentrated on *Jean Bart*, commencing fire at a range of 24,000 yards and open-ing out to 29,000.[15] *Wichita* opened fire on El Hank at 0706 at a range of 21,800 yards, using her own plane spot. *Massachusetts* fired nine 16-inch salvos of six to nine shots each at *Jean Bart*, and made five hits. One penetrated an empty magazine. A second pene-trated below the after control station, completely wrecking it, and the nose made a large hole below the waterline. The third and

14 Capt. Barthes of *Jean Bart* informed Maj. Rogers that she had no radar, only two 8-meter CL range finders temporarily installed; and four radar antennae observed were not operational.

15 Rear Admiral Stanford C. Hooper stated at a meeting of the Institute of Radio Engineers 28 Jan. 1943, as reported in the New York *Times* next day, that the *Massachusetts* got home a salvo on *Jean Bart* at a range of 26 *miles*. The utmost range of *Massachusetts* in any action on this or subsequent days was 31,600 yards, and her utmost range in firing at *Jean Bart* was 29,000 yards or about 17½ miles.

fourth did not meet sufficient resistance to detonate an armor-piercing shell. The fifth, at about 0720, hit the forward turret (then firing at *Massachusetts*), ricocheted against the top of the barbette, and then into the city, where it was recovered and set up as a trophy at the French Admiralty building. The impact of this shell on the barbette jammed the turret in train, silencing *Jean Bart's* entire main battery for about eight hours. Thus, one of the primary defenses of Casablanca, whose guns at extreme elevation might have been able to reach the transport area off Fedhala, was eliminated in sixteen minutes.[16]

Throughout this action, heavy stuff was whizzing over *Massachusetts* and splashing in the water close aboard. Admiral Giffen and Captain Whiting disdained the protection of the armor-cased conning tower, and directed battle from the open flying bridge. The Admiral once remarked, as an enemy salvo passed close overhead, "If one lands at my feet, I'll be the first to line up to make a date with Helen of Troy!"

Tuscaloosa concentrated on the submarine berthing area in Casablanca, then shifted to the Table d'Aoukasha shore battery, while *Wichita*, having fired twenty-five 9-gun salvos at El Hank, and silenced it temporarily, took over the submarine area in the harbor at 0727. The range was then 27,000 yards. At 0746 the Covering Group changed course to 270° and commenced a westerly run past the targets, firing on El Hank, Table d'Aoukasha, and ships in the harbor. This action was broken off at 0835 in consequence of a telephone message relayed from the Army ashore, "For Christ's sake quit firing — you are killing our own troops," and "This is from Army — you are killing townspeople, no opposition ashore."[17] Subsequent investigation proved that these casualties were caused

[16] As a result of wildly erroneous statements made at the time on the performance of the 16-inch AP ammunition, a thorough investigation was made of the *Jean Bart*. The results are reported in the Bureau of Ordnance *Bulletin of Ordnance Information* No. 2-43 pp. 62–66. Other details from memorandum of Capt. L. L. Strauss to Capt. J. E. Gingrich 20 Aug. 1943, and from files of the Bureau.

[17] So received by various ships in the Center Attack Group between 0818 and 0828; Admiral Giffen received the second part only at 0830.

by the Batterie du Port, Cape Fedhala, when firing on our troops at the upper edge of Beach Red 2.

Up to that time, the only certain damage inflicted by either side was on the *Jean Bart*. The French scored no hits on the Covering Group, although they made several straddles and near misses, and one shell passed through the flagship's commissioning pennant. Around 0745 bombing planes' and warships' projectiles sank three merchantmen in Casablanca and also three submarines, *Oréade*, *La Psyché* and *Amphitrite*. Anyway, somebody sank them at anchor.[18] Yet, in spite of all the efforts by Covering Group and carrier planes, eight submarines sortied successfully between 0710 and 0830, and some of them were shortly to be heard from. The shore battery at Table d'Aoukasha — whose guns were described by a French officer as "*tout ce qu'il y a du plus vieux*" — was silenced only temporarily,[19] and the modern El Hank battery remained completely operational.

3. *The Morning Naval Battle*

The Covering Group had become so interested in pounding *Jean Bart* and El Hank that its mission of containing the enemy ships in Casablanca Harbor was neglected. At 0833, when they checked fire, *Massachusetts*, *Tuscaloosa* and *Wichita* had reached a point about sixteen miles northwest of the harbor entrance, and twenty-five miles from our ships engaged in unloading troops at Fedhala. Admiral Michelier, anticipating that this westward run would place the big ships at a safe distance, ordered the destroyer squadrons under his command to sortie from Casablanca and sneak along the coast to break up the landing operations at Fedhala. This was his one desperate chance of defeating the "invasion."

Beginning at 0815, the following French ships sortied from Casablanca: —

[18] Dive-bombers from *Ranger* sank the submarines, and were responsible for sinking most of the merchantmen.

[19] *Wilkes* Action Report and conversation with one of her officers, who is positive that this battery and no other fired on her 9 Nov.

*Destroyer Leaders of 2500 tons, 423 feet long, five
5½-inch guns, four torpedo tubes, 36 knots*

MILAN	Capitaine de Frégate Costet
ALBATROS	Capitaine de Frégate Periès

*Destroyers of 1400 tons, 331 feet long, four 5.1-inch
guns, six torpedo tubes, 36 knots*

L'ALCYON	Capitaine de Corvette de Bragelongue
BRESTOIS	Capitaine de Frégate Mariani
BOULONNAIS	Capitaine de Corvette de Preneuf
FOUGUEUX	Capitaine de Frégate Sticca
FRONDEUR	Capitaine de Corvette Bégouën-Demeaux

This force was under the command of Contre-Amiral Gervais de
Lafond in *Milan*. Light cruiser *Primauguet* sortied last, at 0900.
Admiral Lafond later informed Admiral Hewitt that when the
first sortie commenced he was still ignorant of the nationality of the
ships he had been ordered to fight. Other officers later confirmed
this surprising fact.[20]

Spotting planes reported the sortie to our Center Attack Group
as early as 0818.[21] There then began an anxious twenty minutes for
the transports. Wildcats and Dauntless dive-bombers from *Ranger*
strafed and bombed the ships, but they continued on their course,
and knocked one of the bombers down; its entire crew was lost.
Fedhala is only twelve miles by sea from Casablanca, not much to
cover for destroyers capable of thirty-six knots; and the transports
at that moment were so many sitting ducks for a torpedo attack,
or gunfire for that matter. At 0828 the French destroyers began
shelling landing boats that were seeking Beach Yellow west of Cape
Fedhala, making a direct hit on one,[22] and also firing on *Wilkes* and
Ludlow, who were patrolling a few miles to the westward of the
Cape. *Ludlow* delivered a salvo that started a fire on the *Milan*,
then retired at flank speed, and at 0834 was hit by a shell which entered the wardroom country and exploded on the main deck, start-

[20] Conversations with Admiral Hewitt and of Maj. Rogers with Capt. Sticca
and other French officers at Casablanca 18 Mar. 1943.
[21] Admiral Hewitt's Preliminary Report 28 Nov. p. 7.
[22] Observed by *Wilkes* (information from Lt. Andrew Hepburn Jr. USNR)
and reported by other ships.

ing fires which took her out of action for three hours. Splashes and straddles followed her out to 24,000 yards range, and *Wilkes* too fell back on the cruisers. The French sailors must have believed that they had us on the run.

Admiral Hewitt now ordered *Augusta, Brooklyn, Wilkes* and *Swanson* to intercept the French force.[23] Anxiety on board the transports was dispelled by what one of their officers pronounced to be "the most beautiful sight he ever saw." The four ships went tearing into action like a pack of dogs unleashed: *Wilkes* and *Swanson* with their main batteries yap-yapping, dancing ahead like two fox terriers, followed by the queenly *Augusta* with a high white wave-curl against her clipper bow, her 8-inch guns booming a deep "woof-woof"; and finally the stolid, scrappy *Brooklyn*, giving tongue with her six-inchers like ten couple of staghounds, and footing so fast that she had to make a 300-degree turn to take station astern of her senior. At 0848, when the enemy was not more than four miles from our transports, action opened at 18,500 yards, rapidly closing to 17,600; French shells came uncomfortably close but failed to hit; at about 0900 range was opened by the enemy retiring toward Casablanca, to draw us under the coastal batteries.

Admiral Hewitt at nine o'clock ordered Giffen to close and take care of the French ships. The Covering Group came in at 27 knots, and at 0918 opened fire at 19,400 yards, closing to 11,500. *Augusta* and *Brooklyn* broke off and returned to guard the transports, while the fire support destroyers engaged the Batterie du Port on Cape Fedhala, which had reopened fire, and quickly silenced it for the third time. In the meantime the French destroyers sent up a heavy smoke screen and followed the excellent defensive tactics of charging out of it to take a crack at their formidable enemy, then in again to throw off the spot planes and range finders. "Our enemy deserves much credit," reported the gunnery officer of *Tuscaloosa*, "for superb seamanship which permitted him to maintain a continuous volume of fire from his light forces while exposing them

[23] Capt. Emmet's Narrative of Events says at 0829; *Brooklyn* War Diary at 0839.

only momentarily. One well-managed stratagem observed was the laying of smoke by a destroyer on the unengaged bow of the enemy cruiser, which effectively obscured our 'overs.' " [24]

These French destroyers did indeed put up a fight that commanded the admiration of all. The Covering Group was unable to polish them off; hurling 8-inch and 16-inch ammunition at these nimble-footed light craft was a bit like trying to hit a grasshopper with a rock.[25] At 0935 Giffen changed course to 280° "because of restricted waters," [26] and began another run to the westward, exchanging shots with the French destroyers and El Hank.

The minutes around 1000 were the hottest part of this action. Several things happened almost simultaneously. The beautiful French light cruiser *Primauguet* (7300 tons, 600 feet long, eight 6-inch guns and twelve torpedo tubes) sortied to assist the destroyers, two of which peeled off from the smoke screen group and headed north to deliver a torpedo attack on the Covering Group.[27] *Massachusetts*, at a range of about 11 miles, and *Tuscaloosa*, at a little less, landed a couple of salvos on the van destroyer *Fougueux*. She blew up and sank in lat. 33°42′ N, long. 7°37′ W, about 6½ miles north of Casablanca breakwater.[28] About the same moment a

---

[24] *Tuscaloosa* Action Report, Enclosure G (Lt. Cdr. P. W. Mothersill) 19 Nov. 1942. He probably mistook one of the destroyer leaders for a light cruiser.

[25] Admiral Giffen reports (p. 16): "At about 0925 one of the DLs which the flagship had been engaging was last seen with only her bow projecting from the water. This ship presumably sank." From the check-up of French ships made after the action it seems that this must have been an optical illusion.

[26] *Massachusetts* Action Report. What is meant by "restricted waters" I do not know. There were no mine fields reported in the neighborhood of the French force, and this change of course brought the Covering Group closer to El Hank.

[27] *Wichita's* War Diary states, "0942 commenced fire on *Primauguet*, range 24,000 yards, visibility 14 miles." The French sources state that this cruiser opened fire on *Massachusetts* at 0935.

[28] This is the writer's interpretation of some rather puzzling and conflicting data. From the information that Maj. Rogers obtained from French officers after the battle, *Fougueux* blew up and sank at the position mentioned in the text at 1000, and she was hit by green-dyed and no-colored shells. Green was the color of *Wichita*, *Brooklyn* and *Massachusetts*; *Tuscaloosa* fired no-color. The Action Report by Capt. Gillette of *Tuscaloosa* states: "1001, a French destroyer under fire of *Tuscaloosa* was observed to be sinking." Capt. F. E. M. Whiting, in the same Action Report, states: "On only one occasion did I observe a salvo from this vessel land directly on a ship. When the smoke and splash had cleared away that ship was no longer present." On the other hand, Lt. J. D. Elliot Jr., pilot of a spotting plane of *Tuscaloosa*, states in his report (Enclosure E to Action Report):

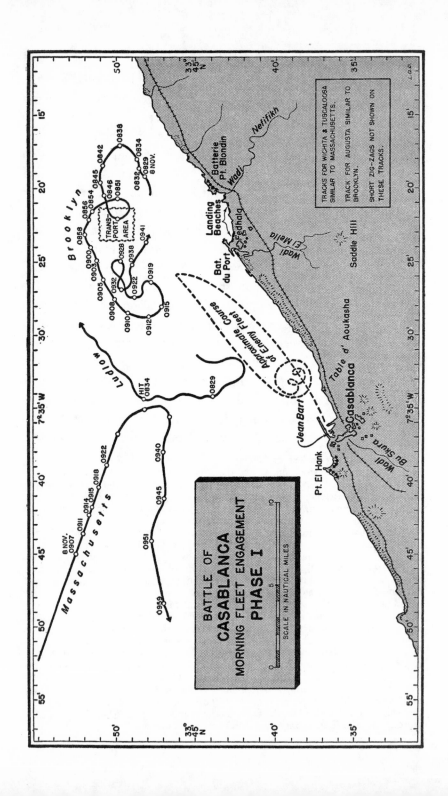

TRACKS FOR WICHITA & TUSCALOOSA
SIMILAR TO MASSACHUSETTS.

TRACK FOR AUGUSTA SIMILAR TO
BROOKLYN.

SHORT ZIG-ZAGS NOT SHOWN ON
THESE TRACKS.

BATTLE OF
CASABLANCA
MORNING FLEET ENGAGEMENT
PHASE I

SCALE IN NAUTICAL MILES

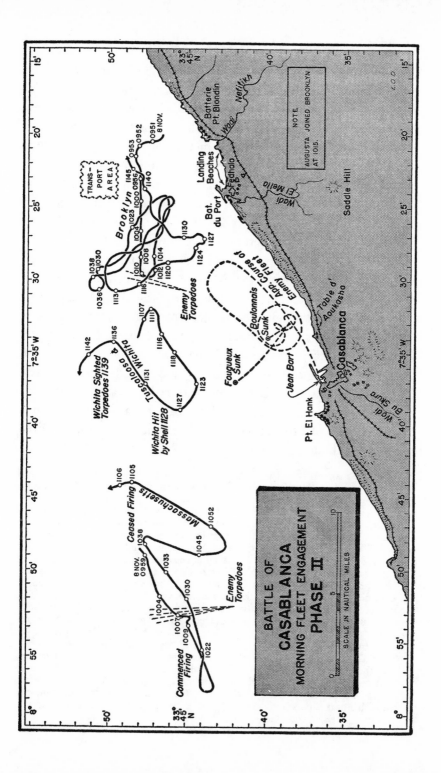

BATTLE OF
CASABLANCA
MORNING FLEET ENGAGEMENT
PHASE II

SCALE IN NAUTICAL MILES

NOTE.
AUGUSTA JOINED BROOKLYN
AT 1015.

shell from El Hank hit the flagship's main deck forward and exploded below, injuring nobody. Within three minutes *Massachusetts* sighted four torpedo wakes about 60 degrees on her port bow, distant under one thousand yards. The big battleship was maneuvered between Numbers 3 and 4 of the spread, and just made it; Number 4 passed about fifteen feet away along her starboard side. Four minutes later four torpedoes, from submarine *Méduse*, narrowly missed *Tuscaloosa;* and at 1021 another torpedo wake was sighted, passing 100 yards to port. The French just missed sweet revenge for their too impetuous *Fougueux.*

While the Covering Group was making this run to the westward, sinking ships and dodging torpedoes, three French destroyers began to edge along shore toward the transports. Our big ships were now well below the horizon, as seen from the transport area, so Admiral Hewitt at 0951 ordered his two cruisers and three destroyers to intercept the enemy. When the *Brooklyn* received this order, she was operating to the eastward of the transport area. Captain Denebrink in his eagerness steered a straight course for fifteen minutes, and just managed at 1010, by a timely 90-degree turn, to dodge five torpedoes from the submarine *Amazone*, fired at a range of about three thousand yards.[29] *Augusta*, who was fueling

---

"We scored a hit on one destroyer, which hauled for the harbor smoking, and the *Brooklyn* split a destroyer in two," but he mentions no time. Lt. (jg) A. M. Barclay of the *Tuscaloosa's* other spotting plane says: "One DD was definitely sunk by being split in half. Fire from the *Brooklyn* I believe being mostly responsible." A junior officer of *Tuscaloosa* confirmed this when I visited her in Dec. 1942. But the *Brooklyn* was not firing at 1000. The hypothesis that the hour of *Fougueux's* sinking was given to Maj. Rogers in French time, one hour later than ours, will not hold; for *Brooklyn* at 0900 was at an excessive range from the spot where the *Fougueux* sank. *Wichita* also fired green dye. She looks like *Brooklyn,* and had been firing on DDs since 0947, but claimed no hit. To add to the confusion: (1) Capt. Sticca, the former captain of *Fougueux,* informed Maj. Rogers at Casablanca 18 Mar. 1943 that his ship was sunk by red-dyed shells, probably 8-inch. If his memory was correct, the *Augusta* must have been responsible. (2) *Wichita's* War Diary states, "1110. One French destroyer hit by torpedo from carrier-based plane and capsized." See also note 33, p. 106.

[29] Cdr. G. G. Herring, the executive officer who advised this change of course, sighted the submarine's firing impulse bubble. The captain of the *Amazone* lunched on board *Brooklyn* at Philadelphia in Apr. 1943 and reported firing six torpedoes one of which stuck in the tube. He could not understand why he missed such a near shot, and like a true fighting man remarked, "I wish I could say I was sorry I fired at you, but I am not."

a plane and preparing to set General Patton and staff ashore, catapulted the plane, cut adrift the waiting landing craft [30] and stood
over to support *Brooklyn*, handsome as a bridal bouquet with her
guns spouting orange bursts of flame.

The second morning engagement, which commenced at 1008
when one of the French destroyers opened fire on *Brooklyn*, became general when *Augusta* came in at 1020. On the one side were
the two cruisers screened by *Wilkes, Swanson* and *Bristol;* [31] on the
other, light cruiser *Primauguet*, two destroyer leaders, and four
destroyers. *Augusta* and *Brooklyn* steered radically evasive courses:
ellipses, snake tracks, and figure eights — dodging shells every few
seconds, and footing so fast that their screening destroyers with
difficulty kept out of the way. *Brooklyn* was very impressive, reported an observer in *Augusta*. "Her fire consisted of ranging salvos with one or two guns, followed by one or more full salvos,
spotted, and then a burst of rapid fire lasting a minute or so." [32] Her
adversary was then steering northwesterly to open the range, so as
to give her guns the advantage; at seven and a half to nine miles
from the enemy one could see little more than black specks of ships
constantly emerging from and submerging in the smoke, and gun
flashes snapping out of the screen. At 1046 *Brooklyn* received the
only hit suffered by either cruiser, a 5-inch dud.

So intent was *Brooklyn* upon the task at hand that she forgot
about the Covering Group; and when the superstructures of three
ships appeared over the horizon to the westward, firing, and large
geysers of green water, far higher than anything she had been
dodging, shot up off her starboard bow, officers on the bridge
thought for a few seconds that the enemy had led us into a trap —
that these ships were the *Richelieu, Gloire* and *Montcalm* from
Dakar. It turned out that the green splashes were from El Hank,

[30] This experience was one of the arguments for the new class of AGC,
amphibious command ships. Capt. Hutchins had to fight the *Augusta* with two
rear admirals, a major general, and their complete staffs on board. See, in Part II,
the success of the R.N. Headquarters Ships *Largs* and *Bulolo*.
[31] These destroyers were engaged only part of the time, as their attention was
drawn by the shore batteries at Cape Fedhala.
[32] Capt. Shepard's Report p. 18.

making a few passes at *Brooklyn*, and that the three ships hull-down were, of course, the Covering Group returning. Great relief on the bridge! At about 1035 *Massachusetts* signaled her re-entry into battle by opening fire on *Boulonnais*, who, hit by a full salvo from *Brooklyn*, rolled over and sank at 1112.[33]

By 1100 *Massachusetts* had expended approximately 60 per cent of her 16-inch ammunition, and decided that she had better save the balance in case that bad dream, the *Richelieu*, came true. Accordingly she pulled out of range with three screening destroyers, while Captain Gillette in *Tuscaloosa* assumed tactical command of the two heavy cruisers and *Rhind*, with orders to polish off the enemy fleet. They closed range to 14,000 yards, closer than our light cruisers were at the time.

At about 1100, just before the reduced Covering Group swung into action, cruiser *Primauguet* took a bad beating from *Augusta* and *Brooklyn*. Holed three times below the waterline, and with an 8-inch shell on No. 3 turret, she retired toward the harbor, and anchored off the Roches Noires. *Milan*, with five hits, at least three of them 8-inch, followed suit.[34] Almost at the same moment, destroyer *Brestois* was hit by *Augusta* and a destroyer. She managed to make the harbor jetty. The planes from *Ranger* strafed her near

[33] The time given in Mordal *La bataille de Casablanca*. Earlier reports said *Boulonnais* was sunk by red-dyed ammunition. *Augusta* was the only ship using that color to my knowledge; but *Augusta's* Action Report mentions no hits made at this time. It notes an enemy "destroyer" hit and sunk at 1107, and *Brooklyn's* spotting plane reported an enemy ship on fire at 1109. (This was undoubtedly *Boulonnais*.) On the other hand, the log of *Massachusetts* has this entry for 1035: "Main battery went to rapid fire. Engaged destroyer of *L'Alcyon* class." Cease-firing was given when four hits were observed to burst on her stern. But all missed her. The *Massachusetts* gunnery officer, Cdr. L. E. Crist Jr., with whom I have corresponded on this matter, saw the *Boulonnais* in that position himself. He says that another green-dye ship, a cruiser, was firing at her and may have given the *coup de grâce*, when *Massachusetts* shifted her attention to the *Primauguet*. However, one of the battleship's aviators, Lt. (jg) T. A. Dougherty USNR, who had been taken prisoner ashore but was given a front-row seat for the battle at Table d'Aoukasha, said his ship sank the *Boulonnais*. Professor R. G. Breckenridge of M.I.T., after reading this and note 28, observed that flourescin, the dye for green coloration, shows red in the splash when viewed by transmitted light, which may well resolve this dilemma.

[34] Memo. of Cdr. C. L. Tyler (who examined her) to Bureau of Ordnance 2 Dec. 1942. Her bridge area also was devastated by plane machine-gun fire; she lost 29 men killed on the bridge.

the waterline with .50-caliber bullets, but did not hasten her end. Holed below the waterline, she sank at 2100.

There were now only three French ships in action outside the harbor, destroyers *Frondeur* and *L'Alcyon*, and destroyer leader *Albatros*. They formed up about 1115, apparently with the intention of delivering a torpedo attack on the cruisers, but were soon reduced to ineffectual zigzagging behind a smoke screen by the fire of *Tuscaloosa* and *Wichita*. They had good support, however, from El Hank. After a number of straddles and near misses, this shore battery scored one hit on *Wichita* at 1128, which detonated in a living compartment on the second deck, injuring fourteen men, none of them seriously; the fires were quickly extinguished. Ten minutes later the same cruiser dodged a spread of three torpedoes from one of the French submarines. *Wichita* and *Tuscaloosa*, however, gave back far more than they got. *Frondeur* took a hit aft and limped into port down at the stern; like *Brestois*, she was finished off by aircraft strafing. *Albatros* was hit twice at 1130, once below the waterline forward and once on deck; with only three of her guns functioning she zigzagged behind a smoke screen, shooting at *Augusta*. At that moment *Ranger's* bomber planes flew into action, and laid two eggs amidships. The fireroom and one engine room were flooded, and the second engine room was presently flooded by another hit from *Augusta*.[35] *Albatros* went dead in the water.

Immediately after, around 1145 or 1150, action was broken off by reason of two rumors, one false and the other misleading. News reached Admiral Hewitt from a plane that an enemy cruiser had been sighted southwest of Casablanca, and he ordered *Wichita* and *Tuscaloosa* to steam down the coast in search of her. From one of our communication teams ashore came word "Army officers conferring with French Army officers at Cape Fedhala. Gunfire must be stopped during this conference."[36] Such a conference was being held, but Admiral Michelier knew nothing about it, and the senior

[35] Maj. Rogers's Report, confirmed by Capt. Shepard's Report. *Albatros* casualties were 25 killed and 80 wounded.
[36] *Brooklyn* War Diary.

French officer present, a lieutenant colonel, had no authority to decide anything except to surrender Fedhala, where all resistance had already ceased.

Out of the eight French ships which took part in this morning engagement, only one, *L'Alcyon*, returned to her berth undamaged. But Admiral Michelier had a few cards still up his sleeve, and proceeded to play them well.

4. *The Afternoon Engagement*

The eighth of November had developed into a beautiful blue-and-gold autumn day, with bright sunlight overhead, a smooth sea almost unruffled by light offshore wind, and a haze over the land to which smoke from gunfire and smoke screens contributed. Sea gulls with black-tipped wings were skimming over the water, and so continued throughout the action apparently unconcerned by these strange antics of the human race.

At 1245 *Brooklyn* and *Augusta* were patrolling around the transports; and their crews, who had been at battle stations for twelve hours, were trying to grab a little cold lunch. General Patton at last had managed to get ashore from the flagship. Admiral Michelier chose this opportune moment, when the Covering Group was chasing a ghost cruiser to the westward, to order a third sortie from Casablanca, led by an *aviso-colonial* named *La Grandière*.[37] At a distance she resembled a light cruiser. She was followed by two small *avisos-dragueurs* (coast-patrol minesweepers) of 630 tons, armed with 3.9 inch anti-aircraft guns, called *La Gracieuse* and *Commandant Delage*. The three vessels steamed along the coast as if headed for the transports. The French, as ascertained later, were simply trying to pick up survivors from the sunken destroyers, but their course then looked aggressive. At the same time two destroyers who had not yet sortied, *Tempête* and *Simoun*, remained near the harbor entrance, milling around temptingly in order to

---

[37] *La Grandière* was 2000 tons, 340 feet long, diesel-powered, carrying three 5½-inch guns in her main battery.

attract some of our vessels under the fire of El Hank. *Albatros* was still outside, but dead in the water.

Again it was *Brooklyn*, *Augusta*, destroyers and bombing planes to the rescue. Action commenced at 1312, range 17,200 yards, rapidly closing to 14,300. Again the enemy put up a smoke screen, through which the cruisers were unable to find their targets. *La Grandière* was damaged by one of the bombing planes, but returned to harbor safely, and the two small *avisos* were not touched. During this short action a brave little tug was observed towing in *Albatros*, who was bombed and strafed on the way, and finally beached at the Roches Noires near the *Primauguet* and *Milan*. This was a bad move on the part of the French, because in that position they were easily attacked from seaward by carrier-based planes who were not bothered to any great extent by the harbor anti-aircraft defenses. *Primauguet* that afternoon suffered several fierce bombings and strafings from *Ranger's* planes, and her whole forward half was completely wrecked. A direct hit on her bridge killed the captain, the executive, and seven other officers; Rear Admiral Gervais de Lafond was seriously wounded, but recovered.[38]

By 1340 the Covering Group was coming up again fast from the westward, and for the third time that day Admiral Hewitt handed over the duty of engaging the enemy to Admiral Giffen, while Captain Emmet's command resumed patrol duties. *Massachusetts* fired one salvo at the small ships, and was promptly engaged by El Hank, but ceased firing after ten minutes in order to conserve ammunition. *Wichita* and *Tuscaloosa* stood in toward the harbor, and engaged *La Grandière* and *Albatros*.

At the height of this action Colonel Wilbur, accompanied by a French guide and Colonel Gay and driven by Major F. M. Rogers, made a second auto excursion into Casablanca in the hope of dissuading the French from further resistance. The advance post let them pass under flag of truce after disarming the party. They called at army headquarters in Casablanca, and after ascertaining

[38] Capt. Shepard's Report states that *Primauguet* had 300 casualties. Although most of the damage was done by aërial bombs, she sustained one 16-inch hit in a boiler room and two 8-inch hits. Report by Cdr. C. L. Tyler to Bureau of Ordnance.

that the Colonel's friend General Béthouart was in jail, and that Michelier was in command, proceeded to the Admiralty on the waterfront. As they passed through the streets of Casablanca, flying the American flag, the population waved and cheered, and a friendly crowd gathered whenever they halted to ask the way. About 1400, word was sent in to Admiral Michelier requesting an interview. An aide came out, saluted, remained at attention, and declared that the Admiral refused to receive them. As Major Rogers was beginning to argue in his best Harvard French, El Hank let fly a salvo at *Wichita*. "*Voilà votre réponse!*" said the Admiral's aide.

The last ruse of Admiral Michelier had succeeded. *Wichita* and *Tuscaloosa*, although not hit, were so frequently straddled by gunfire from El Hank that they broke off action at 1450. Dive-bombers from *Ranger* also engaged this shore battery, but inflicted no lethal damage. At 1530 Admiral Giffen signaled Admiral Hewitt, "Have seven loaded guns and will make one more pass at El Hank." So this day's furious shooting ended in a well-earned tribute to "Old Hank," as the bluejackets named this French shore battery.

The final score of the Battle of Casablanca is very one-sided. The United States Navy suffered one hit each on destroyers *Murphy* and *Ludlow*, cruisers *Wichita* and *Brooklyn* and battleship *Massachusetts*. Three men were killed on board *Murphy* and about 25 wounded, by the Sherki battery. Approximately 40 landing boats were destroyed by enemy action, most of them by airplane strafing when on the beach. The Army casualties ashore that day were very slight. The French Navy lost 4 destroyers and 8 submarines sunk or missing;[39] *Jean Bart*, *Primauguet*, *Albatros* and *Milan* disabled. Casualties to all French armed forces were stated

---

[39] Of the 8 submarines that sortied from Casablanca, *Méduse* was bombed by carrier planes on 8 and 9 Nov., damaged, and subsequently beached near Mazagan; *Orphée* returned to her berth unscathed; *Le Tonnant* made Cadiz, and was scuttled by her crew rather than fall into Franco's hands; *Amazone* and *Antiope* made Dakar safely; *Sidi-Ferruch*, *Conquérant*, and *Sybille* were missing, at least one of them as a result of depth-charging by our planes and destroyers. Three others were sunk by plane bombing or naval gunfire at their berths in the harbor.

by the War Department on 23 November to be 490 killed and 969 wounded. All coast batteries at Fedhala were in our possession at the end of D-day, but those at Casablanca were still in French hands, and operative.

Admiral Michelier still had his two principal assets, the four 15-inch guns of *Jean Bart* and the four 194-mm and four 138-mm coast defense guns of Batterie El Hank. As long as these, and the several mobile and fixed batteries of 75-mm field guns around Casablanca, were undamaged, the Admiral was in a good position to bargain. French naval and air power in Morocco had been irretrievably damaged, but the main American objective, securing Casablanca, was far from being attained; and until we could get the transports and cargo ships into Casablanca they were highly vulnerable to submarine or air attack and also in danger of foul weather damage.

In general, it may be said that the results were respectable, considering that this was the first major action of the Atlantic Fleet; but no more than might reasonably be expected from American local superiority in gun and air power. Nothing had occurred to upset the principle that coastal batteries have a great advantage over naval gunfire. *Brooklyn* to be sure had done a good job on the Sherki, but even her bombardment technique could not have silenced a determined and well-trained crew of gunners. The value of naval air power was well demonstrated; for the speedy destruction and driving down of French planes left the cruiser-based planes free to spot fall of shot, while carrier-based bombers and fighters delivered attacks on ships and shore batteries.

The French observed their traditional economy in the use of ammunition; but the American ships were lavish, considering that they had no place to replenish their magazines that side of Hampton Roads. If the dreaded Dakar fleet had turned up next day, it is questionable whether the Covering Group would have had enough shells to defeat them.[40]

[40] There are two sides to this ammunition question, however. We had to get a quick decision, or get out of the ring, and the aggressive school of action in

Of individual ship performances, that of *Brooklyn* was typical for intelligently directed and courageously sustained aggressive action. Her men remained at battle stations from 2215 November 7 to 1433 November 8, with a single forty-minute interval at noon, and no hot food, without showing signs of discouragement or fatigue. The teamwork and morale of that ship was outstanding. Even the smallest mess attendant, when questioned after the action as to what he had done, since the anti-aircraft gun for which he passed ammunition had never fired, said, "I mostly kept out of people's way, sir — but I did an awful lot of that!"

Equipped with the latest devices to keep main battery trained on a target while steering evasive courses at a speed of thirty-three knots, *Brooklyn* delivered an amazing shower of projectiles, and as she zigzagged and pirouetted, delivering 15-gun salvos and continuous rapid fire from her main battery, her appearance, with great bouquets of flame and smoke blossoming from her 6-inch guns, was a delight to the eye, if not to the ear. *Brooklyn* went far to prove, in this action, that the light cruiser is a most useful all-around fighting ship. She expended almost 1700 rounds of 6-inch common and about 965 rounds of 6-inch high-capacity, on this joyful day of battle, without a single misfire. At the end of the day Admiral Hewitt sent this message to Captain Denebrink: "Congratulations on your gunnery as evidenced by silencing Sherki battery and on your aggressive offensive action shown throughout the day."

Augusta also put in an outstanding performance. Although much of her space and communication facilities were taken up by the two admirals and two generals on board, and their staffs, Captain Gordon Hutchins fought his ship cleverly and well. Her 8-inch guns could not, of course, shoot as rapidly as the 6-inch of *Brooklyn*, but they probably did more damage.

The Covering Group destroyed the *Jean Bart* as a fighting ship,

---

which our naval officers have been trained believes that the way to get results is to throw in everything you have, promptly. Capt. Shepard in his Report condemns the Task Force for squandering ammunition, and discusses the reasons for their so doing. See Appendix II for table of expenditures.

(LEFT) Captain Denebrink in pilothouse of U.S.S. *Brooklyn*. The boxlike gadget
is the "Intercom" telephone
(RIGHT) Near miss on U.S.S. *Wichita*

A 2-gun salvo from El Hank misses destroyer *Mayrant*

Battle of Casablanca

(TOP) The one hit on *Brooklyn*
(ABOVE) *Brooklyn's* No. 3 gun crew relaxes

Bluejackets swabbing out 8-inch guns, *Augusta*

After the Battle

and probably accounted for the *Fougueux* and *Boulonnais. Massachusetts*, on her shakedown cruise, was full of fight and tip-top in morale; her turret men showed unusual endurance in handling the 16-inch shells for hours on end; out of her 113 officers and 2203 men, only three were in sick bay during the action. If she did little damage to the battery on El Hank, that was because of her ammunition. She carried only armor-piercing (AP) 16-inch shells, with a view to engaging enemy battleships. It was well known that AP projectiles would be of slight use in shore bombardment, for which high-capacity (HC) shells with instantaneously acting fuses are required, and Admiral Hewitt's staff made every effort to procure a supply of these for her; but at that time the Bureau of Ordnance could furnish none. The AP simply drove the gunners of El Hank temporarily to cover; only a direct hit on one of the emplacements could have silenced the battery permanently.

The destroyers too were well handled. They acted as all-around utility ships, shepherding the landing boats to the line of departure in dangerous proximity to the shore batteries, delivering accurate and powerful fire on ship and shore targets, and screening the capital ships and transports from torpedo attack. Many of their officers will appear again and again in this history, especially in Pacific Ocean operations. One of several commended by their skippers was Lieutenant Franklin D. Roosevelt Jr. USNR, gunnery officer of *Mayrant*, "for controlling and spotting main battery with skill and good judgment under highly adverse spotting conditions." [41] These conditions were partly due to the inexperience of plane pilots, partly to the glare of sunlight on the water between our ships and their targets.

Perhaps the best story of the battle comes from destroyer *Wilkes*, when screening *Brooklyn* and *Augusta* in their fight with *Primauguet* and the French destroyers. The officer at the engine-room telephone heard loud reports, and more speed was called for. "What's going on up there?" he inquired. "Enemy cruiser chasing us," was the reply. Before long he was almost thrown off his feet

[41] Cdr. E. K. Walker's Action Report of *Mayrant*.

by a sudden change of course, and even more speed was called for. "What's going on now?" he asked. "We're chasing the enemy cruiser!"

Leaving to a later chapter the events around Casablanca on 9–12 November, we may now examine what went on at Mehedia and Safi on D-day.

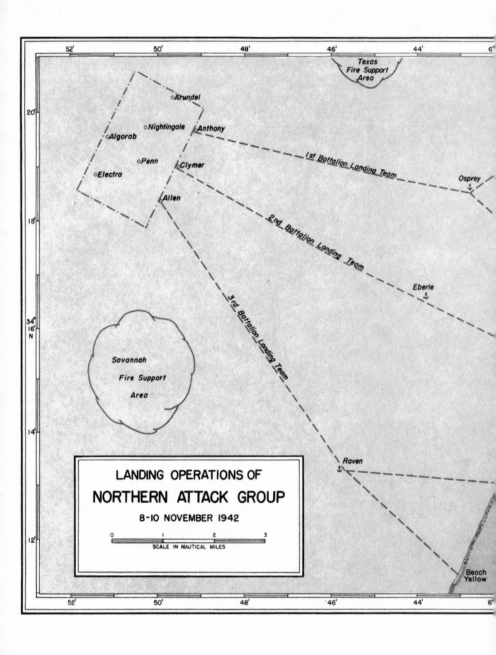

LANDING OPERATIONS OF
NORTHERN ATTACK GROUP
8-10 NOVEMBER 1942

0   1   2   3
SCALE IN NAUTICAL MILES

Texas
Fire Support
Area

Arundel

Nightingale   Anthony

1st Battalion Landing Team

Algorab

Osprey

Penn   Clymer

2nd Battalion Landing Team

Electra

Allen

Eberle

3rd Battalion Landing Team

34°
16'
N

Savannah

Fire Support

Area

Raven

Beach
Yellow

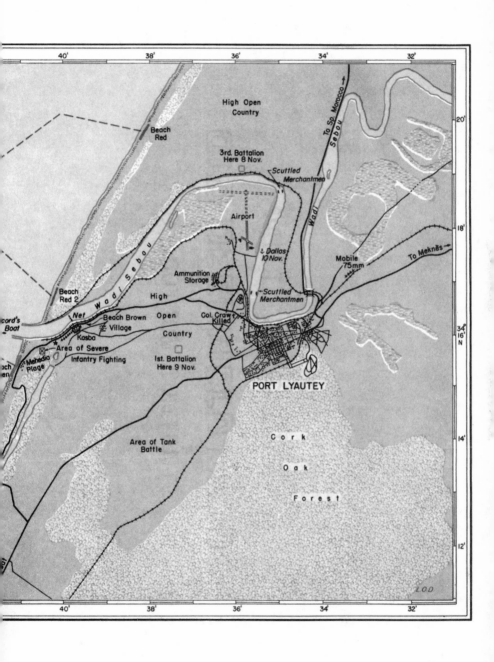

CHAPTER V

The Northern Attack[1]

7–11 November 1942

1. *Conditions and Objectives*

ALTHOUGH the Northern Attack like the others attained its
objective, it was subject to more accidents and misfortunes
than either. French resistance was more determined, American
casualties greater, and, owing to the loss of surprise and early reverses, more fluidity was required in operations.

General Eisenhower's original plan was to land the Northern
Attack Group at Rabat. This would have placed the capital of
Morocco immediately in our possession, secured the Salé airport,
and afforded the French tank regiment no time to deploy. But the
planners of the Amphibious Force had strong objections to Rabat.
Admiral Hewitt pointed out that it was a bad place for an opposed
landing; the approach is so silted-up that landing boats would have
stranded well off shore. Air-minded members of his staff were intent on seizing Port Lyautey, which had the only concrete, all-
weather strip in Northwest Africa; and General Patton, who remembered the Philippine Insurrection, wished to avoid stirring up
the natives in their holy city of Rabat. General Eisenhower accepted their proposed substitute, a landing at Mehedia to capture

[1] Principal sources for this Attack Group are the Action Report of the Commander (Rear Admiral Monroe Kelly) 26 Nov. 1942, and the Report of the
Army Observer (Maj. Carl E. Bledsoe USA) who sailed in *Clymer;* Action Reports
of *Savannah,* and of the screen commander, Cdr. D. L. Madeira. The best of the
transports' Action Reports is that of *Clymer.* The writer has also profited by
conversations with Maj. Bledsoe, Lt. Peddicord, and Col. E. S. Johnston of the
Amphibious Force staff. A copy of Gen. Truscott's Summary of Plan and Operations is included with Maj. Bledsoe's Report.

Port Lyautey. For political reasons, there is reason to believe that his original plan was the better. There were no coast defenses at Rabat as at Mehedia. General Béthouart had everything fixed for an unopposed landing at Rabat, in which case the shoals could have been negotiated; but General Mathenet gave us a hot reception at Mehedia. The danger of a native uprising was largely imaginary; vigorous French opposition was real. And with General Noguès "in the bag" our political and diplomatic troubles would have been less. He might conceivably have then issued orders to cease fire on D-day if there had been a landing in force at his front door. But of course these political factors were variables in the equation; from the military point of view Mehedia was the correct decision.

The orders of the Northern Attack Group were to establish General Truscott's 9000 troops of the 9th Division ashore by simultaneous landing assaults on five widely separated beaches on either side of Mehedia, to capture the Port Lyautey city and airfield for the use of naval anti-submarine and patrol planes, to obtain control of the river, the Wadi Sebou, and subsequently to capture the Salé airfield. A glance at the general map will show the strategic importance of Port Lyautey as a key position on the roads and railroads from Casablanca through Fez to Algeria. If the French had not ceased fighting on the eleventh, it would have been up to General Truscott to clear the way to the Taza Gap, the gateway to Algeria.

The local chart shows the immediate problem to be a very different one from that at Fedhala. The Wadi Sebou, after a hairpin turn through flat country, passes Port Lyautey, makes a wide bend like a staple around open high ground called the Koudiat Hamri, and enters the ocean close by the village of Mehedia. Its mouth is partially protected from silting by two jetties that confine the current. A fifteen-foot draft can be carried up the river to Port Lyautey at high water. Ridges wooded with scrub pine parallel the ocean, but suitable beaches for landing are fairly numerous. The five chosen were selected more for their nearness to objectives than because of superior facilities. The troops to land on Beach Red had as a mission to cross the Wadi Sebou in rubber boats and capture and occupy the Port Lyautey airdrome. The one at Red 2 was to take possession of the north bank opposite Mehedia, cross in rubber boats, and capture Beach Brown inside the river; while the landing team at Beach Green (on which there was a small bathing resort called Mehedia Plage) was to capture the Kasba, or citadel. That old masonry fortress had been built by the Portuguese centuries ago on the edge of a high cliff above the river mouth, about a mile inside the jetties. The Kasba had no military importance in itself, but adjoining it, on the same plateau, the French had placed a battery of six 138.6-mm (about 5½-inch) coast defense guns that commanded the river and the sea for about twelve miles out.[2] Below the cliff, on the river's edge, were a couple of 75-mm field guns mounted on flat cars, as well as sundry machine guns and anti-aircraft weapons. The garrison at Mehedia and on the Kasba amounted to very little, but reinforcements could be rushed in from Port Lyautey and Rabat before General Truscott was ready to attack.

The troops landing at Beaches Blue and Yellow had as their primary mission to control the road from Rabat and Salé, in order to prevent reinforcements coming through from the Moroccan capital.

Naval vessels in the Northern Group were eventually given a number of fire support missions, which they executed very well; and communication was established with shore fire control parties as early as 0620 November 8.[3] Much more naval gunfire could have been used on targets that were holding up the ground forces, if General Truscott had permitted. The General, unfortunately, had strong doubts (to some extent justified by earlier performances) of the accuracy of naval gunfire on shore objectives; and as he embarked in a transport instead of accepting quarters in the flagship, Admiral Kelly had no opportunity to convert him. When a member

[2] Col. E. C. Burkhart's Report of Visit to French Coast Defenses November 14–15, 1942. The Colonel calls four of those guns "obsolete," and they were in the open without armor; the other two, in sunken position with armor, were new German guns.

[3] Action Report of Desron 11 (Comdr. D. L. Madeira). *Savannah* made her first contact at 0824.

of the amphibious staff begged to be allowed to draw up a gunfire support plan for knocking out the Kasba, the General replied that he preferred to capture it by assault before the defenders knew what was up. And he made very sparing demands on the Navy for call fire, for specific shoots at definite targets on demand. Under these conditions and inhibitions naval gunfire support functioned only as counter-battery fire instead of saturating the area and pulverizing the Kasba, as Admiral Kelly was eager to do.[4]

Air power for the Northern attack was wielded primarily by the fighter and bomber squadrons of the escort carrier *Sangamon*. Her sister ship *Chenango* was ferrying Army planes and merely stood by waiting for an opportunity to land them on Port Lyautey airdrome. Owing to the light wind, *Sangamon* used her catapult for all launchings. Planes from *Ranger* also made several strikes on this area in order to supplement the work of the hard-pressed *Sangamon* air groups.

2. *The Landings at Mehedia*

The Northern Attack Group under command of Rear Admiral Monroe Kelly in U.S.S. *Texas*, with Captain Augustine H. Gray in U.S.S. *Henry T. Allen* commanding transports, parted company with the Center Group at 1500 November 7. The northern transport area, about eight miles off the mouth of the Sebou, was approached in two columns; *Texas* heading the right-hand one and acting as guide, light cruiser *Savannah*[5] leading the other. Minesweepers *Raven* and *Osprey* swept ahead, and destroyers patrolled around the formation. Escort carriers *Chenango* and *Sangamon* and oiler *Kennebec* followed in the rear, remaining well over the horizon until called upon to perform their special tasks. The group was tardily joined on the eighth by the Honduran fruiter S.S. *Contessa* with a British master and a polyglot crew. Fortunately Lieutenant

---

[4] CTG 34.8 (Admiral Kelly) Action Report, Intelligence Annex, p. 14.

[5] *Savannah* and *Brooklyn*, sister ships and often sailing in company, have developed mutual affections; their pet names for each other are "The Virgin of Sands Street" (*Brooklyn*) and "The Streetwalker of the Atlantic."

Commander A. V. Leslie usnr, an old square-rigger seaman, had been placed on board as naval liaison officer. When her merchant crew discovered at Newport News that she was to carry a highly lethal cargo for aviation supply, some jumped ship. Mr. Leslie sought seamen volunteers in the Norfolk city prison, and got them; the *Contessa* by that time had missed the convoy but she crossed unescorted and finally made it.

Destroyer *Roe*, who had SG radar equipment, went ahead of the main group at 1800 to locate beacon submarine *Shad*. That vessel had been patrolling off the coast since the evening of 4 November, and had even taken moving pictures of the jetties and near-by beaches; but apparently her station was so far off shore, about fifteen miles, that she was not sighted until 2325.[6] *Roe* arrived in the area two hours before midnight, searched for *Shad* without success, fixed her own location by radar at a point 3000 yards bearing 222° from the jetties, and then charged toward the convoy like a dog running back to his master. And she found "master" to be in need of a guide.

At 2203 November 7 flagship *Texas*, not quite sure of her position, ordered the formation to change course at slow speed from 80° to 60°, and before completion changed it again to 50°. During this wheel the group was brought to a stop, transports got out of position, and never did get back.[7] *Roe* reported the relative position of the transport area to Admiral Kelly at 2246, then again took station off the jetties to help the formation in by reporting their bearings on her radar screen. Fifty minutes later the Admiral informed his commanding officers that the transport area lay two miles to the westward (which was not far wrong), gave over tactical command of the group to Captain Gray, and steamed off with *Savannah* and

[6] *Roe* Action Report. *Shad* patrol report states that at 0412 she was informed by CTG 34.8 that a boarding officer was on his way to her, but he never turned up.

[7] Action Report of Comtransdiv 5 (Capt. Gray). There had just been a 20° change of course at 2254. A northerly set of current, not predicted on the Coast Pilot, was partly responsible for this uncertainty; but as Capt. Gray justly remarks, "At night transports should approach the debarkation areas with a steady course and speed. Otherwise irregularities in formation are likely to result in inability to assume proper stations without undue delay."

a few destroyers to assume fire support positions. Captain Gray signaled visually from the *Allen* a change of course to 270°, but the transports were so far out of position that few saw it. He then signaled *Susan B. Anthony*, the leading transport, who had a local pilot on board, to take her station in the transport area, hoping that the others would guide on her; but his signal was misunderstood. At this juncture the Admiral instructed *Roe* to coach *Allen* into position, but she was unable to find her. *Clymer* arrived at her station in the front line nearest the beach exactly at midnight;[8] *Allen* at 0036 November 8; *Anthony* at 0040.

The system worked out for getting the troops ashore was the same as at Fedhala, but the details were slightly more complicated, owing to the large number of beaches selected for the initial landings. Transports *Anthony*, *Clymer* and *Allen*, in the front line, were served by *Osprey*, *Raven* and *Eberle*, who conducted their assault waves to points known here as the jumping-off places instead of line of departure. A crucial point of the attack was the wire net and boom that blocked the Wadi Sebou inside the jetties. This had to be cut before anyone could ascend the river. First Lieutenant Lloyd E. Peddicord usa, in *Clymer's* scout boat, was ordered to take position off the jetties, both to guide in the net-cutter detail and to help landing boats find Beaches Green and Red 2.

The wind in this area was easterly, sometimes blowing along shore rather than off shore, but it was a light breeze that did not affect the operations. Lieutenant Peddicord shoved off on his mission, guided by the stars, at 0030.[9] A dark cloudbank obscured the transport area and seemed to close in right behind him. At 0230 his boat reached a point 1000 yards from the river mouth. The north jetty could be seen with the aid of night glasses, as well as a faint loom of city lights from Port Lyautey. After killing time for an hour, Peddicord took position off the jetties, turned on his guide light, and awaited the boat waves. Other scout boats in the meantime were

---

[8] Action Report; Maj. Bledsoe says at 0030.
[9] Rough draft of Lt. Peddicord's report to CTG 34.8 and conversation with him in Dec. 1942.

locating and marking Beaches Red, Blue and Green. In this area they actually marked them, too, by lighting flares ashore.

The position of the Northern Force was given away shortly after its arrival at midnight. A coastal convoy of four lighted steamers blundered into the transport area, and the escort, S.S. *Lorrain*,[10] was seen to signal by blinker in French: "Be warned. Alert on shore for 0500." Supposing that this message was meant for us, we assumed that she was a friendly vessel sent there to help, and allowed her to pass unmolested. One of our boats near shore observed the Kasba signal station blinking to *Lorrain*: "*Quels sont les bateaux?*" She evidently told them.

Debarking men from the transports took much longer than had been expected, for the same reasons as at Fedhala. *George Clymer*, a well trained and admirably organized transport, had three boat waves ready by 0200; but the other two front-liners, *Anthony* and *Allen*, were one to two hours behind.

Minesweeper *Raven*, acting as a control boat, left *Allen* at 0410 with the first three waves. General Truscott, who had made the rounds of the transports in a scout boat, now came on board *Allen* and called a staff meeting shortly after 0430, to discuss the situation. It was agreed that surprise had been lost by reason of the delay, the *Lorrain*, and the repeated broadcasting of the President's message,[11] which everyone on board had been profanely listening in on for the last two or three hours. The General nevertheless determined to go ahead with his original plan.

H-hour, the landing hour set at 0400, was delayed by the same

[10] Maj. Bledsoe's and General Truscott's Reports. *Lorrain* was approaching Fedhala at 0450, making 10 knots. She ignored a challenge, and beached herself at Bouznika after having her masts cleaned off by a shot from U.S.S. *Tillman*. Later that morning she got off, and joined a French convoy; on being challenged, she beached herself a second time. Lt. Harrie James USNR, who was on board *Texas*, informed the writer that a small French vessel, apparently a trawler, approached the flagship within 50 yards at 2300 and then steamed off toward Mehedia. This vessel did not give the alarm.

[11] Maj. Bledsoe states that our officers found evidence at Port Lyautey that the President's message to North Africa was picked up in this area, and resulted in the early dispatch of reinforcements to Port Lyautey from Meknès and Fez. The President's message, however, said nothing about specific landing points, and we now know that Port Lyautey was alerted by orders from Casablanca received at 0325.

amount as off Fedhala. Lieutenant Peddicord blinked for almost an hour and a half off the jetties before any boat showed up. At length the first wave from *Susan B. Anthony* hove in sight at 0515. They had no idea where they were, and were starting upriver when contacted and directed to Beach Red 2. *Anthony's* second and third waves shortly followed. At 0530 *Clymer's* waves started coming in, and the first three (24 boats with about 860 men) were successfully landed on Beach Green, where the surf was five to six feet high, by 0540.[12] These boats were beautifully handled; they retracted promptly and returned to the transports. In the meantime the net-cutting party in a scout boat, consisting of fourteen bluejackets and two naval officers, commanded by Lieutenant Colonel Henney of the Engineers, was on its way to cut the obstruction.

So far, all had been quiet ashore,[13] but at 0545 things started to happen. Shots were heard, a red flare was lighted, a searchlight on the north jetty illuminated Lieutenant Peddicord's scout boat; presently he saw flashes and heard dull detonations upriver; then, turning seaward, observed to his surprise that a destroyer was firing toward shore. This was *Eberle;* the detonations were the coast defense battery near the Kasba opening on her.[14] At about the same time, five to ten minutes after six o'clock, machine guns at the foot of the cliff fired on the net-cutting party so vigorously that Colonel Henney ordered a retreat before the mission was accomplished; and another machine-gun battery at Mehedia Plage commenced shooting at landing boats. The Kasba fired only a few rounds at this time, probably because it was still very dark; but at 0630 it opened up seriously on destroyer *Roe.* U.S.S. *Savannah,* playing the same rôle here as her sister *Brooklyn* off Fedhala, undertook to silence the shore battery, and *Roe* almost was silenced herself; when steam-

[12] Maj. Bledsoe says at 0515.

[13] Except that at Beach Blue a searchlight was turned on around 0523, and small-arms fire was heard — probably the scout boat shooting it out.

[14] Lt. J. N. Ferguson of *Dallas,* who lay near shore, clocked the opening gun of the Kasba at 0610, but *Savannah's* action report notes *Eberle* returning the fire at 0606, and *Eberle* Action Report says 0603. *Roe,* acting as control destroyer off Beaches Blue and Yellow, reports "0606 shore battery opened fire on troops and us. 0607 *Eberle* opened fire on shore. 0609 *Eberle* ceased firing."

ing parallel to the shore, less than 6000 yards off, she was closely straddled four times. She bent on thirty knots, maneuvered violently, and opened range.

As early as 0630 hostile planes, fighters, and two-engined bombers from the Rabat-Salé airfield began to strafe and bomb our landing boats; and about twenty minutes later, *Roe* and *Savannah* were attacked ineffectively by two Dewoitine fighters. At 0730 Admiral Kelly asked for air support, and in seventeen minutes' time at least twenty Wildcats from *Sangamon* and *Ranger* were in the area. By 0900 they had shot down about nine enemy aircraft and scared off the rest. They then transferred their attentions to the Port Lyautey and Rabat-Salé airfields, to such good purpose that the northern landings were never again disturbed from the air.

Shortly after sunrise, at 0700, the Kasba battery began to shell the boat waves and the transport area, missing *Clymer* by only six feet. Captain Gray then led a procession of transports to a point fifteen miles offshore, a maneuver which seriously interrupted landing operations. The Kasba's fire was promptly returned by *Savannah* and *Roe* and temporarily silenced; but it resumed spasmodically throughout the day.

To quote General Truscott: —

"The combination of inexperienced landing craft crews, poor navigation, and desperate hurry resulting from lateness of hour, finally turned the debarkation into a hit-or-miss affair that would have spelled disaster against a well-armed enemy intent upon resistance." [15]

The Army had a justifiable complaint of the hit-or-miss methods by which they were put ashore. Sections of the beaches had been properly marked, but this sort of thing happened: Waves 1 and 2 of the 1st Battalion Landing Team, 60th Infantry, destined for the Blue and Yellow beaches, were landed one mile north of Beach Blue. The 3rd Battalion Combat Team was landed at 0630 five miles north of Beach Red, where it should have been before daylight.

[15] Summary of Plan and Operations p. 7.

Not everyone, however, was set ashore at the wrong place. The 2nd Battalion Landing Team 6oth Infantry reached Beach Green from *Clymer* about 0530 and promptly attempted to execute General Truscott's orders to take the Kasba by assault. It was held up by gunfire from the destroyers and *Savannah*. These ships were attempting to silence the two 138-mm guns before they could molest the transports.[16] Thus a cardinal feature of the General's plan, to capture the Kasba by assault before the French knew we were ashore, was frustrated. The French had been alerted too early, and our troops got ashore too late. It would have been better to have withheld cold steel until hot shellfire accomplished the object. Lacking orders for call fire, Admiral Kelly had to follow his general orders with respect to shore batteries: not to fire unless fired upon — check fire if the enemy checked; orders based on the happy assumption that the French would quit when they knew who we were. The French did not quit, but lay low until some tempting target entered their sights, when they resumed fire again, and were silenced again by the ships. This went on for two days. Thus, we had the absurd situation of six 5½-inch coast defense guns holding out for 48 hours when the combined fire power of a 14-inch battleship, a 6-inch cruiser, and several destroyers was available.

3. *Difficulties Ashore*

The troops of this Northern Attack Force did not expect to do much fighting. For some occult reason the word went around that they were to be welcomed "with brass bands," as one sergeant put

[16] The original plan worked out at Amphibious Force headquarters to meet General Truscott's wishes was to land a raider force specially trained for night fighting in the first wave on Beach Green, and take the Kasba and the adjoining battery by stealth, before the defense was aroused. This was discarded by General Truscott, and the raiders were placed on board *Dallas* to be landed inside the river to take the airdrome, while the 2nd BLT got the Kasba assignment. Once the 138-mm guns near the Kasba opened up, the Navy had to attempt to silence them; and this support gunfire made military operations around the Kasba as dangerous for American troops as for the enemy.

it. Instead, they were received with bullets, bayonets and 75-mm shells wielded or fired by some three to four thousand troops of the 1st and 7th Regiments Moroccan Tirailleurs, the Foreign Legion, and naval ground units.[17] Strafing planes, machine-gun fire and other opposition made the men fighting mad and reckless. A Frenchman taken prisoner said, "You brave crazy! You go by front, why you no go by flank?" Moreover, a rumor to the effect that American paratroopers from England would drop on the airfield, circulated among the troops. This attack had originally been planned, but given up.

As part of the prevailing idea that the French could be talked into surrender, Colonel Demas T. Craw, taking Major Pierpont M. Hamilton as interpreter, proceeded in a jeep toward the French headquarters at Port Lyautey. Stars and Stripes, Tricolor and flag of truce were all displayed on the car. But on reaching an outpost of the city a French machine gun opened fire and killed the Colonel instantly. Major Hamilton was then taken prisoner to Port Lyautey, where he did some valuable "persuading" of French officers who came to talk with him.

Thus, D-day brought little but disappointment and frustration to the Northern Attack Group. *Dallas* was to proceed upriver to the airdrome with a raider detachment before daylight; but the boom was not cut, and when *Dallas* attempted to steam in and ram it, about noontime, she was twice driven off by the shore batteries. The 2nd Battalion Landing Team captured the Mehedia lighthouse that morning; but by a misunderstanding of orders advanced toward the airdrome before the Kasba had been captured. French infantry with tanks and artillery, advancing from Port Lyautey, drove this BLT back to the slopes south and west of the lighthouse, inflicting many casualties. Owing to the transports' retiring offshore to escape shots from the Kasba, the 2nd Battalion did not receive its field artillery and anti-aircraft weapons until next day; at one time there was even danger of its being cut

[17] Estimate by Lt. Harrie James USNR. (Admiral Kelly's Action Report, Intelligence Annex, p. 10.)

off from the beach. It was here that General Truscott gathered up crews of stranded landing boats to reinforce the troops, and fought beside them himself with a rifle. His plan may have been faulty, but he was courageous and versatile, a front-line fighting general of the sort that troops admire and respect.

In the meantime the 1st Battalion Landing Team of the 60th Infantry established anti-tank blocks on the road leading from Rabat, and took up positions on the ridge east of the lagoon; while the 3rd Battalion, the left flank landing team, by noon had occupied a hill overlooking the northerly bend of the Wadi Sebou. Unable to remove vehicles from the improvised beach where they had been dumped, this landing team had no rubber boats in which to cross the river and make their next objective, the Port Lyautey airdrome; nor had they artillery that could talk back to the Kasba.

All day *Savannah* had been firing intermittently on the Kasba battery. It was the same story as at Casablanca: salvos, silence, check fire; enemy renews fire, more salvos, silence again. The 14-inch shells of *Texas* were not wanted in the vicinity of troops, so General Truscott never permitted her to shoot at the Kasba; but in the early afternoon he called for battleship gunfire on an ammunition dump near Port Lyautey. Taking station 4000 yards offshore, 16,500 from the target, she fired 59 rounds of 14-inch bombardment ammunition. This particular mission was ineffective because the target consisted of a number of "beehives" on a reverse slope.[18] By sunrise on 9 November the two most active 138-mm guns near the Kasba had been silenced by *Savannah*, but so many reinforcements had arrived in the old fort that a bayonet assault was no longer practicable.

Conditions on the southern beaches during the night of 8–9

[18] *Texas* Battle Report, and Admiral Kelly's Action Report; Col. Burkhart's Report for damage. The word got around that the trouble here was a high proportion of duds. That is not true. The bomb-disposal people later found under 10 per cent duds; the trouble was partly the nature of the target, partly use of AP shells instead of HC, as in the case of *Massachusetts* on El Hank. (Information from Capt. C. W. Moses, who was then gunnery officer of *Texas* and made an investigation on the spot in January 1943.)

November presented a distressing scene of apparent confusion. Surf was rising so that about half the landing boats were unable to retract. Exits from the beaches were possible only for tracked vehicles. Trucks, jeeps, light tanks and stores were "piling up so fast that the Army shore party could hardly keep them above high water mark." Elements supposed to land on Beach Green, or inside the Wadi Sebou later, "were landing on Beach Blue, wandering around seeking their respective units in darkness broken only by the glare of naval signal lights and flashlights to seaward. Crews of stranded landing craft wandered aimlessly or tinkered ineffectively with stranded craft. To find an individual or unit on the beach presented a problem of first magnitude, and was a time-consuming proposition." [19]

Thus reported the Commanding General. His picture is not much exaggerated, but needs interpretation. Bluejackets are not necessarily aimless or ineffective when not in military formation. As for the soldiers, their confusion was due to the failure of Army Shore Parties to direct them to their proper assembly areas. The landing craft crews suffered, as elsewhere, from lack of training, exhaustion after their repeated trips beginning before dawn, and rising surf. On the whole they showed exemplary courage and tenacity.[20]

A recently developed wrinkle in amphibious warfare was tried out this day, with great success. That was the bombing of tank columns from the air with anti-submarine depth charges, whose fuses had been altered to detonate on impact. *Savannah's* five SOC–3s averaged over eight hours' flying time daily, dropped 14 325-lb. and 35 100-lb. depth charges on shore targets, as well as keeping anti-submarine patrol. The effect of a depth charge on a tank was devastating. It did not destroy the shell, but reduced the interior and all its contents to scrap and powder.[21]

[19] Gen. Truscott's Summary p. 10.
[20] Expenditure of landing craft was 70 damaged or destroyed out of 161 used, or 43 per cent, about the same as at Fedhala. Of these 70, 16 were subsequently salvaged. (War Dept. "Lessons Learned from Recent Amphibious Operations in North Africa" 12 Feb. 1943, Annex G–1.)
[21] *Savannah* Action Report and conversation with Col. Johnston.

Progress was made by the soldiers on 9 November. The 3rd Armored Landing Team, which had debarked on Beach Blue by nightfall on the eighth with six or seven light tanks, moved up to the Rabat road southwest of the lagoon at daybreak, dispersed some French infantry, and was then attacked by a column of fourteen tanks which had rumbled up from the Moroccan capital. These belonged to the 1er Régiment de Chasseurs d'Afrique, a famous regiment of the French Colonial Army, full of fight. The Shore Fire Control Party attached to our 3rd Armored Landing Team called loudly for naval gunfire, and the Naval Air Liaison Party attached to the 1st Battalion Landing Team also called for air support. Both obtained it very promptly, from *Savannah* and *Sangamon*. Four of the French tanks were destroyed by naval gunfire. The rest retired into a eucalyptus grove, whither Lieutenant R. Y. McElroy of the *Sangamon* followed them in his Avenger plane, flying so low that his wings smelled of eucalyptus oil afterwards. He located the tanks and supervised an aërial attack that routed them, receiving thirteen hits on his plane.[22] At 0900 more enemy tanks appeared, but were defeated after a running fight of several hours, the open country thereabouts lending itself to tank warfare. In this action a request for naval dive-bombers to break up an enemy road block was answered within fifteen minutes.[23]

The 1st Battalion Landing Team, now reinforced by tanks, reached the ridge halfway between the Kasba and Port Lyautey by dark on 9 November. The 2nd Battalion Landing Team, still badly disorganized despite reinforcements received in the night, made several ineffective assaults on the Kasba, whose original garrison of about seventy men had now been heavily reinforced. The 3rd Battalion Landing Team got its artillery up from the northern beach to a hill overlooking the Sebou. But as yet less than half the troops had been put ashore, and in the late afternoon further landing operations had to be suspended owing to the surf, which

[22] *Sangamon* Action Report.
[23] Admiral Hewitt's Comments 22 Dec. 1942 p. 10.

had reached alarming proportions — fifteen feet high, it is said, on some of the beaches.[24] Yet hard fighting was going on, and fresh water, ammunition and medical supplies were badly wanted by the Army. Three salvage boats were sent ashore by the *Clymer* to try to reach the Army with urgently needed supplies; one was swamped and another returned without landing.

4. DALLAS *Wins Through*

General Truscott realized that the Kasba must be taken, and the Wadi Sebou must be opened without further delay, so that the Port Lyautey airdrome could be occupied. A naval detail had been organized and equipped back in Norfolk to cut the net at the mouth of the river, in case Colonel Henney's party did not succeed in so doing. *Dallas* prepared to move upstream in the early morning of 10 November.

The exploit of *Dallas*, an old "four-piper" of 1920 vintage, shorn of her masts and much of her superstructure to save weight and accommodate troops on deck, was the bright light of the Northern Attack. On the eighth she had taken on board from the *Susan B. Anthony* a raider detachment of seventy-five men, and a French pilot, René Malavergne, a native of that region who had been imprisoned for De Gaullist sympathies, helped by O.S.S. to escape to England, and had there been engaged in this enterprise.[25] The net-cutting party, under command of Lieutenant Mark W. Starkweather USNR, successfully cut the inch-and-a-half wire of the boom inside the jetties at about 0230, despite injuries inflicted by machine-gun fire on every member of its crew.[26] As high water was at 0300, *Dallas* had to go up against an ebb tide, but she had to have light to navigate the upper reaches.

[24] *Clymer* Action Report..
[25] There is an article on Malavergne by Lt. (jg) Raoul Tunley USNR in *Sea Power* V No. 1 Jan. 1945. He was a great pilot, and without his aid we could never have got *Dallas, Contessa, Barnegat* and other ships up this narrow, twisty river.
[26] *Clymer* Action Report.

Dallas started toward the jetties at 0400, in heavy rain and darkness, Lieutenant Commander Brodie in command. Her hand lead had been left ashore at Bermuda when stripping ship, but she had improvised another with a heavy shackle. By 0530 she was between the jetties, and pilot Malavergne took the wheel. The channel runs so near the south jetty that one almost scrapes the stone, and seas were high and breaking, making the destroyer yaw badly; machine-gun fire opened up on her at that juncture. The destroyer's mission was to land the raiders at Port Lyautey airdrome. Commander Brodie decided to live up to his own name, and to his ship's code name, "Sticker." After they had passed through the jetties, it was light enough to see the boom; but as it had been cut on the north side, where the water was too shoal for the *Dallas*, she had to ram the boom where it crossed the channel in the hope that it would part. Before reaching that point she ran aground and began to pound in the swell that washed in from the sea. By turning up maximum revolutions, she just moved through the soft mud; and the Kasba selected that moment to open fire. A big shell hit the water dead ahead as *Dallas* approached the boom, and another lifted her stern off the mud; she turned up eighteen knots, hit a point on the boom midway between two floats, swept it aside, and promptly reduced to fifteen knots to ascend the river.

The next leg, to the top of the staple-like loop of the Wadi Sebou, was uneventful; except that a 75-mm gun from somewhere near Port Lyautey drew a bead on her, dropping a few in the river, and a machine gun on the ridge to the southward tried to rake her decks. *Dallas* answered with her 3-inch guns, and silenced that. She silenced something else too: next day an American Army officer thanked Commander Brodie for knocking out a French anti-tank gun that was holding up the 1st Battalion's tanks. That was done inadvertently by *Dallas's* "overs."

At the east end of this reach the French had scuttled two small steamers to block the passage, but pilot Malavergne steered *Dallas* neatly between them. A detachment of the 3rd Battalion, crossing Wadi Sebou in rubber boats, cheered *Dallas* along; and two planes

Air view of jetties and mouth of Wadi Sebou

Photo by an officer of the ship

The Kasba as seen from deck of *Dallas*

The Wadi Sebou, 10 November 1942

Scuttled French freighter in river

Dallas off Port Lyautey airdrome. Army P–40s have already landed, at right

U.S.S. Dallas *Sails up the Wadi Sebou, 10 November 1942*

from *Savannah* flew out to cover the game little ship. It was half ebb, depth of river nine feet — not enough for *Dallas*. Around the next sharp bend she made contact with the river bottom, but managed to move ten knots by driving her engines full speed, with her keel cutting a trench in the soft mud. As she approached the airport it appeared to be deserted. She came to a stop in midstream at 0737 and began landing the raiders from rubber boats.

At this point, "Sticker" stuck up from the surrounding flat country like a Dutch canal boat; she was a tempting target, as occurred to a French 75-mm battery located northeast of Port Lyautey. At a range of 2600 yards it began dropping shells close to *Dallas*, on her port side away from the landing operations; they churned the river water to a froth, but never touched her. *Dallas* replied with her 3-inch guns, and one of her attendant planes located the battery and laid a couple of depth charges, which silenced it after ten minutes' fire. The troops were placed ashore without a single casualty to them or to the ship. Truly, as one of *Dallas's* officers remarked, "The hand of God was right around us!"

The Army, too, was right on the ball that morning. The 1st Battalion Landing Team had moved up under cover of night, and seized a position on the high ground above the airdrome. The 3rd Battalion, the northernmost jaw of the pincers, had a company across the Wadi Sebou and was ready to coöperate with *Dallas's* raiders. French defenders wisely moved out as we moved in. By 1030 November 10, Army P-40s from the *Chenango* were using the Port Lyautey airport; and during the afternoon flood tide, S.S. *Contessa* moved upriver with her cargo of gasoline, bombs and other aviation supplies. She, too, ran aground below Port Lyautey, but her valuable cargo was safely landed by lighters. Next day the seaplane tender *Barnegat* steamed up with more supplies and repair facilities for the U.S. Navy Patrol Squadron 73, eleven Catalinas, which flew down from England and began landing at Port Lyautey on the thirteenth.

In the meantime the Kasba had fallen. The 2nd Battalion Landing Team, after receiving its howitzers, attacked from the native

village southeast of the fortress at 0625 November 10. At the gates
of the fort they were held up by heavy machine-gun and mortar
fire. French defenders stood right up on the crenellated stone walls,
shooting down at the Americans; an observer said that it reminded
him of the film "Beau Geste." However, this was war and not a
spectacle, so the Naval Air Liaison Party with the 2nd BLT called
for naval aircraft support; and, only four minutes after the first
signal had been sent, Dauntless planes from *Sangamon* delivered an
accurate bombing attack on the fort. The garrison then came out
with their hands up, and our infantry walked in. They found that
one of the newer 138-mm coast defense guns near by had received
a direct 6-inch hit from *Savannah,* which rendered it inoperative;
but no other guns were damaged.[27]

The last action in this area afforded another example of effective
naval deep supporting fire. About seven miles inland a column of
trucks carrying soldiers was observed to be moving toward Port
Lyautey from the direction of Petitjean and Meknès. Army command called for naval gunfire support. Battleship *Texas* opened
fire on the road at 0842 from a distance of 17,000 yards and fired
intermittently until 1131, expending 214 rounds. Spotting planes
reported that she broke up the truck column and made five direct
hits on the road.

Immediately after this bombardment, Admiral Kelly broadcast
from his flagship a message to the people of Port Lyautey, urging
them to put an end to their useless resistance, and concluding: —

"Join with us. Stop this useless waste of lives and use them later
in the fight against your real enemy — Germany."

Resistance had already ceased in that area. As soon as the Kasba
fell, the transports commenced to move in from their remote positions, and anchored from 1500 to 3000 yards off the mouth of the
river. Unloading of vehicles and supplies started immediately and
with gusto, lighters and landing craft boating their cargoes to the
protected Beach Brown inside the Wadi Sebou. Both space and personnel available for unloading at that point were so limited that

[27] Col. Burkhart's Report of Visit to French Defenses 14–15 Nov. 1942.

many boats were sent up to Port Lyautey to discharge their cargoes, and it took as much as eight hours for landing craft to make the round trip. In the shoal spot between the jetties, the swell rose so high in the ebb tide that two LCMs capsized, drowning most of the men on board. *Osprey* and *Raven*, the industrious minesweepers, were given a new job acting as river lighters.

Before midnight General Mathenet, the French Army commander in this sector, received orders from Admiral Darlan to cease resistance immediately. Major Hamilton, the officer who had been detained when Colonel Craw was killed, sent a message by courier that Mathenet desired an interview with General Truscott as soon as possible. This message was sent on board *Dallas* at 0128 November 11. By voice telephone the word was passed to *Texas* off shore and by her to General Truscott's headquarters at Mehedia Plage; and the meeting was arranged for 0800. As in the other areas, nothing could be definitely settled, awaiting word from General Eisenhower; but General Mathenet agreed to quit fighting, and to place the Rabat-Salé airfield at our disposition. We had already captured the other objectives; this completed the bag.

Salvage operations by a party from the *Texas* started immediately on the numerous small vessels that the French had sunk, or attempted to scuttle, in the Wadi Sebou. The Dutch S.S. *Export* was raised in time to perform service transferring stores from the transports to Port Lyautey; and three other steamers were well along on their way to being serviceable on 15 November, when the Northern Group pulled out.

On that day eight transports proceeded to Fedhala, Casablanca and Safi to unload in protected harbors (*Electra* being torpedoed en route), while *Texas*, *Savannah* and seven destroyers escorted *Sangamon*, *Kennebec* and four transports of the Center Group to Hampton Roads.

Thus an operation which began under difficult circumstances, and encountered sundry unexpected twists and turns, was effectively concluded.

Before the *Texas* and her consorts departed, ground had been

broken in one corner of the Kasba for an American military cemetery. The bodies of Colonel Craw and of 84 officers and men lie
there overlooking the broad reaches of the Atlantic, facing the
country for which they gave their last measure of devotion.[28]

[28] Capt. A. T. Moen's Action Report of *Clymer*. There were 125 seriously
wounded who were evacuated to the transports, and 125 lightly wounded who
were retained ashore. (Col. E. C. Burkhart's Report.) The Navy lost 11 dead
and 26 wounded in the Northern Attack. (Dispatch File, AFAF.)

CHAPTER VI

The Southern Attack[1]

7–11 November 1942

1. *The Problem*

IN THE southern attack, on Safi, everything clicked. The landing was effected promptly with a minimum of loss; Army-Navy coöperation could not have been better; French resistance developed early, yet was quickly neutralized; and by the afternoon of 8 November all objectives had been attained. The story of this well timed and brilliantly executed operation is an amplification of Rear Admiral Lyal A. Davidson's crisp summary: —

That the Southern Attack Group was able to land at Safi with but two naval casualties and no material damage other than the loss of eight landing craft stranded and one burned, and with comparatively light casualties (estimated ten killed, seventy-five wounded) among the Army assault troops, is attributed to Divine Providence, good weather, surprise, retention of the initiative, and accurate and overpowering gunnery.

Follow the Moroccan coastline to the southward, around Cape Blanco and Cape Kantin, and you reach a point, about one hundred and fifty miles from Casablanca, where the coast becomes

---

[1] Sources for this chapter: the comprehensive Action Report by CTG 34.10 (Admiral Davidson); the Report of the Army Observer, Major James Y. Adams; the Action Report of Capt. Wallace B. Phillips commanding Transdiv 7; and the Report of Ensign John J. Bell to Admiral Hewitt 29 November 1942. The writer has also profited by conversations with Capt. Phillips, Capt. C. G. Richardson, Capt. Umstead of *New York*, Cdr. Palmer of *Cole*, and Ens. Bell. Two articles on the Safi landing: "Africa, We Took It and Liked It," by Ens. Robert Wallace USNR, who commanded one of the boat waves, appeared in *Sat. Eve. Post* 16 and 23 Jan. 1943. They are excellent for the spirit and atmosphere of the occupation, but unreliable as to details.

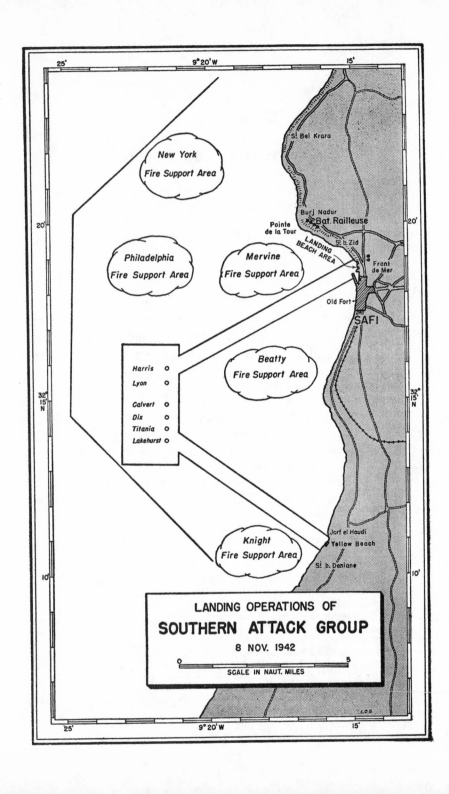

LANDING OPERATIONS OF
SOUTHERN ATTACK GROUP
8 NOV. 1942

0   5
SCALE IN NAUT. MILES

steep-to and cliffy. At a gap in the cliffs the Arabs centuries ago perched the small fishing town of Safi, facing west but somewhat protected from northerly gales. Subsequently the Portuguese built a masonry fort on the waterfront to protect their trade; and in the present century the French constructed a small artificial harbor just north of the old town to serve as an export point for phosphate rock. Highways and a railroad lead down to Safi harbor from the interior metropolis of Marrakech, which is also the site of a large airdrome and of a French Army base.

Safi was selected as the objective of the Southern Attack Group, partly to box off the French forces in Southern Morocco, but mainly because it offered the only facilities for landing medium tanks. The harbor is only half a mile long, tapering from a width of 580 yards near the entrance to only 170 yards at Petite Darse, the fishing-boat harbor and wet basin at the head. One quay, how-ever, was long enough and the water deep enough to berth the tank carrier *Lakehurst,* a former Port Everglades–Havana train-ferry steamer.[2] The 28-ton General Sherman tanks that she car-ried were too big to be landed in lighters, at least in such lighters as we had; there was no other harbor in Morocco that she could enter except Casablanca; and it was for the capture of Casablanca that those tanks were wanted.

Beaches in the Safi area were few. Beach Blue, as we called it, adjoining the north breakwater of the harbor, was the best. Beach Green, inside the harbor, was well protected. Less than a mile to the north was Beach Red, a mere pocket in the cliffs that only rock climbers could get out of. Nine or ten miles to the southward, adjoining the Jorf el Houdi, was Beach Yellow, thought to be a good starting point for an advance on Safi from the rear.

The harbor and all these beaches except the last were covered by artillery; the harbor was also defended by machine-gun nests. On a

[2] Described in the Standard Nomenclature List as "ex-APV 3, ex-*Seatrain New Jersey,* Auxiliary – Mechanized – Artillery Transport APM 9." We always re-ferred to her as "the Seatrain." She was built in 1940, 8,108 tons gross, 465 feet long. She had to be used, as no LSTs had been completed in time to take part in the operation.

300-foot cliff at the Pointe de la Tour, about two and a half miles north of the harbor, was the Batterie Railleuse [3] of four 130-mm coast defense guns. At the Front de Mer, the French sea frontier headquarters in a house commanding the harbor, was one section of 75-mm; a second was stationed in the town cemetery. None were in the old Portuguese fort within 600 yards of the harbor head. About two miles to the southward and near the coast was a mobile battery of four 155-mm guns well camouflaged. The mobile defenses were sufficiently manned by Foreign Legionnaires, and Moroccan Infantry.[4] All this ordnance could be brought to bear on the harbor, but in order to permit the Seatrain to enter and disembark these tanks, it was necessary for us to capture the harbor promptly and hold it securely. Naval tug *Cherokee,* one of the most useful vessels in the entire Task Force, was assigned to this group in the expectation that *Lakehurst* might need aid in berthing.

To effect prompt capture the assault destroyer game was used, as at Port Lyautey. Two old four-pipers, U.S.S. *Bernadou* and *Cole* (which had once made a speed of 41.7 knots and was then rated fastest ship in the world), were razeed and deprived of their torpedo tubes to minimize visibility and lessen weight. The plan was to get them inside the harbor ahead of the first four waves of landing boats, and take over.

2. *The Assault*

Southern Attack Group, under command of Rear Admiral L. A. Davidson in *Philadelphia,* was the first to peel off from Task Force

[3] So called from a French destroyer whose guns had formerly been mounted there. Only two of the guns were operational.

[4] Capt. Deuve, in enumerating the French casualties at the taking of Safi (27 killed, 44 wounded) says that these amounted to almost one sixth of the forces engaged, which would mean a total under 450. The general opinion in the American Army was that the French had about 1000 armed personnel on hand; some of the mobile forces were still maneuvering in the interior. General Harmon's Report states that the units present were two batteries 2nd Foreign Legion Artillery, two companies 2nd Foreign Legion Infantry, two companies 2nd Moroccan Infantry. It is now certain that the total was 450.

34 at daybreak 7 November.[5] A southerly course was laid toward Safi, and between 1300 and 1618 evasive courses were steered while the transport *Lyon* transferred approximately three hundred and fifty assault troops, who had been trained in night raider tactics, to *Bernadou* and *Cole*. An hour later all ships formed in single column. Sweepers *Howard* and *Hamilton* screened the van, which was led by the gallant old battleship *New York* and, six hundred yards in her rear, the light cruiser *Philadelphia*. Tug *Cherokee* plugged cheerfully along their flank, flaking her towlines against eventualities. Abaft the flagship, at intervals of six hundred yards, steamed the transports *Harris* (flagship of Captain Wallace B. Phillips), *Lyon*, *Calvert*, *Dorothea L. Dix* and *Titania*. Minelayer *Monadnock* and Seatrain *Lakehurst* brought up in the rear; escort carrier *Santee* and tanker *Merrimack* hovered discreetly behind. Four destroyers patrolled each flank. In order to make the approach with combat ships between the transports and Pointe de la Tour, Admiral Davidson brought this column into the transport area by two 90-degree wheels, so that its track looked like an inverted question mark. As the interval between the ships was not great, and all were in one column, nobody straggled. Signal *stop* was made at 2345, approximately in the assigned transport area, eight miles distant from Safi.[6] A few faint lights to the eastward, conspicuous in a very black night, marked the town. The sea was smooth with a moderate ground swell, and a light offshore breeze was blowing. Well trained *Harris*, who reached her position at 2355, lowered a landing boat before midnight; and all her boats, including a tank lighter, were in the water alongside at 0039 November 8.

U.S.S. *Barb*, the beacon submarine for this area, had been patrolling it for forty-eight hours. Her special mission was to put off

[5] Admiral Hewitt's Preliminary Report p. 5 gives the time as 0653.

[6] The Southern Group appears to have done a better navigation job during the approach than the others. Although the bearing of the breakwater turned out to be 83° instead of 63° at 0345, this was probably because an allowance had been made for a southerly drift which did not exist, though predicted by the Coast Pilot. Capt. O. M. Forster in *Harris* Action Report says that navigational fixes proved there was no drift in this area, unless westerly.

1st Lieutenant Willard G. Duckworth usa and four amphibiously trained army scouts in a rubber boat. Their mission was to take station by the bell buoy off the Safi breakwater in order to coach in *Bernadou* and *Cole* with radio and blinker; but everything went wrong. Lieutenant Duckworth and his men shoved off from the *Barb* about two hours before midnight at a point which the submarine skipper assured them to be three-and-a-half miles off shore, but which subsequent events proved to have been at least twice that distance. The scouts paddled continuously for six hours on the direct course for Safi, arrived off the breakwater exactly when the firing began, and attracted more than their share of enemy attention. As a rubber boat has no defense and no maneuverability, these unfortunate scouts, after paddling all night, had to go over the side and hang on to avoid machine-gun bullets that were whizzing a couple of feet over their vulnerable craft. They finally made the shore safely.[7]

In anticipation that something of this sort might happen, Ensign John J. Bell, who had been associated with Lieutenant Duckworth in Amphibious Force training activities, was assigned one of the beach-marking boats in which to act as pinch-hitter for the Lieutenant. He departed from *Harris* at 0200, in quest of the submarine and of whatever intelligence she might have picked up. Unable to locate her, he proceeded to take the place of the *Barb's* rubber boat, and moved in toward the breakwater, taking position off the bell buoy shortly after 0400. All this in black darkness.

In the meantime, boats were being loaded with troops and equipment alongside transports *Harris* and *Dix*, boat waves were being formed, and the control destroyers were standing by, signaling "Where are your babies?"

There was no straggling here to cause delay, but the usual trouble arose through boats' being separated from the troops they took ashore; *Harris* only received the last of the boats from *Lyon* and *Calvert* at 0200, although they were next astern of her in the

[7] Lt. Duckworth's Report is appended to that of Ens. Bell to Admiral Hewitt.

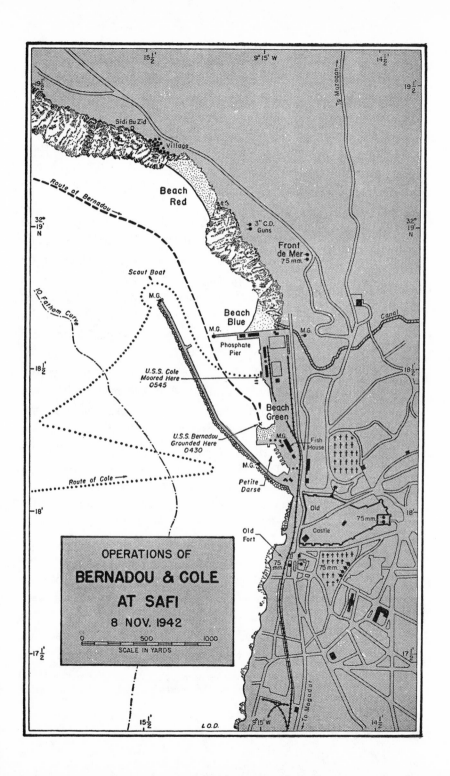

OPERATIONS OF
**BERNADOU & COLE
AT SAFI**
8 NOV. 1942

SCALE IN YARDS
0   500   1000

column formation.[8] But the greatest delay factor in the Southern Group was in embarking personnel. There was quite a roll on, and the soldiers with their 60 pounds of equipment hated to go over the rail and down the net ladders until the fellow ahead was safely in the boat. It took some boats a full hour to load 36 men and their equipment at the transport's side.[9] Consequently, H-hour, the date for the rush of landing boats from the departure line, had to be postponed from 0400 to 0430.

During the unloading there occurred the only example in the entire operation of an occurrence common in night warfare — firing on your friends. The tanker attached to each attack group carried on deck, athwartship, two 63-foot gasoline speedboats armed with machine guns and intended for use in aircraft rescue. These "crash boats," as we called them, were fragile but unwieldy, very noisy, and of little use except to deliver messages. They were all more or less wrecked by three days' rough usage, and the two belonging to the Southern Group were nearly expended before daylight. That happened around 0430. A motor truck being lowered from *Dorothea L. Dix*, into a tank lighter alongside, swung with the ship's roll and ruptured a five-gallon gasoline tank that was stowed topside. The gas spilled into the lighter below, caught fire from its engine, igniting both gas tank and ammunition. The lighter exploded with a flash that was seen and a loud roar that was heard by the other transports. Some officious radioman began transmitting, "*Dix* torpedoed, *Dix* torpedoed." Just then, the two crash boats belonging to this group, which had been laboriously lowered from tanker *Merrimack*, came charging into the transport area from *Dix's* direction. Everyone jumped to the conclusion that they were French motor torpedo boats that had hit the *Dix* and were looking for other targets. *Lyon's* and *Calvert's* gun crews let go with everything they had, and afforded the crash boats a somewhat earlier baptism of fire than they had expected. Fortunately, the

[8] *Lyon* required 96 minutes to lower 18 boats as against 40 minutes for *Harris* to lower a larger number — an excellent demonstration of what training means to a transport. Capt. Phillips's Report.

[9] Capt. Forster's Action Report of *Harris*.

transports' shooting was so wild that nobody was hurt. The crew of the tank lighter, blown overboard by the explosion, were saved through quick and courageous work by a landing craft from *Titania.*[10]

The first assault waves from *Dix*, carrying the 2nd Battalion of the 47th Regiment, were to have landed at Beach Yellow, some nine miles south of Safi, in order to take the town from the rear in case anything went wrong elsewhere. Her scout boat located this beach after considerable search, and had marked it with a yellow flare by 0430. But the boat explosion so disconcerted *Dix's* crew that by 0523 only one incomplete boat wave was ready to go in with the control destroyer *Knight.* Captain Phillips therefore decided to postpone that particular landing until after daylight. His decision was most fortunate, because Beach Yellow proved to be a dangerous landing place with a heavy surf; and owing to our success in the harbor area, no troops were needed there anyway.[11]

Now came the great moment when *Bernadou* and *Cole* were to make their dash for the harbor, each carrying 197 raider-trained soldiers in addition to her own crew of 150. Every precaution had been taken. Three-inch 50-caliber ammunition for the main batteries was point-detonating. Fuel oil had been removed from outboard tanks above the waterline. Locker tops, mattresses and bedding from the living compartments were stowed aft in the crew's washroom on deck so that no combustibles were left below; and in order to afford the crew sufficient working space on deck, most of the soldiers had to lay below. From their rendezvous near the *Harris* the course for Safi Harbor mouth was supposed to be 63°. Lieutenant Commander Palmer, skipper of *Cole*, believing that they were farther north than that bearing would indicate, took a sight on the "lighthouse" situated at the base of the transverse jetty and found it to bear 83°. That happened to be the correct bearing of the lighthouse, but its light was not lit; the one Palmer

[10] *Dix, Titania* and *Lyon* Action Reports. Coxswain Henry B. Kulizak was particularly commended.
[11] The troops that landed there after daylight reached Safi at 1400.

saw was in a house overlooking the harbor, which happened to be on the same bearing. So, by committing one error, he compensated for another. The correct course was also given him by *Mervine*.

Shaping a circuitous course based on this true (though false) bearing, *Bernadou* left the rendezvous at 0345 and *Cole*, with boat waves following, at 0403. Their plan of approach was to steam close under the cliffs in order to escape observation; it is surprising how invisible a destroyer becomes when you clear off her masts and cut down her stacks.[12] From observing the lights of motor cars hastening toward the Batterie Railleuse the men on board suspected, and from the records[13] we now know, that the French were already alerted. Casablanca had telegraphed *"Danger"* at 0130 and *"Alerte"* at 0227. Captain Deuve, the local commander, had alerted every strong point but one by 0340. At 0400 spotters at the Front de Mer saw a ship which at first they thought to be an expected steam fisherman, approaching the harbor mouth. Ten minutes later, *Bernadou* was challenged by blinker and naturally gave the wrong answer.[14] Although the element of surprise was technically lost, actually it was not, for "in the complete darkness the French were unable to visualize the attack or to gauge the size or composition of our forces."[15] Had this assault been postponed until daylight, our losses would have been severe.

Guided by Ensign Bell's scout boat, *Bernadou* neatly rounded the bell buoy and was just entering the narrow harbor mouth at 0428 when "hell broke loose." The 75-mm battery at Front de Mer (only 1500 yards away), the machine-gun nests all around the

[12] On the way across, one vessel in the convoy requested that an assault destroyer be ordered to the rear, as she was continually running afoul of her in the darkness.

[13] From the radio log at the Front de Mer, captured by our troops, and a translation of the report on this action by Capt. Deuve, French commander at Safi, to his commanding general Marrakech Division, 14 Nov. 1942, in Admiral Davidson's Report.

[14] She replied with the same letter as the challenge. A French prisoner afterwards said that if she had replied with anything else she would have got by, as the code had recently been changed; and as they thought she was a fishing steamer coming in, they would not then have opened fire.

[15] Admiral Davidson's Report.

harbor, and even the 155-mm battery two miles to the southward, opened up on her. *Bernadou* shot off an American Flag flare [16] in the hope of persuading the French not to fire. The French threw up star shell, and the little harbor became light as day. Batterie Railleuse at the Pointe de la Tour took destroyer *Mervine* under fire, its shells appearing "as a white luminous glow whipping toward us, whistling overhead and then smoking in the water." [17] *Mervine* broadcasted "Batter Up!" at 0428; Admiral Davidson replied with the earliest "Play Ball!" of the Moroccan front at 0439, and within a minute *Philadelphia* and *New York* were throwing 6-inch and 14-inch hardware at Pointe de la Tour.

Nicest little pyrotechnic display ever seen in Morocco.

It was a miracle that *Bernadou* came through unhurt. In the darkness she entered a harbor that nobody on board had ever seen, and almost point-blank fire from an arc of 200 degrees converged on her. In that narrow harbor she could not employ a destroyer's chief defenses, speed and maneuverability. An anchored coaster was sighted dead ahead, and two other small craft on her port bow blocked access to the pier where she intended to land the troops. Yet, the one fear of her officers was being sunk in the fairway, which would prevent the Seatrain from coming in. Here is the gist of what the *Bernadou* gave back to the French. She swept the jetty on her starboard hand with Number 1 20-mm, and Number 5 3-inch 50-caliber; swept the dock and phosphate pier with Numbers 2, 3 and 4 20-mm and Numbers 1, 2, 4 and 6 3-inch 50. Number 1 3-inch fired two rounds into the old Portuguese fort, which scored two direct hits and prevented any guns there being manned. Number 2 3-inch made two direct hits on the 75-mm which first opened fire at Front de Mer, and silenced it. A grenade launcher took out a machine-gun nest on the long jetty. All oppo-

---

[16] This was a star shell with a flag attachment. The Admiral thought that it only helped the French by illuminating our ship, but a French gunner later told one of our men that he saw the Stars and Stripes when ready to fire a 75, and held his hand.

[17] Capt. Hartman's Action Report of *Mervine*. La Railleuse straddled her repeatedly, but made no hits.

sition being silenced, the order to cease fire was given at 0514.[18]

While dishing this out, *Bernadou* bent on more knots, dashed by the small craft that screened the quay, which was her first choice for berthing, and at 0430 executed her alternate plan, grounding so gently that her bottom was uninjured, alongside some rocks at the end of the Petite Jettée near the harbor head. The assault troops (Company K, 47th Infantry) clambered down a landing net over her port bow onto the rocks and a few minutes later were chasing members of the famous Foreign Legion away from the harbor.

"*Cole! Cole!* Come on in!" was heard for some time over the voice radio before *Cole* appeared. The one-time Speed Queen of the Atlantic Fleet was lost temporarily in the darkness. Shepherding the first boat waves from the *Harris,* she was still well offshore when the shooting started. From the bridge a vague shape was seen in the darkness crossing her bow. This was destroyer *Beatty,* on anti-submarine patrol, but *Cole* mistook her for *Bernadou* and by following her missed the harbor mouth and headed straight for the long jetty. Ensign Bell, observing this from his scout boat, blinked briskly and got *Cole* on his radio. Just in time to avoid the jetty, she reversed engines, turned west and then northeast, cut between the buoy and the jetty, and entered the harbor at 0517. The landing boats following her showed fine discipline in keeping up. They were destined for Beach Blue and some of them actually reached it before *Cole* was berthed. This delay may be counted another "Spetial Prouidence," as Cotton Mather would have said, because if *Cole* had brought her boat waves in right after *Bernadou,* at the height of the shooting, some of the troops would have been hit. Her appearance, to be sure, was the signal for a renewed burst of enemy fire, but it was feeble compared with what had greeted *Bernadou,* as so much of the source of that had been shot out.

Cole had been directed to moor at the merchandise pier on the eastern side of the harbor. Anticipating the difficulties of maneuver-

[18] Boiled down and corrected as to identity of targets from *Bernadou* Action Report. Gunnery Officer Lt. (jg) William R. Brewster Jr., who had just celebrated his twenty-first birthday, "displayed a coolness and courage which was heartening to me and to the gun crews," reported Cdr. Braddy.

ing in that narrow space — difficulties enhanced by the presence of the three small craft — the planners had invented a new gadget. In place of a depth charge for one of the Y-guns, she had placed on the arbor a 50-pound grapnel with a 4-inch hawser bent to it, and flaked along the sheer strake. Having arrived off her quay, yet too far for a heaving-line to reach shore, the Y-gun shot out the grapnel, which caught neatly in a railroad track. But one of the soldiers on board spoiled it all. Helpful Joe, mistaking the hawser for a device of the enemy, whipped out his sheath knife and cut it. So the *Cole* had to back and fill after all; but soldiers already landed from *Bernadou* caught her heaving lines, and by 0545 she was snugly berthed. Before day broke at 0600, her raider detachment (Company L, 47th Infantry) was ashore and fighting.

The two destroyers and their troops came through this ordeal with but a single casualty — one man aboard *Cole* was shot through the lungs, and he reported for duty a month later. A bold, original, and complicated plan, made by Admiral Hewitt's staff away back in Norfolk, worked perfectly.

A part of Headquarters under Lieutenant J. W. Calton USA, who had had commando training in England, landed on Beach Blue with the first wave and promptly seized the town telephone exchange. Other assault troops of Company "A" moved northward toward the Pointe de la Tour. Light tanks came ashore in LCMs on Beach Green as early as 0530, and infantry used the same beach. At dawn the 1st Battalion 47th Regiment 9th Division deployed and attacked French units that were firing from the hillside; later waves of troops fanned out on either side; and with the capture of Front de Mer at 1000, the initial beachhead was secured.

"General Harmon gave it as his fixed opinion that, had not the port and town been taken by surprise during darkness, he would have had as heavy a fight as at Port Lyautey, with consequent heavy losses. The assault destroyers were of inestimable worth." [19]

From daylight on, the troops and bluejackets in the harbor area

[19] General Harmon's verbal report included in Col. E. C. Burkhart's Report.

were shot at from the hill slopes to the eastward; few were hit and none killed. When the Army asked for fire support on the Front de Mer, the sniper headquarters, the *Cole* with one salvo knocked off one corner of the top story and forced its surrender. *Bernadou* floated at high water and moored alongside *Cole*. In the early afternoon, Seatrain *Lakehurst,* for whom all this business cleared the way, made her entry. Followed by tug *Cherokee,* she suggested a dignified queen entering a captured castle with a tiny maid of honor. And she was appropriately followed by *Titania,* who promptly began unloading at the phosphate pier. By 1600 the landing forces controlled a beachhead extending ten thousand yards to the rear.

3. *Fire Support and Air Support*

Batterie Railleuse, the strongest coast defense unit in the Safi region, started shooting in the direction of the harbor, as soon as the "fireworks" occasioned by *Bernadou* attracted its attention. *New York, Philadelphia* and destroyer *Mervine,* at about 0436, commenced firing back,[20] in order to draw the battery's attention away from the harbor. It ceased firing shortly, and our fire support group, unable to locate it in the darkness, checked at 0450. Shortly after 0600, when day was breaking, *New York* catapulted a spotting plane and stood by expecting something to happen. At 0640 it did; the four 130-mm guns of Batterie Railleuse opened upon her. This thirty-year-old battlewagon steered north-and-south courses at ranges of 16,000 to 18,000 yards,[21] daintily zigzagging like a dowager dancing a minuet as she dished out 14-inch projectiles. The shore battery fired fast and accurately, making several straddles but no hits. After an expenditure of 60 rounds of 14-inch by *New York* and approximately three hundred by the battery, a

[20] It should be remembered that our ships had instructions not to fire unless fired upon.
[21] The actual distances were 2000 yards less, as the battery was on a cliff 525 feet above sea level.

(LEFT) Fire Control Station of battery, after 12-inch shell had plowed furrow in foreground and ricocheted through observation slot

(RIGHT) Batterie Railleuse at the close of the action

Courtesy Commander Benjamin L. Talman

Bernadou aground, debarkation net over bows

Batterie Railleuse and U.S.S. Bernadou, 8 November 1942

From landward, afternoon of D-day. U.S.S. *Cole* and *Bernadou* are alongside quay in center, *Lakehurst* can be seen over dock roof, and *Titania* alongside pier at right. An SBD is in flight. Beach Green is near head of the harbor

From seaward, 10 November. The two conspicuous beaches are the Red and the Blue; Safi town is at extreme right. The ships, left to right, are U.S.S. *Dix, Calvert, Harris, Lyon* and *Housatonic*

Safi Harbor

lucky shot around 0800 hit the ground in front of the fire control station on the edge of the cliff and ricocheted through the observation slot, killing everyone within and wrecking the instruments. Batterie Railleuse ceased fire at 0850. Later that morning our troops came in, took possession, and spiked the guns by spreading the muzzles.[22]

Admiral Davidson observes in his report that but for the effective fire delivered by *New York*, the Batterie Railleuse could have made the Safi harbor untenable for the American attack forces. She had also helped disprove the popular notion that battleships had become obsolete and useless.

Another effective bombardment was performed by the *Philadelphia* on a battery of three 155-mm guns located a short distance back of the coast, three miles south of Safi. General Harmon, believing that this battery was molesting his troops operating in that area, called for naval gunfire support; at 1035 the flagship commenced fire on the position indicated in the chart at hand. *Philadelphia*'s spotting plane reported shortly that no guns were there. Fire was checked, and the spotter, by flying low, located the well camouflaged battery about half a mile east of its supposed position. At 1110 action was renewed and 109 rounds of 6-inch bombardment were fired at a range of 12,000 yards. Plane spotter reported that no direct hits had yet been made, although the area had been well peppered.[23] Admiral Davidson then decided to send in float planes to try for direct bomb hits. Four 325-pound demolition and two 100-pound fragmentation bombs were dropped by the *Philadelphia*'s own planes, after which General Harmon signaled that the battery was neutralized. The guns were put out of commission

[22] In some of the Action Reports (notably that of Capt. Phillips) and in an illustration of this battery that appeared in the press, it is said that the guns were spiked by the French. This is not true. Lt. Col. Deutsch, who was on board *Philadelphia*, witnessed the spiking through his binoculars, and other eyewitnesses have confirmed him, including Col. E. H. Randle USA who gave the order.

[23] The battery occupied a space of only 600 square feet; and as the pattern of the 6-inch 47 salvo at 12,000 yards is approximately 450 feet, "it can be readily seen that with perfect fire control and perfect spotting the getting of a direct hit on a gun pit is largely a matter of chance." (Report of Capt. Paul Hendren of *Philadelphia*.)

by the French cannoneers, by loosening the recoil mechanism from the barrel of each piece and then firing a light charge.[24]

Fortunately the original air-operation plan, which contemplated an early destruction of aircraft on the fields at Bou Guedra, Marrakech, and Agadir, was abandoned; because of a false report that General Henry-Martin, the French sector commander for Safi-Mogador, would not oppose the landing at Safi if his planes and fields were not attacked. Consequently only *Santee*, greenest of the carriers, was attached to the Southern Group in order to furnish combat air patrol and anti-submarine patrol for the landing force. One of the five escort carriers converted from tankers, she "shook loose" from the Navy Yard, in the graphic phrase of Captain W. D. Sample,[25] on 13 September 1942, but even then was unable to shake off the yard workmen or, for another month, to make practice cruises and flights. She had only five experienced aviators on board, and very few of her officers and men had previously smelled salt water. On the passage to Morocco she was allowed but one flight operation of six planes. Only nine of her planes had operated for more than ten days prior to 8 November. And the wind was even lighter off Safi than farther north, so that taking off from a low-speed carrier was difficult and sometimes impossible.

In consequence *Santee*, making fewer combat sorties than any the four carriers, suffered almost half our total plane losses. Twenty-one out of thirty-one that she carried were lost or missing by 11 November; only one of them, possibly, by enemy action.

The first flight of seven Wildcats left *Santee* at daybreak 8 November, to provide protection for the transports and landing craft. One pilot radioed that his oil-line had been cut, whether by enemy action or otherwise he did not say, and nothing more was heard of him or seen of his plane. Five pilots could not find the carrier on their way back. One crashed in the sea (the pilot in his rubber

[24] Report of Lt. (jg) O. W. Corrie, who examined the guns after the bombardment.

[25] Enclosure A in Admiral McWhorter's Report on Operation Torch; conversations with Lt. Corrie (Observer on board *Santee*).

boat was picked up by a destroyer sixty hours later), four landed on or near Mazagan airfield, were taken prisoner and lost their planes; only one returned safely to *Santee*. Later in the day another flight ran out of gas and tried to land on Safi airfield, which was too soft and bumpy for Wildcats. All bogged down, but others tried the same thing later until nine planes had been wrecked on that field. Fortunately, only one plane was wanted for reconnaissance by General Harmon ashore, "and Lieutenant Commander Joseph Aloysius Ruddy USN, our group commander, responded and commenced his excellent exemplification of a one-man air force. . . . Joe landed only once for refueling and spent over eight hours in the air that day and over nine hours the next day. . . . Joe had equipped himself for any eventuality . . . he was loaded down like a porter starting on a long safari. Extra gear included a murderous-looking knife, pistols, a rifle, a shotgun, a garrot, a special knapsack of home comforts, a small camera and 7 by 50 binoculars." [26]

Admiral Davidson, not impressed by the carrier plane performance, relied on the planes belonging to *New York* and *Philadelphia* for close air support missions; and it was one of the flagship's SOCs that bombed the French submarine *Méduse* after she had beached near Cape Blanco.

Weak air power at Safi might have had serious subsequences if the enemy had taken advantage of his opportunity. The harbor, with *Lakehurst, Titania*, three or four transports, several destroyers, and mountains of stores concentrated in a space a mile square, offered an ideal target for air attack. Fortunately none developed on the eighth, and on the ninth a heavy blanket of fog protected the harbor from high-level bombers. In the meantime, one of *Santee's* aviators had stirred up the French by dropping bombs on their Marrakech field without orders,[27] and General Martin sent

[26] *Santee* Action Report.
[27] Conversation with Capt. W. B. Phillips. *Santee* Report describes the incident thus: the aviator reconnoitered Marrakech airfield, observed a plane landing and two tuning up, and was fired on by AA; he then let go two bombs which did not detonate.

a bomber squadron to retaliate shortly after daylight on the ninth. Only one French plane got through the overcast; it dropped one bomb which hit the roof of a fish-house in the Petite Darse and started a fire, but that was quickly brought under control and the anti-aircraft batteries of *Lakehurst* and other transports in the harbor shot the bomber down.[28] This was the only enemy air attack on Safi; although the fog lifted at 0800, the bombers did not return.

Now that Marrakech was aroused, we could no longer afford to ignore the enemy planes based there; and *Santee's* pilots were active on 9 November, led by "Joe" Ruddy. Admiral Davidson called for a bombing attack on the airdrome. On its way, the squadron's attention was called by Army radio to a column of trucks carrying soldiers from Marrakech toward Safi. Three planes peeled off, delivered an attack, and believed that they had destroyed twelve out of fourteen trucks, but an Army observer reported that the trucks were only dispersed.[29] French troops certainly got through as far as Bou Guedra, 26 kilometers from Safi, where they collided with elements from the 2nd Armored Division United States Army and withdrew. The other planes of this squadron destroyed 15 grounded planes at Marrakech and attacked another column of 40 trucks on their way home.

Next day (10 November) the French advanced again toward Bou Guedra. Ensign Jacques from *Santee* shot down a French reconnaissance plane. Another aviator attempted to pilot an Avenger, a type in which he had had less than three hours' flying experience. He was shot down by anti-aircraft fire, but survived. His fellows did some useful strafing of ground troops in the foothills. The final exploit of the *Santee* pilots was to destroy a dozen aircraft on the Marrakech field 11 November, after the armistice had been declared.

[28] Admiral Davidson's Report; Major Adams's Report says 3 killed, 12 wounded, 3 or 4 vehicles burned.
[29] Major Adams's Report.

4. *Unloading and Fueling*

Less heroic than the assault but no less indispensable was the work of unloading. All fighting men and tanks were ashore by 1800 November 10,[30] and Captain Phillips's transports were completely discharged five days and eighteen hours after their arrival off the beach. Unloading was effected largely by sailors; for as soon as the Army landed it was — "Good-bye, Jack, thanks for the trip; rush that stuff ashore, I've got to go and fight." General Harmon did his best to help the Navy by assigning Army details to the docks, but the officers were constantly being changed, the noncoms knew nothing about unloading, and men trained to fight resented being given a stevedore job.

During the first three days of unloading, the naval details were a good deal bothered by snipers, but the Army finally cleaned them out and engaged a considerable number of natives to help, the price being one cigarette or a hunk of Navy bread for each case handled, plus five Moroccan francs per day.

An extract from the log of the transport *Lyon's* beach party will show the vicissitudes of this inglorious but necessary part of amphibious operations.[31]

8 *Nov.*, 2000.   Relieved by *Harris* beach party. Slept in foxholes on beach, for protection from snipers.

9 *Nov.*, 0530.   Turned-to unloading.

0630.   Bombing attack. Put out fire started by enemy aircraft. Medical section cares for wounded. Unloading resumed.

1500.   Ordered to Beach Blue, which was cluttered up with vehicles. Medical and communication sections set up anew. Worked past midnight getting ambulance and jeep out of water.

[30] Major Adams's Report.
[31] Report of Lt. (jg) A. C. Witteborg Jr. enclosed in *Lyon* Action Report.

10 *Nov.*, 0300.   Turned in, to foxholes again.

Dawn.   Turned-to, unloading vehicles and removing stranded ones. Joined by *Dix* beach party.

2100.   Turned in, to air-raid cave on shore.

2200.   All hands roused out and sent to *Bernadou* to load ammunition and gasoline.

11 *Nov.*, 0700.   Secured loading *Bernadou* and returned to air-raid shelter to rest.

1500.   Turned-to, raised and repaired sunken landing boat.

1730.   Seaplanes from *Philadelphia* arrived for fueling.

1900.   Secured for day.

And so on, until 1500 November 13, when the log ends with "Unloading finished, returned aboard ship."

This beach party worked without complaint because they knew it had to be done. They slept in foxholes in damp sand and ate when they could. Most of the men had no dry clothes until the night of 11 November. Their devotion to duty received generous praise from the Army Observer: "Boat crews of landing craft performed valiantly, and all the transport crews worked for protracted periods without sleep or rest."

The landing craft crews performed, not only valiantly in this sector, but professionally. Out of 121 landing craft employed, only one was destroyed and eight damaged; these last were salvaged.[32]

A splendid job of discharging cargo was done by *Titania* alongside the phosphate pier in Safi harbor. Her crew, working day and night with very little outside aid, got everything on the beach inside seventy-eight hours. She and other transports served as hospitals for the *Harris* beach party. One detail salvaged landing craft from Beach Blue, another put the sabotaged Phosphate Company's powerhouse in working order so electric cranes could be used on

[32] War Dept. "Lessons Learned" Report 12 Feb. 1943, Annex G–1. It must, however, be remembered that, owing to the decision not to use Beaches Red and Yellow and the prompt securing of the harbor, the boats had a relatively easy time landing.

the dock. Details from other ships mastered the machinery of the two small tugs in the harbor, and got up steam so they could be put to work. As one cruiser captain remarked, "You can always count on the bluejackets for anything. They never let you down."

The concluding exploit of this Southern Attack Group added a new note to amphibious warfare — the use of a destroyer as filling station for tanks. General Patton wanted the medium tanks off *Lakehurst* for the final assault on Casablanca scheduled for the morning of 11 November. But they could not make the journey on only one fill, and General Harmon had no trucks to carry a supply of gas. Accordingly, the versatile *Cole* was employed to conduct a string of landing craft carrying drummed gasoline to Mazagan, about two thirds of the way to Casablanca.

The tank column started north half an hour after the last General Sherman rolled off *Lakehurst*. En route, General Gaffey, who commanded the tanks, had a curious experience that illustrated the French civilian attitude toward Americans. His car was stopped by a large stone in the road with a red lantern on it. An old man was standing by. The General asked what the hell he thought he was doing? Old man said that was a road block, to stop tanks. General: "You couldn't stop a tank with that little rock." Old man: "That's a *symbolic* road block." General: "What's the lantern for?" Old man: "I was afraid you might not see my block and hurt yourselves!"

The tank column arrived at Mazagan ahead of the *Cole* in the early morning of 11 November. The feeble French garrison at Mazagan, before sighting the General Shermans and a flight of *Santee's* planes overhead, had received the order to cease fire from Casablanca headquarters. The tanks were no longer urgently needed, but they still wanted a fill and obtained it from the five-gallon tins that landing craft lightered ashore from the *Cole*. This tank column later moved on to Rabat.

When the word came through from Admiral Darlan on the morning of 11 November, French representatives from Marrakech came down to Safi and arranged with General Harmon and his staff a cessation of fighting.[33] French prisoners to the number of three hundred were ceremoniously released on the morning of the thirteenth, and "the N.C.O.'s of the garrison at Safi expressed their appreciation that the French flag had never been taken down from over the town." [34] The 47th Infantry Regiment remained to garrison Safi, and excellent relations were established with the local population.

[33] Oral report of General Harmon and General Gaffey on Safi, incorporated in Col. E. C. Burkhart's Report.

[34] Report of Col. Edwin H. Randle (C.O. 47th Infantry) 2 Dec. 1942, enclosed in General Patton's First Report.

CHAPTER VII

Morocco Secured

9 November – 1 December 1942

1. *Events at Fedhala*[1]

a. Unloading Progress

WE LEFT the Center Attack Group at the close of 8 November with the French naval forces in Casablanca decimated, but with plenty of trouble ahead.

At Fedhala the great and pressing problem was to unload the transports quickly. The Army was clamoring for reserves and vehicles; the transports were anchored in an open roadstead, protected by a large destroyer screen, but perfect targets for any submarine that might get through. On 8 November *Miantonomah* laid a protective mine field to the north and east of the transport area, but the Center Attack Group had sufficient respect for U-boats to believe they could circumvent it, as they did.

The progress of unloading in this group can best be followed from tables enclosed with Captain Emmet's report. At the time it seemed exasperatingly slow, but anyone who has had to do with discharging cargo by lighter will appreciate that these men, with bouncing landing craft instead of lighters alongside, worked hard and persistently to get Major General J. W. Anderson's 3rd Infantry Division and 67th Armored Regiment ashore.

---

[1] CTF 34 Staff Notes on Torch, compiled by officers on the way home; Capt. O. T. Shepard's "Rough, Partial Estimate of the Situation" to Admiral Hewitt 11 Nov. 1942; Capt. A. G. Shepard Report on Torch Operation to Cinclant 31 Dec. 1942; also documents cited in first footnote to Chapter III.

PROGRESS OF CENTER ATTACK FORCE, IN PERCENTAGES

	TROOPS	VEHICLES	SUPPLIES		
At 1700 November 8	39	16	01.1	*Total No. Troops:*	19,870
At 1700 November 9	55	31	03.3	*Total No. Vehicles:*	1,701
At 1700 November 10	87	54	14.0	*Total tonnage of sup-*	
At 1700 November 11	100	68	24.0	*plies (approximately):*	15,000
At 1700 November 12		88	40.0		

Rest of unloading effected at Casablanca.

All night long, 8–9 November, unloading from the transports continued; no rest for cargo winches, landing boats, or men. Day broke fair off Fedhala 9 November, and morning twilight brought the first enemy air raid on the transport area. The planes hit nothing. Sun rose golden, with showers; the wind was still light and offshore but the swell had risen perceptibly, and under the haze that concealed everything behind the beaches one could see the whole coast ringed with surf. A lone bomber flew across about 0737, dropped four bombs near *Brooklyn* and made off. In order to help unloading, Captain Emmet pulled his transports in until the nearer ones were on the previous day's line of departure, only four thousand yards from shore.

b. Shift of Command

Overall command in an amphibious operation shifts from the admiral afloat to the general ashore when the latter believes that his attack force is firmly established. General Patton spent the night of 8 November on board *Augusta* because, as he jovially remarked, the "goddam Navy" had demolished the kitchen of the house he had selected for his headquarters at Fedhala. On the morning of the ninth he went ashore again, established a command post in the field, and set up headquarters in the Hotel Miramar — which the German Armistice Commission had hastily vacated the previous day. Admiral Hewitt visited him there that afternoon, and thenceforth, since the overall command of troops ashore was General Patton's, the Navy assumed the supporting rôle.[2]

[2] Statement by Cdr. L. A. Bachman (Admiral Hewitt's Intelligence Officer), and the Admiral's recollection. There appears to be no information on the subject in Action Reports.

c. Unloading Troubles

This shift of command did not of course lessen the Navy's responsibility for completing the unloading.

Before the end of D-day, arrangements were made with the local French authorities to take the three smaller cargo ships of the Center Attack Group, *Arcturus, Procyon* and *Oberon,* one at a time, into Fedhala Harbor — where there was only one berth for a seagoing ship. This move had been anticipated in the plan. Every other vessel had to be unloaded by landing boats with the aid of a few small French craft that were pressed into service. When destroyer *Bristol* captured the French trawler *Poitou* on 8 November, Captain Heffernan put a prize crew aboard and ordered them to report to Captain Emmet in *Leonard Wood.* *Poitou* was a tremendous help in getting our men to the beach, taking about 200 soldiers ashore per trip and working steadily for two days and nights. She also released landing craft for unloading supplies. Fedhala Harbor, small as it was, proved a boon in the unloading process; for the surf was rising, the beaches were becoming dangerous, and the removal of supplies from them was difficult for want of vehicles. Consequently, the beachmaster, Commander Jamison, routed all boat traffic to the harbor or to the near-by Beach Red where there was some protection. Two tank lighters which disregarded his orders came in too fast ahead of a wave crest, hit the beach when in the trough, and were turned completely over, end for end.

In spite of the expenditure of landing craft on D-day, there were still enough left to handle the boom capacity of each ship; unloading the stuff ashore presented the first real difficulty. The transports and AKs were supposed to be combat-loaded, but the insistence of the Army in bringing garrison equipment and long-range supplies in the assault transports resulted in congestion and foul-up. Ammunition, provisions, equipment and vehicles came ashore all mixed up, creating extra work to sort it out. We in the Task Force had prepared for this to some extent, but nobody realized how big and complicated a job it would be. The Amphibious Force had a Shore Party School in which soldiers were trained in handling supplies, getting them off beaches promptly and into classified dumps; but not enough men had been trained. The failure of the Army Shore Party to function properly was the most glaring defect in this and future amphibious operations. Officers placed in charge both of Army shore parties and of Navy beach parties [3] were not clothed with sufficient authority to cope with so difficult a situation. Communications equipment was rendered useless by salt water and the natives stole telephone wire as fast as it was laid.[4] There was a crying need for trucks to move the stuff once it got ashore; but General Patton required most of the vehicles to move his army toward Casablanca. A premature whoop of joy went up when the captured French ship *Capitaine Paul Lemerle* was found to contain sixty French Army trucks destined for Dakar; but they lacked essential parts and were of no use. So there was not one bottleneck but a series of bottlenecks: boats, vehicles, labor, communications; and it was providential that the enemy made no attempt to bomb the harbor area, where a few well-placed explosives would have blown bottles and necks alike to bits.

The most admirable feature of this unloading process was the vigor with which it was carried on by bluejackets and coastguardsmen when the Army Shore Parties proved inadequate. Transport officers sent details ashore to help and drove their crews relentlessly on board, where operations continued all night. For instance, be-

[3] A Navy beach party is not primarily concerned with unloading. As organized for this expedition it consisted of (*a*) Hydrographic section to mark obstructions; (*b*) Maintenance section to salvage and repair boats; (*c*) Medical section to set up first-aid stations and evacuate wounded, and (*d*) Communications section, to communicate with ships and with other beaches. Actually, for want of Army coöperation, the Navy beach parties and boat crews did most of the unloading. See previous chapter for a description of what a typical Navy beach party, that of *Lyon* at Safi, had to do.

[4] Capt. Emmet issued an important order about holding up the landing of provisions and expediting vehicles at 0943 Nov. 11. Delivery of this order was completed at 1845. There were many occasions in the operation when runners or men pulling boats could have beaten the radio. Compare Colonel X "African Snafu" *Infantry Journal* LVIII No. 1, Jan. 1946, p. 51.

tween 2100 November 9 and daybreak November 10, *Ancon* landed the 3rd Signal Company, both equipment and personnel; *Thurston* and *Elizabeth C. Stanton* landed Batteries C and B of the 39th and 9th Field Artillery Regiments complete; and *Biddle* put ashore the bulky signal and medical equipment of the 2nd Armored Division.[5] By 0806 November 10, all fighting troops were ashore or moving thither. The exhausted boat crews, who had been working continuously since midnight 7 November with catch-as-catch-can meals and brief snatches of sleep, could stand no more. They fell asleep on the boat trip or when unloading; some even ran their craft aground in Fedhala Harbor at low water so they could "caulk off" until flood tide.

2. *French Hostilities Concluded*

After the early morning air attacks, 9 November was fairly quiet off Fedhala. Destroyer *Wilkes* swapped a few punches with the shore battery at Table d'Aoukasha. The Army was engaged in advancing to positions whence Casablanca could be attacked from the east and south. Such French combat ships as remained intact attempted no sortie. Both sides were taking stock and getting ready for the next move. American air superiority was more definitely asserted when a squadron of six Wildcats from *Ranger* encountered eleven Dewoitine 520s, shot down five, and damaged four more. After this fight and the shooting down of a mysterious black-painted "phantom raider," an ME–109 which had been making low-level strafings on the Fedhala beaches, neither the transports nor the beach were again troubled from the air. The Wildcats broke up a column of fifty French trucks bringing reinforcements into Casablanca, and both they and the dive-bombers set fire to a number of tanks. The *Ranger's* fighter planes also took part in the air attack on Port Lyautey.[6] All day on the tenth, carrier

[5] Capt. Emmet's Narrative of Events.
[6] *Ranger* Action Report; *"Wildcats" Over Casablanca* pp. 125–127, 137. Chapters IX and X of this book have an amusing account of the adventures of Navy aviators who made crash landings or bailed out in Morocco.

planes ranged over the area at will, strafing and dive-bombing troop concentrations and columns of tanks and trucks.

On the early morning of the tenth, plans were drawn up by the Army for an all-out assault on Casablanca next day. The capture of Port Lyautey airdrome and the Kasba removed a great source of anxiety to the northward; now Safi was in the bag, battleship *New York* was ordered up to reinforce the Center Group,[7] and General Harmon's tanks began moving north toward Mazagan.

Admiral Michelier did not intend to let Casablanca fall to us without another fight. Capitaine de Corvette Bégouën-Demeaux, organizing survivors from the four sunken destroyers and a battalion of Senegalese troops, formed a defensive line running inland from the Table d'Aoukasha through the Ainsaba anti-aircraft battery of 90-mm guns. When General Anderson's troops advanced westward in two columns toward this line, they met their first real ground resistance. The French had naval gunfire support from the twin-mounted 90-mm (3.7-inch) anti-aircraft batteries of the *Jean Bart*, and from corvettes *La Gracieuse* and *Commandant Delage*. These latter vessels advanced along the coast shortly before 1100, firing into our troops with their 100-mm anti-aircraft and machine guns. *Augusta* immediately steamed toward the scene of action, accompanied by destroyers *Edison*, *Boyle*, *Tillman* and *Rowan*. *Edison* opened fire on the leading corvette at 1125, while *Tillman* took on the other; at 1139 *Augusta* fired the first of ten salvos at a range of 18,000 yards. Within a few minutes the corvettes, although suffering only slight damage, put back into Casablanca under a smoke screen. Deprived of their help, the French defensive line was breached by the 30th Infantry mortar guns. But Admiral Michelier still had a little surprise for us.

A couple of large, yellow circles appeared on the sea ahead of *Augusta* and quickly developed into geysers of yellow-dyed water some sixty feet high. These were from *Jean Bart's* 15-inch main battery, silent since the hit on the morning of the eighth and re-

---

[7] Also, *Cleveland* was exchanged for *Brooklyn*, who had expended a large proportion of her ammunition on the 8th, and *Brooklyn* joined the offshore group protecting the *Ranger*.

ported to be completely knocked out by our carrier-based dive-bombers. The crew had repaired the turret but cannily left the guns pointing as when jammed in train, so that no one would suspect they were operational. *Augusta* immediately reversed course, ten 2-gun salvos from the French battleship following her out from 19,500 to 29,000 yards; and the last three salvos were close straddles. Officers on the bridge and even "sky forward" were drenched with yellow-dyed sea water. This encounter was not, as we suspected, the result of a ruse to bait the flagship within range; the *Jean Bart* simply saw the *Augusta* and let fly what she had. Fortunately she was unable to fire more than 2-gun salvos.[8]

Jean Bart paid dearly for her fun, however. Almost at the moment this action began, Admiral McWhorter was asking Admiral Hewitt to give him some bombing missions and General Patton was calling for air support to knock out the Ainsaba anti-aircraft battery. Dive-bombers from *Ranger* promptly disposed of that, and at 1500 Lieutenant Commander Embree's nine-plane squadron attacked *Jean Bart* with 1000-pound bombs. They dropped nine of these big ones and got two hits, one opening up an enormous crater in the hull; the squadron leader signaled jubilantly, "No more *Jean Bart!*" She was not too badly damaged to be rehabilitated, however.

Ranger followed this up by a seven-plane attack on the El Hank battery with 500-pound bombs which injured only buildings and accessories.[9]

So far, our bombing and shelling activities on Casablanca had been confined to El Hank and the harbor. Several merchant vessels, unfortunately, had been sunk,[10] but few civilian buildings had been hit, and even the port installations were intact. The naval gunfire and air-bombing plans for the assault on 11 November,

[8] Information obtained by Maj. Rogers from Capt. Sticca and other French officers at Casablanca 18 Mar. 1943.
[9] Capt. Shepard's Report; one of my notes says seven 1000-pound bombs were also dropped on El Hank.
[10] One of these, the *Porthos*, had just evacuated civilians, including many women and children, from Dakar. Fortunately they were all disembarked and in places of safety before she was hit.

providing for ample coverage of every possible point of resistance, and deep supporting fire for our troops, would doubtless have caused considerable loss of life and property, although orders were given not to injure the power plant, harbor facilities, or other civil installations. The Army by now had attained its desired objectives over an arc of about 180 degrees around the city; only the Sherman tanks from Safi were wanting for a complete investiture. The hour of attack was set for 0715 November 11.

At 0600 *Augusta, New York, Cleveland,* and several destroyers got under way for their designated fire support positions, their first mission being to silence El Hank and *Jean Bart.* Shortly before 0700 the French sent General Patton a flag of truce, and at 0655 the attack was cancelled. *Ranger's* planes were nearly over their objective, and it took quick work in communications to call them off. A "peace conference" between the French and American commanders in this region was arranged for 1000 at Fedhala. The order to cease resistance had come to Admiral Michelier at Casablanca from General Noguès. He in turn had received it by telephone from Admiral Darlan, who had been recognized by General Eisenhower as the chief French authority in North Africa.

Admiral Hewitt attended the conference at Fedhala when assured that Admiral Michelier would be there.[11] He held out his hand to the enemy of yesterday, and the French Admiral shook. Hewitt declared he regretted having had to fire on French ships; Michelier said, "I had my orders and did my duty, you had yours and did your duty; now that is over, we are ready to coöperate." Commander Bachman of Admiral Hewitt's staff had brought ashore a draft armistice agreement; but General Noguès, who arrived later in the afternoon, declared he was not ready to sign the document because Admiral Darlan and General Eisenhower were making an agreement that embraced Algeria and Tunisia as well as Morocco.

This agreement, which reached Casablanca several days later,

[11] Most of the details of this and the next two paragraphs were told the writer by Admiral Hewitt.

Those whose faces show, right to left, in the upper photo are Admiral Hewitt, Admiral Michelier, Admiral Hall, Captain Ives, Colonel Wilbur and a French naval lieutenant. In the lower photo, Major Rogers, French lieutenant, Colonel Wilbur, General Patton, Admiral Hewitt and Admiral Hall

Luncheon Conference at Fedhala, 11 November 1942

U.S.S. *Ranger* in action with submarine off shore

Off Fedhala, U.S.S. *Tasker H. Bliss*, near center, has just been hit by two torpedoes. U.S.S. *Edward Rutledge*, at right, is completely hidden by smoke, having been torpedoed a few moments earlier

Submarine Attacks of 12 November 1942

provided for little more than a cease-firing. Nothing was surrendered. The Tricolor continued to fly over ships and over batteries that had held out. All French forces retained their arms and munitions. All prisoners were returned. Nothing was done to assert American superiority or to humiliate the French, for we wanted their help both against the Germans and in keeping the native population under control. Knowing that our real objectives lay to the northeastward, that this operation was mere practice "for getting at the real so-and-so's in Europe" (as General Patton remarked), it was essential to keep the fighting Berbers quiet. Already they were showing an unpleasant habit of sniping at our troops and knifing them in the dark. Nobody was better qualified to deal with these people than the French soldiers and civilians who had pacified the country under the great Marshal Lyautey. It would have been the height of folly to dislocate their authority or injure French prestige and so throw the whole native problem into our lap.

The American forces bit by bit evolved a *modus vivendi* with the French, in which there was a gradual increase of coöperation, without putting anything on paper. The French naval administration at Casablanca immediately placed its entire organization — port facilities, installations, tugs, pilots and divers — at our disposal and moved French merchantmen out to make room for the United States Navy. When Admiral Hewitt paid a visit of ceremony to Admiral Michelier at Casablanca on 12 November, the French commander expressed great solicitude for the safety of our ships and even proposed to take away the anti-torpedo net from *Jean Bart* and place it around *Augusta*. This, despite the fact that four days before Admiral Hewitt had destroyed the better part of Michelier's command and had inflicted heavy casualties on the French Navy.

Thus, after three days' sharp fighting, the traditional friendship was renewed under the happiest circumstance of making a common cause against the Axis powers. But we had not yet heard from the Axis.

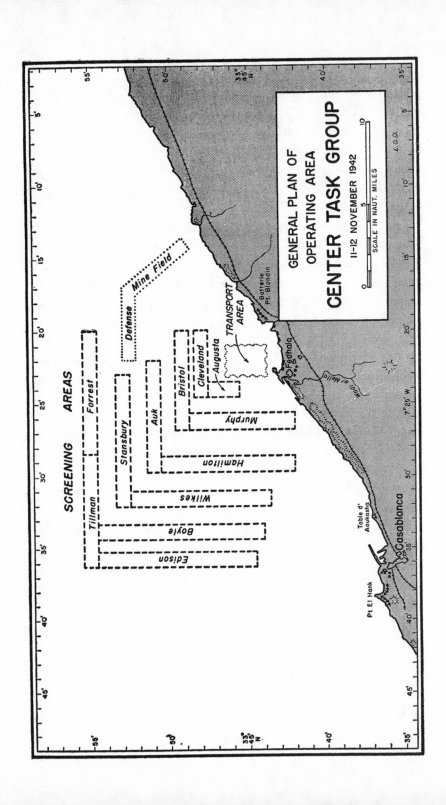

GENERAL PLAN OF
OPERATING AREA
CENTER TASK GROUP
11-12 NOVEMBER 1942

SCALE IN NAUT. MILES

SCREENING AREAS

Forrest
Tillman
Stansbury
Auk
Bristol
Cleveland
Augusta
Murphy
Hamilton
Wilkes
Boyle
Edison

Defense
Mine Field

TRANSPORT AREA

Batterie
Pt. Blondin

Fedhala

Oued el Mellu

Table d'
Aoukasha

Casablanca

Pt El Hank

3. *The Axis Takes a Hand*[12]

It was high time that our luck should change. Up to the evening of 11 November, the American forces had enjoyed almost uninterrupted good fortune. Task Force 34 had reached its destination without a submarine attack. Exceptional weather had permitted a successful night landing with negligible casualties. Our carrier-based planes quickly secured local air supremacy. In the sea battles we made all the hits and the French suffered all the losses. The French Army offered but halfhearted resistance, excepting at Mehedia. The political somersaults in Algeria had brought Darlan on top, much to our advantage, and the enemy of yesterday was our friend today. But the Axis had been heard only over the radio, by which means an Italian, broadcasting in English, assured us that we would never get home alive.

In Task Force 34 it was a matter of wonderment that no air or submarine attacks by Germans had yet materialized. The Luftwaffe, we now know, was too busy covering the rush of Axis reinforcements into Tunisia to bother with so remote an area, but the concentrations of U-boats that we had escaped on the way over would surely close in on such tempting targets as the anchored transports.

On 10 November in the forenoon watch occurred the first samples of what we were to expect. An unidentified submarine fired four torpedoes which passed under the stern of *Ranger*,[13] as she maneuvered off shore around lat. 35°25′ N, long. 07°37′ W. An hour later the big carrier's lookouts saw a submarine's conning tower broach, and one of her screening destroyers, the *Ellyson*, sighted a periscope.[14]

[12] Information identifying the U-boats concerned, from the captured German Admiralty Archives, was forwarded to the writer by Cdr. K. A. Knowles in January 1946.

[13] *Ranger* War Diary. These were fired by submarine *Tonnant*.

[14] Comdesron 10 (Cdr. J. L. Holloway Jr.) "Preliminary Narrative of Operations" (Enclosed H in Admiral McWhorter's Report 3 Dec. 1942). *Ranger* Action Report (Enclosure C in same) is more literary than factual. "*Wildcats*" *Over Casablanca* p. 141 exaggerates this incident.

During the afternoon of the eleventh, when three planes on anti-submarine patrol were returning to the *Suwannee*, they sighted a submarine close to shore about eighteen miles west of El Hank, and sank it with depth charges. Although at the time this was supposed to be a German U-boat, it proved to be one of the three French submarines (*Sidi-Ferruch, Conquérant,* or *Sybille*) which disappeared after they sortied from Casablanca 8 November.[15]

A report was received at Fedhala on the afternoon of 11 November that there were indications that some of the concentrations of German U-boats which we had evaded in the Atlantic were now converging on the Task Force. This turned out to be correct. All ships in the Task Force were warned at sunset to exercise special vigilance, and more Army patrol planes were requested to be flown in from Gibraltar and England.

Fifteen transports and cargo ships of the Center Attack Group were then at anchor in Fedhala Roads. There was no need for most of them to continue unloading there; Casablanca was already available for twelve ships. A member of Admiral Hewitt's staff, a member of General Patton's staff, and Captain H. G. Sickel, commander of the Naval Advanced Base Group, visited Casablanca the morning of 11 November, and, with the aid and countenance of Admiral Michelier, inspected the harbor. They found three berths vacant, together with nine which the French Admiral promised to make immediately available by moving outside the harbor several merchant ships that were still afloat. This was reported to Admiral Hewitt that afternoon as he was leaving the armistice conference at Fedhala, and Captain Emmet was then consulted on board *Leonard Wood.* The transport commander wanted an immediate removal of as many ships as possible to Casablanca Harbor, and drew up a list of priorities, high in which were the *Hewes, Bliss, Scott* and *Rutledge,* which had just commenced unloading.

The subject was discussed between Admiral Hewitt and his staff on board *Augusta* shortly after 1800 that evening. A prompt

[15] *Suwannee* Action Report; *U.S. Fleet Anti-Submarine Warfare Bulletin* Feb. 1945 p. 29. The position of this sinking was lat. 33°35′ N, long. 07°50′ W.

transfer of as many vessels as possible to Casablanca seemed the logical course, but there was one strong argument against it. The D plus 5 follow-up convoy, already approaching the coast, needed space in Casablanca; how could it be accommodated there, if the Center Group transports took up all the berths? The risk from submarine attack to the high-speed D plus 5 convoy, if it had to maneuver off shore, was of course much less than that to the anchored transports; but Admiral Hewitt, after weighing the risks, reluctantly decided to move no ships from Fedhala Roads.

At 1948, within an hour of the time that the Admiral made this unfortunate decision, transport *Joseph Hewes* was torpedoed on her port bow. Then, between 1955 and 1956, tanker *Winooski* and destroyer *Hambleton*, anchored off her starboard quarter, were hit by torpedoes on their port sides, amidships.[16]

Hewes went down within the hour, taking with her Captain Robert McLanahan Smith, several seamen who were killed by the explosion, and over 90 per cent of her cargo. All the troops on board and most of the vehicles had already been landed. Most of her crew were picked up in the water, since every other transport rushed landing boats to the scene and the sea was calm. *Winooski* was hit in a fuel tank that had been ballasted with sea water. The torpedo made a hole 25 feet square, but only 7 men were slightly wounded and the ship was able to resume fueling next day. *Hambleton*, having just arrived off Fedhala, had anchored awaiting an opportunity to fuel from *Winooski*. The torpedo hit her below the waterline, killing 9 men outright; 11 more were missing or fatally wounded. The forward engine room and after fireroom flooded and all power was lost. But enough bulkheads were closed so that *Hambleton* floated, and after the crew had done all they could they gathered on deck and sang, "Don't Give Up the Ship!" and other naval songs. Next day, *Cherokee* towed her into Casablanca, where emergency repairs were effected so that she was able to return home under her own power.[17]

[16] Hewitt Report p. 15.

[17] Cdr. Close, skipper of *Hambleton*, adverts in his Action Report with pardonable bitterness to his being ordered to anchor, which gave him no chance to

Destroyer *Bristol*, of the inner screen to the transports, at 2027 sighted the guilty submarine, *U-173*, making a getaway to the northward at 400 yards' range. The *Bristol* had just stopped and diverted to the beach two lost troop-laden boats; momentarily the submarine was mistaken for another stray landing craft. One shot only was fired before the U-boat submerged; two depth-charge patterns were then dropped, but the boat escaped this time. It was credited by the German Admiralty with sinking the *Hewes* before being sunk itself on 16 November.

Early next morning, 12 November, Admiral Hewitt held a conference on board his flagship. The question was whether the transports should continue to unload from their present anchorage, trusting to the screen's protection in case of new submarine attack; or put to sea, which would upset the already tardy schedule; or seek refuge in Casablanca, which might prejudice the safety of the follow-up convoy, due 13 November.[18] In the meantime two other members of his staff had inspected Casablanca, and confirmed the information already in the Admiral's hands that the French authorities were ready to make room there for twelve out of the fourteen remaining transports. But Admiral Hewitt decided to stay put and accept the risk. The consequences of this decision were very grave.

----

dodge the torpedo. He reported upon arrival in the transport area to screen commander Capt. John B. Heffernan, who ordered him to go alongside *Winooski* at once and fuel. It was already dusk and the tanker refused to receive the destroyer on the ground that she had been ordered to fuel in daylight hours only. Cdr. Close then applied through his division commander (Capt. Wellborn), who was on board, to Capt. Heffernan for orders. Heffernan, then busy organizing his screen for the night, replied, "Remain in area, suggest you anchor," because he feared lest *Hambleton* hit a mine if she steamed out. He hoped to be able to attend to her in a few minutes and to overcome *Winooski's* objection to dusk fueling. Capt. Wellborn assumed responsibility for the order to anchor. (Information from Cdr. Close and Capt. Heffernan.)

[18] Capt. O. T. Shepard's report "Rough, Partial Estimate of the Situation" made to Admiral Hewitt 11 Nov., and information from various members of the staff present at the conferences 11 and 12 Nov. It does not appear that Army members of the staff pled for a continuance of unloading at Fedhala, for the Army was already moving into Casablanca and preferred unloading there; but the interruption of unloading incidental to the change of location may have influenced Admiral Hewitt's decision.

Unloading operations continued off Fedhala all day 12 November, while increasing evidence of submarine activity came in. That morning, when *Ranger, Suwannee* and *Chenango,* screened by *Brooklyn* and six destroyers, were maneuvering well out to sea about fifty miles north of Cape Blanco, *Ranger* was apparently attacked by a wolf-pack of U-boats. Torpedoes were reported to be slipping by, under the overhang forward and below the fantail aft; periscopes were observed from the flight deck; and obscure shapes were sighted under water by the *Brooklyn's* planes. For three hours, guns were firing and depth charges popping.[19]

Chenango's escorting destroyer *Rowan* had a hot submarine contact about halfway between Fedhala and Casablanca at about 1600, and that afternoon *Titania* and *Cole,* on their way to Fedhala to deliver landing craft, were unsuccessfully attacked by a submarine whose conning tower they sighted.

All that day the German submarine *U-130* was approaching Fedhala Roads cautiously from the eastward, observing ships beached at Bouznika on the way, and steaming so close to shore that she scraped the bottom. She did not pass through the Fedhala mine field, but sneaked inside its shoreward end, as we now know from her log, and at 1758 she was in position for a highly successful torpedo attack. *U-130* fired four torpedoes from her bow tubes, then whipped around and shot one more from her stern tube. Every one of these hit. Transports *Edward Rutledge, Tasker H. Bliss* and *Hugh L. Scott* were the victims. All three burst into flames. Landing boats were at once concentrated around the three burning ships, and they were abandoned precipitately, but under ideal sea conditions. *Bliss* burned until 0230 and then sank, tak-

---

[19] *Ranger* Action Report; writer's observations from *Brooklyn.* An amusing incident of this attack, before it really got hot, was the attempt of a Spanish-speaking Marine Corps sergeant aboard *Ranger* to chase away two Spanish fishing vessels, suspected of spotting for the enemy, with a "bullhorn" loudspeaker, his efforts being illustrated by the carrier's navigating officer with frantic gestures "in the international language of pantomime." *Woolsey* later performed the ancient rites of visit and search, as a result of which the fishermen were found to have nothing on board but salt and fish, and were cleared of any complicity. There is no record of this attack in German Admiralty records; it may have been delivered by French submarines that escaped from Casablanca, but the French think not.

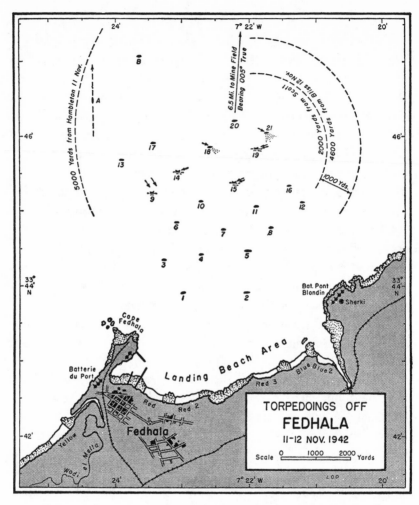

KEY TO CHART

1. *Augusta* – 11 November only.
2. *New York*
3. *Oberon* – 12 November only.
4. *L. Wood*
5. *Cleveland* – 11 November only.
6. *Ancon*
7. *T. Jefferson*
8. *Biddle*

9. *J. Hewes* – Torpedoed, sunk, 11 November.
10. *Stanton*
11. *Carroll*
12. *Arcturus*
13. *Thurston*
14. *T. Bliss* – Torpedoed 12 November. Sank 13 November.
15. *E. Rutledge* – Torpedoed, sunk, 12 November.

16. *Dickman*
17. *Miantonomah*
18. *Winooski* – Torpedoed, not sunk, 11 November.
19. *H. Scott* – Torpedoed, sunk, 12 November.
20. *Procyon*
21. *Hambleton* – Torpedoed, not sunk, 11 November.

A. Approximate position of enemy submarine when sighted on surface 11 November.

B. Approximate position of *Bristol* when firing at the submarine on the surface.

ing the ashes of 34 men down with her. *Rutledge* and *Scott* foundered earlier; if only a tug had been available, they might have been beached. Owing to the efficiency with which survivors were picked up by landing craft, losses of men were limited to those killed by the explosion or trapped below by fires that raged through the flimsy construction of these ex-passenger liners.[20] Well over a thousand survivors were taken ashore and quartered in the Hôtel de Commerce and the Catholic church. Surviving medical personnel, assisted by the rear echelon of the 3rd Division, opened a first-aid station in the casino and treated the wounds, which were mostly burns.

As *U-130* retired safely to the northeastward, Captain Emmet got the rest of the Center Group, except three minesweepers, under way. No further attacks developed as the ships steered evasive courses. But H.M. depot ship *Hecla* was sunk by *U-515* that night off the Straits. Several hundred survivors were picked up by H.M.S. *Venomous* and were brought in to Casablanca.

The last torpedo damage inflicted on the Western Task Force was suffered by the cargo ship U.S.S. *Electra* of the Northern Group. At 0640 November 15, when steaming independently toward Casablanca, she was torpedoed about seventeen miles off Fedhala. The detonation tore a hole 19 by 43 feet on her starboard side, and eleven large holes on her port side. Her port tanks were flooded and her starboard ones had to be filled to prevent capsizing; her engine room flooded, all power was lost, and she seemed likely to founder. Fortunately plenty of assistance was at hand and *Electra* averted the tragedy suggested by her name. All hands except a salvage party were taken off by the destroyer *Cole* at 0720. Naval tug *Cherokee* and minesweepers *Raven* and *Stansbury* stood by, alternately towing and pumping; they held her up all night and beached her outside Casablanca at 0400 November 16. A notable salvage job was done on *Electra*. Divers from *Cherokee*

---

[20] Losses as follows: from *Scott*, eight out of 43 officers, 51 out of 623 men killed or missing, 6 wounded, 609 survivors fit for duty; from *Bliss*, two out of 43 officers and 32 out of 444 men killed or missing, a few died later from wounds; from *Rutledge*, one out of 35 officers and 14 out of 419 men killed or missing.

made temporary patches with mattresses. The biggest hole was covered by steel hatch covers held together by beams secured in place by hogging-lines and, after the hold was pumped dry, cemented from within. The engines, after being under water three weeks, were reconditioned by the ship's own force working three shifts seven days in the week. All wiring was overhauled and tested. In April of 1943, *Electra* was able to proceed under her own power to the United States for permanent repairs.[21]

U-173, which sank *Hewes*, was probably the one that torpedoed *Electra*. In any case, *U-173* hung around Casablanca too long for its own good. Destroyer *Woolsey* made a sound contact on this boat off the harbor entrance at about noon 16 November, and with the aid of *Swanson* and *Quick* depth-charged it out of existence.

4. *The Move to Casablanca*

At dawn 13 November, the French authorities at Casablanca, as they had been ready to do since the eleventh, began very efficiently to move every ship that was afloat outside the harbor and to clear up the docks. The five transports of the Center Group that were nearly empty were ordered into the harbor on the thirteenth, completed their unloading on the fifteenth, and sailed promptly for Hampton Roads under escort. Admiral Giffen's Covering Group, no longer needed after the capitulation, had already departed. At 1000 November 15 the rest of the Center Group, seven transports and cargo vessels, entered Casablanca together with five transports of the Northern Group. Transports of the Southern Attack Group were taken into Safi harbor and sent home as soon as unloaded.

Although the torpedoing of the *Electra* on 15 November marked the end of hostilities in or off the coast of Morocco, three big problems remained: relations with the French; unloading; and the

---

[21] Bureau of Ships *War Damage Report No. 32* on *Joseph Hewes* and *Electra*.

Air view over harbor entrance, 16 November. Outside the harbor, among other ships, is U.S.S. *Electra* with tug *Cherokee* standing by her bow; in the corner are the French warships *Primauguet, Albatros* and *Milan* burned out and beached. Inside with sterns to breakwater, right to left, are a U.S. transport, *Augusta,* a destroyer, *Chenango, Brooklyn, Terror* and two minesweepers

View looking westward across Môle du Commerce, 11 November. Two passenger ships are resting on the harbor bottom; S.S. *Porthos* is capsized at the end berth; and *Jean Bart,* with steam up but badly holed, is on far side

Casablanca Harbor after the Fighting

Pointe El Hank, lighthouse and gun emplacements, December 1942

Fedhala Harbor, 10 November. U.S.S. *Procyon* is at oil dock with tug *Cherokee* alongside

follow-up convoy. The first, as we have seen, solved itself; the French responded so readily to our friendly advances, and coöperated so efficiently in handling the greatest volume of traffic ever known in the port of Casablanca, that we could well afford to await General Eisenhower's pleasure for a formal protocol. On our side, we did not compel the French to disarm or hand over the ships and batteries that had recently been shooting at us, or to replace their flag by ours. The theory was that the French had not surrendered — merely quit fighting; they were now our allies and friends after a brief but bloody misunderstanding.[22]

Unloading conditions in Casablanca, while better than in Fedhala because some ships needed no lighters, were still shockingly bad, owing almost entirely to the lack of help from shore. The docks were heaped up to a height of fifteen or twenty feet with supplies, ammunition, and material of every description just as it came out of the holds — a perfect target for air attack, and insufficiently policed against pilferers and snipers.[23] Here is a good sample: In one heap were three sections of steel mat, a case of wienerwurst, two 10-gallon field containers of aviation gasoline, one case of pistol ammunition, one field container of lubricating oil, one case of strawberry jam and one "clover leaf" of incendiary 105-mm ammunition. On the fifteenth, Admiral Hewitt sent a staff officer to tell General Patton what went on, stating that the conditions on the docks were scandalous. The General then assigned two battalions of infantry and one of engineers to help unloading; but it was not until the night of 18 November, after Brigadier General Arthur Wilson had arranged to employ French

---

[22] Report of Rear Admiral B. H. Bieri USN to Gen. Eisenhower from Casablanca 12 Nov. 1942. Admiral Bieri was then Deputy Chief of Staff Atlantic Fleet, attached to Gen. Eisenhower's staff.

[23] Sniping continued intermittently at Casablanca for a few days after the eleventh, and pilfering by the natives never stopped. The Intelligence data furnished the Western Task Force laid such stress on respecting the dignity of the natives, especially their women, that most of the soldiers and bluejackets had a mental picture of Moroccans as being First Families of Virginia in bathrobes. They were entirely unprepared to find that the natives with whom they first came in contact were beggars, pimps, and thieves.

and native labor, that order and system were established. Until then, the Army was reduced to foraging in the piles on the docks for essential supplies.

Most of the combat ships and transports of the Western Task Force that were still left sortied in the morning of 17 November and reached Hampton Roads safely on the thirtieth after passing through some exceedingly foul weather. Their departure enabled the D plus 5 convoy [24] to enter Casablanca on the morning of the eighteenth. For a week this important convoy (4 transports and 20 merchantmen with 9 destroyers and a battleship as escort, commanded by Captain Carleton F. Bryant in U.S.S. *Arkansas*) had been steering evasive courses offshore in moderate to rough weather, waiting for a chance to enter, and making frequent sound contacts on submarines; yet providentially it was not attacked.[25] Aided by French tugs and pilots, this task force commenced entering the harbor at 1115, November 18.

Two more follow-up convoys were waiting to sail on the other side of the Atlantic as soon as the word was passed. These were UGS–2 (Task Force 37) consisting of 45 ships, including 2 fleet oilers, escorted by 6 destroyers and 3 minelayers; [26] and Task Force 39, known as "the Spitkit Convoy," which crossed via Bermuda. Commanded by Captain R. M. Zimmerli in the tanker *Maumee*, TF-39 consisted of 1 "bird"-class and 9 motor minesweepers, the repair ship *Redwing*, net tender *Yew*, 8 patrol craft (PC) and 9 subchasers (SC), all destined to make up Rear Admiral Hall's Sea Frontier Forces, Northwest African Waters. U.S.S. *Memphis* escorted them to long. 30° W, where they were released, and made Casablanca safely 25 November after experiencing heavy weather.

*   *   *

[24] It was due to arrive off Casablanca on D plus 5 day, 13 Nov. Official designation was Task Force 38 and Convoy UGF–2. The Navy wanted this to be timed for D plus 10, fearing what would happen, but the Army insisted on having the reinforcements earlier.

[25] Minelayer *Terror* peeled off early in order to help *Miantonomah* and *Monadnock* lay a protective mine field outside Casablanca.

[26] A composite convoy with sections for both Casablanca and Oran.

The work of the Western Task Force was already finished.

On Sunday 15 November, the following dispatch from General Patton to Admiral Hewitt was transmitted to every ship of Task Force 34 remaining in African waters: —

It is my firm conviction that the great success attending the hazardous operations carried out on sea and on land by the Western Task Force could only have been possible through the intervention of Divine Providence manifested in many ways. Therefore, I shall be pleased if in so far as circumstances and conditions permit, our grateful thanks be expressed today in appropriate religious services.

Marvelous indeed to reflect on what had happened during the past week, and how completely the whole picture of the European war had been changed by events in North Africa.

The largest amphibious operation or indeed overseas expedition in the history of man had been skillfully planned and admirably executed, in the face of adverse weather, a large concentration of submarines, and fierce fighting by units of the French Army and Navy.

Northwest Africa had been denied to the Axis as a source of supplies and a possible submarine base, the potential menace of Dakar ended, and an Atlantic port secured by which the liberating forces of the United States could enter Morocco and help to drive the Axis forces from North Africa. Bases from which Allied air power could control adjacent waters and protect ships bound for the Straits and the Cape of Good Hope had been brought under United Nations control. Admiral Hewitt as Commander Western Naval Task Force had been the means of opening more light into the Dark Continent than anyone since Marshal Lyautey, thirty years before.

As a fitting conclusion to this brief but vital campaign, combined memorial services were held at Rabat on 21 November, for the French and American dead. In the Cathedral, General Noguès and the Grand Vizier of Morocco stood on one side of a double bier; General Harmon and other American officers stood on the other side. After the services, detachments of the 3rd and 9th Infantry Divisions United States Army and of the 1er Régiment de Chasseurs d'Afrique, with a squadron of native Spahi cavalry, formed a guard of honor at the gate of the Rabat Cemetery. General Noguès and General Harmon passed through lines of Army, Navy and Air Forces, to place flowers on the graves of the French and the Americans who had fallen fighting one another less than two weeks before.

PART II

The Expeditions against Algeria and Tunisia

All times used in the initial landings are Greenwich (Zone Zebra)

CHAPTER VIII

Preparations[1]

October – November 1942

1. Plans and Targets

ALLIED FORCES undertook to seize the ports of Algiers and Oran concurrently with the landings on the Atlantic coast of Morocco, centering on Casablanca. This Mediterranean part of Operation "Torch," mounted in the United Kingdom, was planned to take place simultaneously with the Atlantic effort, yet to proceed regardless of what happened on the outer coast. But the landings at Algiers and Oran were so linked that if one should be prevented for any reason, the other would have to be postponed.

Lieutenant General Dwight D. Eisenhower USA had been appointed Commander in Chief Allied Expeditionary Force on 14 August 1942, and preliminary planning in the higher echelons began at his headquarters in London soon afterwards. He stated: —

I was determined from the first to do all in my power to make this a truly Allied force, with real unity of command and centralization of administrative responsibility. Alliances in the past have done no more than to name the common foe and "unity of command" has been a pious aspiration thinly disguising the national prejudices, ambitions and recriminations of high ranking officers, unwilling to subordinate themselves or their forces to a commander of different nationality or different service.[2]

[1] The overall sources for this chapter include General Eisenhower's official "Dispatch" (Action Report) for the North African Campaign; Lt. Col. Homer L. Litzenberg Jr. USMC "Occupation of French North Africa – Outline History" Dec. 1942; O.N.I. Combat Narrative *Landings in North Africa*; Cincmed (Admiral Cunningham) Operation Torch Report 30 March 1943; War Diary N.O.B. Oran; Comtransdiv 11 (Capt. Edgar) Action Report Operation Torch 23 Nov. 1942.

[2] Eisenhower "Dispatch" p. 1.

The preliminary naval outline plan, issued by Expeditionary Force Headquarters at London on 29 September, set the division of labor between the United States and Royal Navies. Mediterranean landings were the responsibility of the British as those on the Atlantic side of French Morocco were of the United States Navy. Admiral Sir Andrew B. Cunningham RN, Commander-in-Chief Mediterranean, was Allied naval commander of the entire "Torch" operation. Actually he left Rear Admiral Hewitt a free hand in the Atlantic while directing the Mediterranean landings himself.

Admiral Bertram H. Ramsay RN was Admiral Cunningham's top naval planner, and his detailed operation orders, issued between 3 and 13 October, covered all phases leading up to the assault and including the follow-up. The "sound planning and forethought" of Admiral Ramsay's planning staff was acknowledged by Admiral Cunningham as "not easily measured." [3] The United States Army employed the major strength — about 49,000 officers and men as against 23,000 British — in the Mediterranean landings, hence General Eisenhower's planners worked in close coöperation with the British located at Norfolk House in London. Rear Admiral B. H. Bieri and Captain Jerauld Wright were the most important United States naval officers attached to the combined staff.

The question of how far to the eastward landings in the Mediterranean should be effected was much discussed. Although the ultimate goals of the operation were the Tunisian ports, in order to close the Sicilian Straits and box off the Afrika Korps in Libya, it was decided to attempt no initial landing east of Cape Matifou, Bay of Algiers, because of the proximity of Axis shore-based aircraft in Sicily and Italy. Speaking after the event, Admiral Cunningham said: —

It is a matter of lasting regret to me that the bolder conception for initial assault in that area [Bône] or even further eastward was not implemented. Had we been prepared to throw even a small force into

the eastward ports, the Axis would have been forestalled in their first
token occupation and success would have been complete. They were
surprised and off their balance. We failed to give the final push which
would have tipped the scales.[4]

The Admiral, to use his own words, wanted to "snap into Bizerta." [5] He believed that a concentration of assault ships would be
taken by the Germans to be a Malta-bound convoy [6] and thus preserve the necessary surprise element. As to that he was right;
whether he was right in his strategy we can never know. In this
operation there were more than the usual number of imponderables,
because nobody could tell beforehand how the French forces in a
given area would react. Without Allied military support, the Resident General at Tunis, Admiral Jean-Pierre Esteva, found himself
and all his forces at the mercy of the Germans; but we now know
he would have coöperated if Allied forces had landed in Bône. Yet
if they had landed there with insufficient forces and Admiral Esteva
had refused to coöperate, the Allied forces would probably have
been pinned to the beachhead after taking heavy losses from enemy
air attacks in steaming so far east in the Mediterranean. Moreover, if
Tunis had been added to the list of initial objectives to the eastward,
Casablanca to the westward must have been neglected in order to
supply the necessary ships and troops. Some of the British planners
wished the operation to take that form — throwing everything as
far east as possible; but the United States planners, Admiral Cunningham too, refused to countenance any weakening of the Western Task Force. From their point of view, Casablanca must be secured in order to possess an Atlantic port for reinforcement and
supply, and a base for anti-submarine warfare. And if sufficient
force were provided to take Casablanca, only a token force could
have been spared for Bône or Tunisia.

On 6 September it was decided to eliminate Bône and Bizerta in
the initial list of objectives. Algiers was unquestionably the most

[4] Cincmed Report.
[5] Said to the writer at London 19 Dec. 1944.
[6] Actually two Malta-bound freighters were included in one of the initial assault convoys.

important prize for an amphibious operation. This old pirate head-quarters had become, after a century of French rule, a modern city of about 250,000 inhabitants. The harbor was the best equipped of any North African port, with the exception of Tunis and Alexandria. As the largest and most important city in French Africa, Algiers had considerable prestige value. Its occupation by the United Nations was bound to affect the international situation in Europe as well as the strategic situation in the Mediterranean.

As the plans worked out, Allied naval and military units were divided between an Eastern Naval Task Force with target Algiers and a Center Naval Task Force [7] with target Oran. In both sectors American participation was to be stressed, for, as General Eisenhower stated, "German propaganda used incidents of Mers-el-Kebir, Dakar, Syria and Madagascar to inflame French opinion against the British." [8]

2. *La Haute Politique* [9]

Owing partly to better contacts with leading French officials and partly to the subordinate rôle of the French Navy in Algeria, resistance there was far less than in Morocco. Yet even in Algeria there was a comedy of misunderstandings and mistakes.

At the secret conference near Cherchel on 23 October 1942 between General Mark Clark and French leaders, the General was deeply impressed by the loyalty and sincerity of General Charles Mast and he empowered Mr. Murphy to impart full knowledge of the attack plan to him. This he did on 29 October, which gave General Mast nine or ten days to make such disposition of his troops that resistance would be at a minimum. At the same secret conference the question arose of the supreme command over the expeditionary force. Mast urged the appointment of General

---

[7] Not to be confused with the Center Attack Group at Fedhala which was part of the Western Task Force.

[8] Eisenhower "Dispatch" p. 6.

[9] Demaree Bess "Backstage Story of an African Adventure" *Sat. Eve. Post* 3 July 1943 pp. 51–53, checked by Dr. Langer's Report to the Dept. of State.

Giraud, on the ground that he alone could rally the French garrison and population to our side; but General Clark convinced him that to appoint a Frenchman over an Anglo-American army was impracticable, and Mast finally agreed that General Eisenhower was the proper person to command the expeditionary force. It was decided, however, that Giraud should be brought in to take over the government of North Africa, and prepare the way for an eventual assumption of military responsibility by the French Army.

Mr. Murphy then had the delicate task of obtaining the consent and coöperation of General Giraud, who had already been approached but was still in France and ignorant of our plans. This "accord," if anything that produced so much discord could be so called, was concluded on 3 November through a French intermediary. The General accepted his subordinate position in the invasion, on the understanding that the force would be American in composition and in command; that immediately after the initial landings, he would be given the supreme command; that he himself would set D-day for North Africa when satisfied that our preparations were adequate. No more unpromising basis for French coöperation could have been laid.

This diplomatic foul-up was further complicated but eventually straightened out by the presence in Algiers of Admiral Darlan, commander in chief of all military and naval forces under Marshal Pétain. He had come there to be at the bedside of a sick son; but he probably smelled something in the wind.[10] Darlan had a bad reputation for collaboration with the Axis, although in that respect he was in the class with Pétain rather than Laval. He was a political admiral to whom the French Navy was loyal, and eventually the Allies had to deal with him, because he was the one man in North Africa able to deliver the goods.

Lieutenant General Eisenhower, overall Allied commander of

---

[10] According to Captain Butcher's *Three Years with Eisenhower* pp. 145–146, friends of Darlan put out feelers to Mr. Murphy in mid-October to the effect that the Admiral might join our side if suitably encouraged. But these overtures may have been unauthorized by him, and there is no evidence that he was promised anything in return.

the forces to be landed in North Africa, set up temporary headquarters on 5 November in the famous tunnel under the Rock of
Gibraltar. That day the cheering news of the British Army's victory over Rommel at El Alamein arrived. General Giraud, who had
been picked up near Levandou in Southern France by H.M.S.
Seraph (politically under command of Captain Jerauld Wright)[11]
and transferred to a seaplane in mid-Mediterranean, arrived at
Gibraltar about 1600 November 7, the eve of the invasion. General Eisenhower promptly imparted to him the astonishing news
that H-hour was only nine hours away; and the bad news that he,
not the French General, was to command the operation. Giraud
protested and tried to "pull rank" on Eisenhower, who was one
grade lower than he.[12] The conference broke up that night without
an agreement, but next day Eisenhower's firmness and tact and the
logic of the situation prevailed. General Giraud loyally accepted
his subordinate place in the invasion as the military and civil chief
of all French forces and affairs in North Africa. This agreement,
too, could not be kept, because it was found that Admiral Darlan
was the only man able to control the uneasy, touchy and bewildered French officers on the spot.

Easily the busiest man in Algiers the night of 7–8 November was
the Honorable Robert D. Murphy. With infinite pains he had assembled a nicely filled apple cart; but three men were in a position
to kick it over before our troops got the apples — Admiral Darlan,
General Giraud and General Juin. H-hour, he had been informed,
was to be 0100. At that moment the voices of President Roosevelt
and General Eisenhower would broadcast our landings to the
world. Time was short. At 0030 Mr. Murphy told his story to General Juin, military governor of Algeria. Then Darlan was called to

[11] Captain Wright was the U.S. Naval Liaison Officer at Gibraltar. His report
is enclosed with that of Admiral Stark, 31 Dec. 1942. The General stipulated that
the submarine should be American, but we had none available, so a British one
was sent with a temporary U.S. Navy commander as figurehead. An American
flag was kept handy, ready to run up if identification were necessary. The submarine's real commander, Lieutenant N. L. A. Jewell RN, wrote *Secret Mission
Submarine* (Chicago, 1945).

[12] Told to the writer by an American general who was present. French *Général
d'Armée* (five stars) is equivalent to our full General (four stars).

Juin's house and Murphy broke the news to him. The Admiral was, or at least appeared to be, furious. His anger somewhat subsided when he heard with what strength the United Nations were landing, and he decided to cable to Marshal Pétain at Vichy requesting him to order an end to all French resistance. Vice Admiral Raymond Fenard, Secretary General of French North Africa, who was present at this interview, appears to have made no effort to check resistance on the part of French ships or coastal batteries. No one else, apparently, tried to alert them. Their standing orders for repelling attack therefore were simply executed by commanding officers of the ships and coastal batteries. Neither Mr. Murphy nor the Allied generals knew what reception our troops would have from the French.

On the morning of D-day Marshal Pétain received a personal letter from President Roosevelt reminding him what Germany had done to France, requesting his coöperation in the coming operation, and assuring him that neither we nor the British would attempt to annex any part of French North Africa. Pétain replied the same day, declaring that he had learned of the American "aggression" with "bewilderment and sadness," that France was capable of defending her own empire, and would do so even against her old friends. "That is the order which I give." [18]

The United Nations were also very apprehensive of what the dictators of Portugal and Spain might do, particularly of Franco's course. Spain was reported to have about 200,000 troops in Spanish Morocco. She was in a position not only to close the Straits by bombarding the Gibraltar airfield and harbor from Algeciras, but to cut communications between the Moroccan and Mediterranean task forces; for the railway from Casablanca to Oran runs within twenty miles of the Spanish Morocco border. The British Army said that if Franco chose to intervene, there was absolutely nothing they could do about it. General Eisenhower's staff planners estimated that five divisions would be necessary to occupy Spanish Morocco, and that such an operation would require three and a

[18] Text in *N.Y. Times* 9 Nov. 1942.

half months. Thus, our one means of pressure on Franco was diplomatic.

Diplomacy, lubricated by the oil that Spain was allowed to procure from the Caribbean and implemented by our extensive purchases in Spain, was expertly applied at Madrid by the American ambassador, Professor Carleton J. H. Hayes.[14] Franco continued officially to be a "nonbelligerent" ally of the Axis, but he gave them the shell and us the oyster. Here, again, was a so-called appeasement that paid dividends. President Roosevelt tactfully saw to it that General Franco had a few hours' advance notice of the landings, assuring him "that these moves are in no shape, manner or form directed against the government or people of Spain or Spanish Territory," and that "Spain has nothing to fear from the United Nations."[15] Franco was content to stay quiet, and there was never any danger of Portugal being faithless to her ancient alliance with England.

[14] E. K. Lindley and E. Weintal "How We Dealt with Spain" *Harper's Magazine* (Dec. 1944) pp. 23-33.
[15] Text in *N.Y. Times* 9 Nov. 1942. A similar letter was delivered to President Carmona of Portugal.

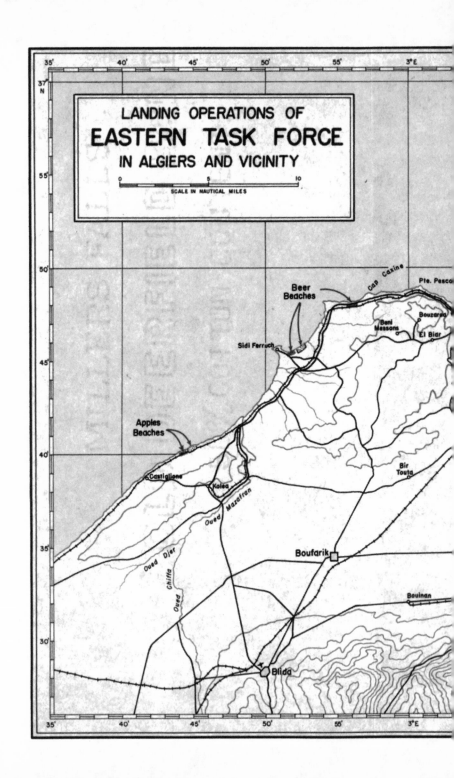

LANDING OPERATIONS OF
EASTERN TASK FORCE
IN ALGIERS AND VICINITY

SCALE IN NAUTICAL MILES

Beer Beaches

Cap Caxine

Pte. Pesca

Bouzarea

Beni Messous

El Biar

Sidi Ferruch

Apples Beaches

Castiglione

Kolea

Oued Mazafran

Bir Touta

Oued Djer

Oued Chiffa

Boufarik

Bouinan

Blida

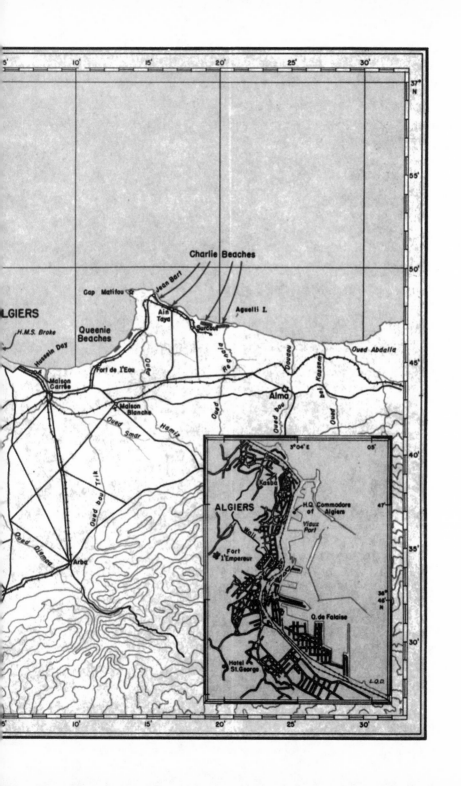

CHAPTER IX

The Winning of Algiers

8–15 November 1942

1. *The Eastern Naval Task Force*

a. Organization[1]

BOTH Eastern and Center Task Forces were covered in the
Mediterranean by Force H of the Royal Navy, comprising
H.M.S. *Nelson*, flagship of Admiral Cunningham, and two other
battleships, H.M.S. *Rodney* and *Duke of York*; battle cruiser *Re-
nown*; carriers *Victorious* and *Formidable*; light cruisers *Bermuda*,
Argonaut, *Sirius* and *Phoebe*; and seventeen destroyers. Theirs was
a heavy responsibility. Force H was charged with covering the attack forces while embarked and during the debarkation and assault.
It had to protect them from Axis submarines and aircraft, and
possibly from the French fleet at Toulon and the French ships
attached to North African bases. There was also the Italian fleet
to guard against, on paper; but the "Dago Navy" had long been
regarded by British tars as a huge joke. According to Admiral Cunningham, "The complaisant attitude of the Italian fleet and the
inactivity of the French main fleet unfortunately gave Force H
no scope for action. This powerful force had in fact to be kept
cruising idly." During daylight through their entire passage, both
the Eastern and Center Naval Task Forces enjoyed air cover from
the two carriers, reinforced by land-based planes from the United
Kingdom, Gibraltar and Malta.

---

[1] No complete Task Organization has been attempted of the Eastern and Center
Forces, as of Task Force 34, because with the exception of a few transports all
the ships belonged to the Royal Navy and various Allied merchant marines.

Rear Admiral Sir Harold M. Burrough RN was in charge of naval operations against Algiers, as Commander Eastern Naval Task Force. His force consisted of the British headquarters ship *Bulolo;*[2] light cruisers *Sheffield, Scylla* and *Charybdis;* carriers *Argus* and *Avenger;* auxiliary antiaircraft cruisers *Palomares, Pozarica* and *Tynwald;* monitor *Roberts,* thirteen destroyers, seven fleet mine-sweepers, seven corvettes, three sloops and miscellaneous small craft. Embarked in the Eastern Naval Task Force was the Eastern Assault Force, commanded by Major General Charles W. Ryder USA, consisting of the 39th Regimental Combat Team of the 9th Infantry Division United States Army, 168th Regimental Combat Team of the 34th Infantry Division United States Army, 11th and 36th Brigade Groups of the 78th British Infantry Division, 1st and 6th Commando Battalions composed of both British and American troops, with miscellaneous attached units. In all there were about 23,000 officers and men of the British Army and 10,000 officers and men of the United States Army in the Eastern Assault Force. The object of this curious set-up was to make the assault force appear to the French to be all American.[3]

For the landings, the Eastern Naval Task Force was divided into three main groups designated "Apples," "Beer" and "Charlie," with a Senior Naval Officer Landing in charge both of the landing and of the ships involved. Group Apples, an all-British outfit, was to effect the westernmost of the Algiers landings on beaches north-east of Castiglione. The 11th Brigade Group was charged with this assault, the 36th being held in reserve. Group Beer, composed mostly of members of the 168th Regimental Combat Team United States Army, was to land fifteen miles farther to the eastward on beaches between Sidi Ferruch and Pointe Pescade. Group Charlie, primarily the 39th Regimental Combat Team United States Army, embarked

---

[2] The prototype of our AGCs.

[3] That is why American personnel were included in British commando formations. On 9 Nov. overall command of Allied troops in Algeria was transferred to Lt. Gen. K. A. N. Anderson of the British First Army whose force was to be increased to a strength of four to six divisions, including the whole 34th U.S. Division. Eastern Assault Force then became known as Eastern Task Force.

in United States Navy transports, was to land on the east side of Algiers Bay on beaches lying eastward of Cape Matifou in the vicinity of Surcouf and Ain Taya.

The commandos and a United States Ranger battalion [4] were to effect "scramble" landings on the rocky coast near Cape Caxine and Pointe Pescade. There was also to be a frontal attack on Algiers harbor by a detachment of the 135th United States Infantry Regiment embarked in two British destroyers. This group was to hold the docks and wharves and prevent sabotage while the main landing teams were to converge in a pincers movement on the city which was the objective of the force.

Assault forces for both Oran (Center) and Algiers (Eastern) landings sailed from the United Kingdom together in two big convoys: a slow division (KMS–O and KMS–A) on 22 October, and a fast one (KMF–O and KMF–A) on 26 October. This timing put both through the Straits of Gibraltar during the night of 5–6 November, and brought the slow convoy to the Algiers landing places about two hours after the assault had begun.

Before passing Gibraltar each of the two convoys broke in half. Once through the Straits all vessels destined for Oran (KMF–O and KMS–O) peeled off to the southward while the Algiers divisions (KMF–A and KMS–A) continued on their way. The last two, which constituted the Eastern Naval Task Force, were further divided when approaching near their objectives into landing groups Apples, Beer and Charlie. Each group had about equal strength and was given an assignment of equal difficulty. The adventures of Group Charlie we shall relate in more detail, since it consisted almost entirely of American troops and was embarked in United States Navy transports.

Group Charlie, commanded by Captain Campbell D. Edgar of Transport Division 11 in *Samuel Chase*,[5] comprised the transports

---

[4] The 1st Ranger Battalion had been especially trained in Scotland by its commanding officer Maj. William O. Darby USA, side by side with the British Commandos, to spearhead an assault. Milton Lehman "The Rangers" *Sat. Eve. Post* 15 June 1946. But they actually landed at Arzeu — see p. 231 below.

[5] Not to be confused with the Liberty ship *Samuel Chase*.

Thomas Stone [6] and *Leedstown*,[7] assault cargo ship U.S.S. *Almaack*, the American merchant ship *Exceller* (chartered by the Army to carry additional equipment) and the Netherlands passenger liner *Dempo*, carrying Royal Air Force personnel and equipment. Two British freighters came in the slow convoy. These vessels carried about 7,600 troops, together with their armor, vehicles and other equipment.[8]

Of the United States transports involved, only *Thomas Stone* had participated in landing exercises in Chesapeake Bay with other ships of the Amphibious Force Atlantic Fleet. Subsequent to these exercises General Eisenhower decided to use one more regimental combat team in the Algiers operation. Accordingly the 39th Infantry Regiment (reinforced) was detached somewhat belatedly from the 9th Division, and without prior amphibious training trans-

---

[6] There was also a Liberty ship *Thomas Stone*.

[7] Not to be confused with a later U.S.S. *Leedstown* (APA–56), ex-S.S. *Exchequer*.

[8] Divided up among the vessels of Group Charlie as follows: —

Type Number	Vessel	Commanding Officer	No. LCMs	No. LCPs	Forces Embarked
AP 56	SAMUEL CHASE (ex-*African Meteor*)	Comdr. Roger C. Heimer USCG	2	24	1st BLT 39th RCT
AP 59	THOMAS STONE (ex-*President Van Buren*)	Capt. Olten R. Bennehoff	2	22	2nd BLT 39th RCT
AP 73	LEEDSTOWN (ex-*Santa Lucia*)	Lt. Cdr. Duncan Cook USNR	2	26	1st Commandos 3rd BLT 39th RCT
AK 27	ALMAACK (ex-*Executor*)	Capt. Chester L. Nichols	4	10	Service and Anti-Tank Companies
S.S.	EXCELLER American	....	2	—	Service Battery 26th F.A.
S.S.	DEMPO Netherlands	....	—	—	1 co. 3rd BLT 39th RCT; Aëro Constr. Party; A.A.
S.S.	MACHARDA British	....	5	—	Light and Heavy A.A. Vehicles
S.S.	MARON British	....	2	—	Light A.A.; R.A.F. Commandos; Vehicles

U.S.S. *Thomas Stone* in Algiers Bay, after torpedoing

U.S.S. *Samuel Chase*

ported to the United Kingdom in U.S.S. *Almaack, Leedstown* and *Samuel Chase*, who had enjoyed very limited training opportunities.[9] Organized as Transport Division 11, these ships departed 19 September from Hampton Roads for New York, whence they sailed on the 26th in Convoy AT-23, escorted by U.S.S. *Arkansas* (flagship of Captain C. F. Bryant) and nine destroyers. Captain Edgar's orders were to report to the Commander United States Naval Forces in Europe (Admiral H. R. Stark) and to the British Admiralty, for duty in connection with Operation "Torch." The three transports arrived 6 October at Belfast, Northern Ireland, where they stayed nine days. This very limited interval was spent in re-stowing army equipment and waterproofing vehicles while the troops, billeted ashore, were drilled in landing craft operations.

On 15 October the 39th Regimental Combat Team was shifted to Inveraray, Scotland, the location of a British training establishment for amphibious operations. Captain Edgar found Inveraray "not well suited for this type of training"; the Scottish coast certainly had little in common with North Africa. In his opinion about all the ships got out of the visit was badly needed practice in hoisting in and lowering boats.[10] The 39th RCT shoved off for the Mediterranean without having had a real landing rehearsal.

The forces which comprised groups Apples and Beer likewise lacked adequate training. The 3rd Battalion Landing Team of the 168th Infantry embarked in *Otranto* at Liverpool and took part in the practice exercises at Loch Fyne. Its commanding officer reported that the "landing crews were somewhat confused," and that the practice actually did more harm than good since a different type of landing craft was used from the one prescribed for "Torch."

In groups Apples and Beer, Senior Naval Officers Landing were embarked respectively in H.M.S. *Karanja* and *Keren*. Apples comprised approximately 7000 men from the 11th British Brigade

[9] Lt. Col. Homer L. Litzenberg Jr. USMC "Occupation of French North Africa — Outline History" Dec. 1942.
[10] Comtransdiv 11 Action Report 23 Nov. 1942.

Group with their equipment in eight fast personnel and cargo ships. Group Beer included the 168th Regimental Combat Team United States Army, with divisional troops of the 34th United States and 78th British Divisions, together with the 6th Commandos and part of the 1st Commandos. Headquarters ship *Bulolo* was attached to this sector. Approximately 10,000 men and their equipment were loaded in a dozen transports and cargo vessels.

The reserve force, about 6000 men from the British 36th Brigade, was embarked in five vessels divided between groups Apples and Beer.

b. The Passage

Captain Edgar's transports made up but a small part of the enormous composite fast convoy of both Center and Eastern Naval Task Forces which sailed from the Clyde on the night of 26 October. By this time the slow convoy had had four days' headstart and was well on its way to Gibraltar. The fast convoy, consisting of almost forty transports and cargo ships, reached the assembly point where the escorts joined, and before dawn on the twenty-seventh took its final departure from the British Isles.

The passage south was uneventful. Soldiers acquired sea legs slowly and did not "beef" at British rations for some days. Gradually, as stomachs recovered and appetites were whetted by the sea air, that aspect of the voyage became all-important; the "limey" cook on board *Keren* was deprived of his coffeepots in favor of more competent hands. Training classes went on continuously but only a chosen few knew the convoy's destination. As the days passed "scuttlebutt" on this subject increased, as did the gripes about the inevitably recurring herring, tripe and mutton. It was unfortunate American troops had to be carried in British ships, for a sea voyage demands sufficient adjustment without superimposing the concoctions of strange sea cooks. But no other shipping was available.

The Center Force for Oran left the composite convoy at 1400 November 4. During the night of 5–6 November, the Algiers convoy [11] slipped through the Straits of Gibraltar and assumed the course usually followed by Malta-bound vessels in the hope that enemy spotters would be fooled. They were. According to Count Ciano's Diary, the Germans believed that this convoy was destined either to relieve Malta, or to land troops in Tripoli behind Rommel's army. Only at the last minute were the ships turned south for their actual destinations. Groups Apples, Beer and Charlie were to be unscrambled later.

The first hostile incident occurred at daybreak 7 November, at lat. 37°31′ N, long. 00°01′ E, about thirty-three miles off Cape Palos, Spain, and one hundred and fifty-five miles from Algiers. At a time when the convoy was not zigzagging and the anti-submarine screen was disposed about the transports, an explosion on the port side of *Thomas Stone*, well aft, disabled her propeller and rudder and forced her to drop out of the convoy.[12] The explosion was so loud that people in H.M.S. *Keren* steaming abreast of *Stone* thought they were hit. A torpedo wake was sighted from *Stone*, and it was at first thought that she had been hit by a drop from a plane which came up from astern and passed from starboard to port. This plane, however, proved to be a friendly one coming in for a bomb attack on the U-boat which fired the lethal torpedo. Another torpedo missed *Samuel Chase* by about fifty yards. H.M. corvette *Spey* was detached to screen the crippled *Thomas Stone* while the rest of the convoy stood on its course.

Commander Roger C. Heimer USCG of *Samuel Chase* proposed

[11] After the separation of the Oran Section from convoy KMF–1, the Eastern Naval Task Force convoy (KMF–A) consisted of the following United Nations vessels: —

    H.M.S. *Bulolo*, flagship of Rear Admiral Sir H. M. Burrough, RN, Convoy commodore;
    S.S. *Strathnaver* (British), Convoy vice-commodore;
    S.S. *Viceroy of India* (British), Convoy rear-commodore;
    U.S.S. *Samuel Chase, Thomas Stone, Leedstown, Almaack;*
    H.M.S. *Royal Scotsman, Royal Ulsterman, Ulster Monarch, Keren, Karanja;*
    S.S. *Leinster* (British), *Awatea* (British), *Sobieski* (Polish), *Cathay* (British), *Marnix van St. Aldegoude* (Netherlands), *Dempo* (Netherlands), *Exceller* (American).

[12] Report of Torpedoing and Salvage of U.S.S. *Thomas Stone*, enclosed in War Diary of Transdiv 11 for November. Nine bluejackets were killed or wounded.

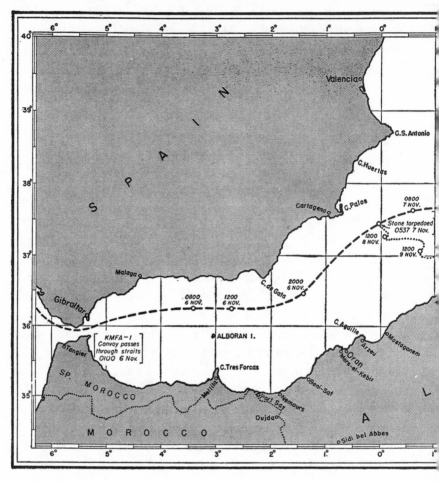

to take the *Stone* in tow, but his request was denied by Captain Edgar as contrary to his orders.[18] Commander Heimer proposed as an alternative to take off the troops, but this suggestion was likewise rejected, and rightly so. The operation order was clear: vessels damaged in convoy must be left behind.

During the afternoon of 7 November, both the convoy and Admiral Cunningham's covering force, which was steaming about ten miles to the northward, brought Axis observation planes

[18] *Samuel Chase* War Diary 7 Nov. 1942.

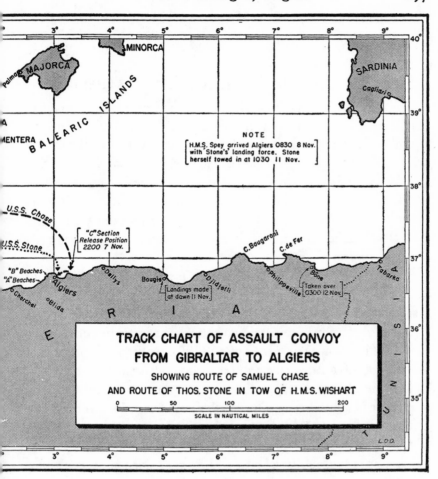

NOTE
[H.M.S. Spey arrived Algiers 0830 8 Nov. with "Stone's" landing force. Stone herself towed in at 1030 11 Nov.]

["C" Section Release Position 2200 7 Nov.]

[Landings made at dawn 11 Nov.]

[Taken over 0300 12 Nov.]

TRACK CHART OF ASSAULT CONVOY
FROM GIBRALTAR TO ALGIERS

SHOWING ROUTE OF SAMUEL CHASE
AND ROUTE OF THOS. STONE IN TOW OF H.M.S. WISHART

0   50   100   200
SCALE IN NAUTICAL MILES

under heavy anti-aircraft fire. At 1815, Group Charlie was detached and proceeded to the rendezvous, which was marked by a
British submarine.

The disabling of the *Thomas Stone* was a serious blow to Group
Charlie. The best trained of the transports, she carried a whole
battalion landing team, numbering about fourteen hundred assault
troops, as well as much wanted landing craft. For the moment we
shall have to leave her, as the convoy did, and follow Group
Charlie through its landing phase.

2. The Landings

a. Group "Charlie" Lands East of Algiers [14]

Group Charlie of the Eastern Naval Task Force under command of Captain Edgar, transporting the United States 39th Regimental Combat Team 9th Infantry Division, under the command of Colonel B. F. Caffey Jr. USA, was assigned to land on four beaches about five miles east of Cape Matifou, and twelve miles east of Algiers.[15] Two of the beaches, designated Red 1 and 2, extended from Surcouf to the Oued Reghaia, and were reserved for landing vehicles. Beaches Green and Blue to the westward were set aside for landing troops.

This group included United States Transport Division 11 and two British merchant ships of the slow convoy, protected by H.M. auxiliary anti-aircraft cruiser *Tynwald*, destroyers *Cowdray* and *Zetland*, three minesweepers, two trawlers and two motor torpedo boats.[16] These ships left the Apples and Beer sections of the Algiers convoy at 1815 November 7 and made contact with the beacon submarine H.M.S. *P-48*, at about 2130, when they deployed and commenced debarkation. The weather was fair, with a force-three NE wind. *Leedstown's* troop contingent, the reserve, stepped into the breach left by the torpedoing of the *Thomas Stone*.

On Cape Matifou was a battery of four 7½-inch guns, constituting the greatest threat to Group Charlie. The successive boat waves moved in without opposition, and since the landings were receiving no attention from the fort, Captain Edgar at about 0200 shifted his troopships to a line about four thousand yards from the beaches. Although the wind set them towards Cape Matifou the risk had to be accepted, since it was impracticable to maneuver while unload-

[14] Transdiv 11 Action Report.

[15] The initial release point of the landing boats from the transports was about 8 miles offshore.

[16] At 0300 (H plus 2) November 8, the slow convoy joined up with the freighters *Macharda* and *Maron*, escorted by three corvettes.

ing. The risk proved to be worth taking, since the French cannoneers left the transports alone in favor of H.M. destroyers *Cowdray* and *Zetland*. They answered in kind, and the battery ceased fire at about 0400, after an exchange lasting only twenty minutes.

Night landings on the Charlie beaches proceeded without much delay or confusion. The *Chase* took fifty-five minutes and the *Almaack* sixty-seven to get their boats into the water. H-hour was set for 0100. The first boat wave left the *Chase* at 0015 and the *Almaack* at 0145. The *Chase's* first wave landed at 0118, slightly delayed because it could not find its guiding motor launch. The second wave landed at 0120 and the third, delayed by slow loading, at 0200.

At about daybreak, pursuant to plan, the ships moved to the assigned anchorage 1500–2000 yards off the Red beaches, and proceeded with the unloading. A screen of white smoke or fog effectively concealed them from the fort, but, unhappily, also concealed the beaches from the boat crews. And the weather was deteriorating. The American commandos who had been assigned to take the battery at Cape Matifou had been unable to do so. Supporting fire was requested by an artillery observation officer with them, who was in radio communication with H.M. destroyer *Zetland*. Captain Edgar referred the request to Rear Admiral Burrough, recommending that if the battery were to be bombarded, a heavy ship be used. Bombardment was later effectively conducted by H.M.S. *Bermuda* both on Cape Matifou and on near-by Fort d'Estrées, which also proved recalcitrant.

Once the beachhead was consolidated, the 39th Infantry set out overland for its assigned objectives. This force was the eastern prong of the giant nutcracker designed to squeeze Algiers. Initially, its most important task was to take the airdrome of Maison Blanche. This capitulated at 0827, and soon afterwards played host to Allied aircraft staged in from Gibraltar.

Data on the loss of landing craft are fragmentary. *Chase* lost six of her twenty-three boats participating in the first landing. At the

time of the air-bombing attack ten were left moored to her side —
at about 1700 on 8 November. Near misses caused three of these to
break adrift, and they were lost. Some of the *Almaack's* boats were
intact at the close of landing operations on the afternoon of 8 November, but rising seas in the night caused their coxswains to beach
them to prevent swamping. Sixty-eight "useful" trips had been
made, and three out of the eleven beached boats were still usable.[17]

In the early part of this landing, there were many mistakes by inexperienced sailors and much breakdown of equipment. It was the
same story as off Fedhala. Lack of proper training[18] caused delay
in loading the boats.[19] Some of *Leedstown's* boat cranes blew their
fuses, and efforts to squeeze two or more vehicles instead of one
into the *Almaack's* tank lighters, in order to make up for the loss
of *Stone's* boats, caused further delay. After boat waves left the
ships, they had trouble in finding the motor launches assigned as
guides, never having worked with them. Coxswains were green and
boat compasses "went haywire" as usual. Boat waves which lost
sight of those ahead had great difficulty in finding the right beach
in the dark. Boats were stranded, even though the rise and fall of
tide was only six inches. Until 0900 November 8, the breeze was
light and the swell measured only one to two feet from trough to
crest; yet some boats were swamped from overloading and others
sank offshore because ramps were lowered too soon.

Both wind and sea began to make up after 0900. Between 1400
and 1600, urgent appeals from the Army for its communication
equipment and anti-aircraft guns, and from the Royal Air Force
for gasoline stores in the *Dempo*, required more boats and crews
to be jeopardized.

[17] Report by Lt. Cdr. J. W. Buxton 10 Nov. 1942.
[18] Comtransdiv 11 in first endorsement to report of loss of *Leedstown* states
she had little or no training, had never fired a target practice, her captain had
never had any active training since World War I, none of her officers were of
the regular Navy. In spite of these disadvantages, "the vessel did much better
throughout the operation than could be expected."
[19] Lt. Charles L. Carville of the 15th Engineers of RCT 39, whose men were
delayed seven hours in leaving the *Chase*, saw many idle landing craft and dryly
observed that "it seems that the Army and Navy could improve this situation
considerably."

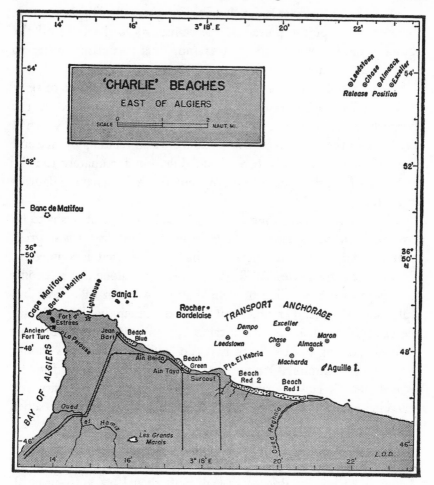

All landing on beaches had to be called off at about 1800; and it was never resumed, because next morning most of the French quit fighting and Allied ships could then use the harbor.

The commanding officer of *Samuel Chase* attributed the loss of boats in the Matifou landings to their "poor design for even slight surf." However, a boat is like a mule and will serve you well if treated properly. Many of the boats would have been all right, had they not been loaded so deeply that they shipped water over the stern, which snuffed out their gasoline motors and swamped them. Others were lost for such trivial reasons as having inadequate painters improperly secured to the transports, or backing off the beaches before closing the bow ramp, thus permitting water to rush in and swamp them.

At the end of the operation, only two of ten LCMs, five of sixty LCPs, and one LCV remained of the landing craft carried by the *Samuel Chase, Almaack, Leedstown* and *Exceller*. And, as we shall see, most of the *Thomas Stone's* boats were lost. Landing of men and equipment was seriously behind schedule, but fortunately the absence of strong shore opposition prevented this from having damaging effect.

The loss of some landing craft in amphibious operations is to be expected, but in the Eastern Task Force the mortality was so great that the Army felt that the Navy had proved itself incompetent. Major General Charles W. Ryder USA was not alone in his recommendation that "the line of demarkation, wherein the Navy has full control of the operation until the troops reach the shore, should be changed so that the Army takes control when the troops get into the landing craft,"[20] and that the landing craft crews should be soldiers. Admiral Cunningham, accepting the blame for the Royal Navy's lack of training, occasioned by the necessity for carrying out the operation when we did, wrote words of sober counsel: —

Although I am fully in sympathy with the spirit of the proposals of the Commanding General Eastern Assault Force and of the 1st Engineer Amphibian Brigade that all craft should be Army-manned, this is not the real answer. The solution is that, whatever uniform the crews wear, they must be *trained seamen* with special practice in the technique of landing operations, and in close touch with the requirements of the troops they have to land and maintain.[21]

He further stated that: —

It was only possible to give very brief training to officers and men from general service who were required to make up the numbers re-

[20] Compilation of Reports, Eastern Assault Force U.S. Army, p. 6.
[21] Dispatch of 7 Feb. 1943, para. 6.

quired for the landing craft crews and beach parties. Some of the latter landed on the North African coast without ever having fired even one practice round from their rifles or revolvers.[22]

General Eisenhower also admitted that lack of training had been inevitable and therefore saw no reason for the Army to take over a function which has been traditionally that of the Navy. "The Navy is and will be in control of landing operations until troops are ashore, when such control passes to the Commanding General," said he.[23]

As the handling and navigation of the boats were criticized, so was the unloading. Here again, as in Morocco, the poor functioning of Army Shore Parties was largely responsible, and boat crews found themselves saddled with the added task of unloading. In the confusion, cargo was dumped helter-skelter and many units were separated from their equipment. Vehicles were loaded in one boat, and their drivers in another. Even if it had been broad daylight and on familiar soil, bringing them together would have been difficult enough. At night and amid other confusion, the drivers naturally took a long time to locate their vehicles, if indeed they ever found them.[24]

The assault troops were too heavily burdened for tactical efficiency upon landing. General Ryder admitted that they carried far too much equipment. It was the age-old problem of deciding what must be left behind that confronts all human beings when they move, and to which no hard-and-fast formula can be applied.

b. Groups "Apples" and "Beer" Land West of Algiers

While United States transports were engaged in landing American troops east of Algiers, the Royal Navy was debarking British troops on the Apples beaches and American troops on the Beer beaches west of the capital city.

The Apples as an all-British sector we shall pass over briefly. Its

---

[22] Cincmed Report, Annex X para. 3.
[23] "Dispatch" of 15 Feb. 1943, para. 1*a*.
[24] Report of Gen. Ryder in Compilation of Reports, p. 5.

beaches lay near the town of Castiglione, twenty-two miles west of Algiers. After consolidating the beachhead the primary mission of the 11th British Brigade was to strike southeastward to capture the airdrome of Blida fifteen miles away, and then northeastward to Bir Touta to cut off communications with Algiers from the south. This they well performed against sporadic resistance. As elsewhere, so on the Apples beaches there was unnecessary disorder, confusion and loss of landing craft. Evidently a westward sweep of current along the Algerian coast was not considered, for a considerable number of Beer landing craft wound up on the Apples beaches.

Beaches near Sidi Ferruch, a small town fifteen miles west of Algiers, were selected for a primary landing by Group Beer, partly in order to assist Apples in the securing of Blida airdrome, and partly to coöperate with Charlie in a pincers movement on Algiers. The United States Navy had no part in Group Beer, but the troops involved were primarily United States Army. This attack force consisted of the 168th Regimental Combat Team of the 34th Infantry Division, commanded by Colonel John W. ("Iron Mike") O'Daniel USA. The 34th Division, originally an Iowa National Guard outfit, arrived in Northern Ireland in echelons between February and April 1942. It had been given amphibious training at Inveraray in H.M.S. *Ettrick*. The Beer Group, embarked in H.M.S. *Keren* and nine other ships, broke formation at about 1800 and proceeded to the designated release position shortly before midnight 7 November.

The first forces disembarked were detachments of the British 1st Commandos, who effected "scramble" landings on both sides of Fort Sidi Ferruch, and detachments of the 6th Commandos and Rangers, who landed in the neighborhood of Cape Caxine and Pointe Pescade. They were followed by waves of the 168th Regimental Combat Team United States Army on the assigned Beer beaches. No resistance was offered by shore batteries or other French elements at Sidi Ferruch. The assault wave of Company A

168th Infantry met General Mast near Fort Sidi Ferruch and received his assurance that they would meet no opposition, nor did they. This same Company A landed in considerable confusion at 0130 from LCAs of the *Winchester Castle*. All went well until the landing craft touched down on Beach Green. Some boats grounded well off shore and men were landed in water over their heads. Other craft broached and beached broadside to, while others steamed in over the heads of the heavy-laden swimmers. Captain James J. Gillespie's report does not present a felicitous picture: —

We received no opposition whatsoever from the beach and if we had, in that condition of landing, it would have been a complete failure in my opinion, as the troops in the wallowing boats and those in the water would have been helpless against enemy fire.[25]

Some initial resistance was encountered on the Beer beaches where a few units landing were badly shot up. But most of the trouble in this sector was caused by the inability of British landing craft coxswains to locate the correct beach. Colonel O'Daniel and his staff, to their great annoyance, were set down on one of the Apples beaches seven or eight miles on the wrong side of Sidi Ferruch. Company H of the 168th Infantry, embarked in an LCM from the Belgian freighter *Jean Jadot*, milled around the Mediterranean for hours and then landed fifteen miles west of Sidi Ferruch. They identified their position, reëmbarked in the LCM, and at 0700 were finally set ashore on an Apples beach. Company C took six hours and a quarter to reach the shore twelve miles from its destination. One could cite many similar instances which unnecessarily complicated the Army's task of assembly and deployment to assigned shore objectives. Only the fortunate lack of resistance on the part of the French saved this landing from a hopeless foul-up.

Colonel O'Daniel pushed his troops hard, once they were ashore and assembled. One column marched eighteen to twenty miles to

[25] Report of Co. A 168th Infantry.

the southward and assisted in the capture of Blida airdrome before noon. Another, the 2nd BLT of the 168th Regiment, made a forced march eastward to a height overlooking El Biar, one of the western suburbs of Algiers. On the way they passed the Beni-Messous farm, which was occupied by Indo-Chinese troops. It was typical of our relations with the French that these colonials were puzzled as to their duty; in the end they did nothing, as their commanding officer had gone to town and the Americans prevented the second in command from following to inquire whether or not to shoot. During the afternoon the 2nd BLT had some sharp street fighting in El Biar with a Moroccan regiment whose commander rightly did not heed Admiral Darlan's Algiers nonresistance order. But by nightfall that had ceased, and the American troops had only snipers to deal with. They camped in olive groves on the outskirts of the city and moved into barracks at the École Normale in Algiers about 12 November.

No sooner was this battalion snug in barracks than it was routed out on a night alarm. A message came through from Allied troops occupying Sidi Ferruch that an amphibious counter-invasion was on. A combat patrol was promptly formed and drove hell-bent for Sidi Ferruch, where complete quiet reigned. Daybreak revealed the fact that this "amphibious counterattack" consisted of about ten abandoned British landing craft floating with wind and current. Six of these empties, as if still obedient to military command, beached themselves in a perfect line on Sidi Ferruch beach, and another floated into a small harbor near by. The want of proper training which caused their crews to abandon these perfectly good boats was very apparent in the Beer sector. Ninety-eight out of 104 boats used in the three sectors of the Eastern Task Force were casualties. This percentage of loss (94.2 per cent) was appallingly high comparing with 34.3 per cent for the Western Task Force on the exposed Moroccan coast, boated by United States Navy landing craft, and 20 per cent for the Center Task Force, boated by the Royal Navy.[26]

[26] War Dept. "Lessons Learned" 12 Feb. 1943.

c. H.M.S. *Broke* and *Malcolm* Attempt a Frontal Attack [27]

In each of the three task forces a direct frontal attack was planned on an important harbor which it was desired to secure promptly. On the Atlantic coast the operation of United States destroyers *Cole* and *Bernadou* at Safi was eminently successful. In Algiers H.M.S. *Broke* and *Malcolm* did not fare so well. And at Oran the attempt of H.M.S. *Hartland* and *Walney* was disastrous.

The Eastern Task Force plan contemplated forcing an entrance into Algiers Harbor and landing a picked detachment to seize installations and prevent sabotage to ships and port facilities. Two Royal Navy destroyers, *Broke* and *Malcolm*, were selected for this mission. The American contingent, a detachment of the 135th Regimental Combat Team under Lieutenant Colonel Edwin T. Swenson USA, began training 15 October at Sunnylands Camp, Carrickfergus, Northern Ireland. This force was equally divided between the two vessels when it joined the fast assault convoy at Gibraltar. By the early morning of 8 November the destroyers were standing by off Algiers Harbor. At 0220 they received word that the landing of the combat teams had been successful, and immediately stood in towards the harbor entrance. Both ships missed the boom; when circling for another try they were picked up by searchlights. Shore batteries immediately gave tongue, and on board *Malcolm* "all hell seemed to break loose." [28] She was badly holed in the engine room, three boilers being knocked out, which cut her speed to four knots. *Malcolm* retired as *Broke* maneuvered for a second try at the boom. On the third attempt she crashed through. She finally secured alongside the Quai de Falaise on Môle Louis Billiard. She had disembarked her troops at 0520 on the Quai de Fécamp.

Although the troops were pinned to the dock, it was noted that the French were shooting more to restrain than to kill. Ultimately

[27] Cincmed Report para. 10, 11; 135th Infantry Regiment Report.
[28] Report of U.S. Forces on board *Malcolm.*

the Americans were surrounded and led off to a French military prison. Meanwhile the position of the *Broke* was becoming untenable, and as it would have been suicidal to attempt to recall the troops, she cast off and, under cover of a smoke screen laid by destroyer *Zetland,* steamed out of the harbor at 1030. Although Captain Fancourt stated simply, "We failed in our mission," his handling of the crippled destroyer evoked the respect of French naval officers who described the feat as *magnifique.* Outside the harbor *Zetland* passed her a towline. Apparently the serious nature of her damage was not appreciated, for although there was time to beach the *Broke,* she sank on 10 November while still under tow.

d. Diplomacy Ashore

While *Broke* and *Malcolm* were preparing to steam into the harbor and American and British troops were landing at three different points adjoining the Bay of Algiers, Mr. Robert Murphy was endeavoring to persuade Admiral Darlan to assume responsibility and order French armed forces to cease resistance. Darlan saw which way the wind was blowing, and wished to go with it rather than be gone with it. But he knew that unless he had, or could claim to have, Pétain's orders to that effect, many subordinate officers would refuse to obey him. In the early hours of the morning, 8 November, he consented to cable Marshal Pétain requesting the Chief of State to give, or authorize him to give, the required order. It seems clear from the evidence now at hand that the Marshal's real attitude was favorable to the idea of not resisting the landings.[29] There is much reason to believe that his reply to President Roosevelt's message, declaring that French forces would be ordered to resist the invasion, was for public consumption only. Laval, over his protest, gave the Germans permission to pour troops into Tunisia. Even though the Marshal did secretly favor the Anglo-American expedition, he was so surrounded by collaborators as to make him helpless.

About noon on 8 November Darlan issued orders on his own

[29] Information from Service Historique de la Marine, 28 Aug. 1952; see p. 219, below.

responsibility to the French troops and ships in the Algiers sector to cease firing. It did not apply to the Oran sector, nor, as we have seen, to Morocco.

Major General Ryder, commanding the Eastern Assault Force, made contact with Darlan and at 1600 accompanied him to Admiral Fenard's house. In conjunction with General Juin, Darlan and Ryder concluded an oral armistice, which applied only to the Algiers sector; and it is believed that all resistance ceased there by 1900 November 8.

3. *The* THOMAS STONE *Flotilla*

We left the United States naval transport *Thomas Stone* torpedoed and abandoned by the rest of Group Charlie, 150 miles from Algiers at daybreak 7 November. Only H.M. corvette *Spey* stood by. It was soon evident that the *Stone*, although in no immediate danger of sinking, could not regain propulsion. She received word that a tug had been ordered from Gibraltar and that two destroyers, H.M.S. *Wishart* and *Velox*, were on the way to assist. The sea was smooth, with a light breeze from the northwest. Why not boat the troops then and there, and let the ship's landing craft cover the trip to Algiers under their own power?

Captain O. R. Bennehoff of *Thomas Stone*, and Major Walter M. Oakes of the BLT embarked,[30] decided to adopt this unorthodox solution in order not to miss the assault. As the ship's boats could not accommodate the entire battalion, Major Oakes and about 800 officers and men, comprising three assault waves, were embarked in the 24 most seaworthy landing craft. They were ordered to land the troops at their original destinations on Algiers Bay unless otherwise directed by Captain Edgar, who was duly notified.

As Admiral Cunningham said, this was a "notably courageous decision." The landing craft had not been designed for long voyages and the weather, favorable at departure, could not be depended on to remain fair until they reached their destination one

[30] 2nd Battalion Landing Team 39th U.S. Infantry 9th Division.

hundred and fifty miles away. There was as much risk for those who stayed as for those who departed. *Thomas Stone* had been torpedoed, probably by a U-boat which was standing by submerged for a favorable chance to finish her off. H.M.S. *Spey*, her only protection until aid could arrive from Gibraltar, now must escort the landing craft in order to afford the troops a fair chance of reaching land. Necessary changes in loading plans delayed the departure of the troops. Even so, the *Stone* lay dead in the water without protection for almost two hours until destroyers *Velox* and *Wishart* closed.[31]

Captain Bennehoff's courage was rewarded by good fortune, and no further attack was made on his ship. H.M.S. *Velox* passed a cable to the stricken transport. *Stone*, with her rudder carried away, yawed drunkenly at the end of the towline, which ultimately parted. *Wishart* maneuvered, picked up another line, and again the group proceeded. At daybreak on 8 November, H.M. tug *St. Day* joined and took lines from the stern of the *Stone* in order to help the steering problem; but this did not work very well. Soon after, *St. Day* took over the tow from *Wishart*. With mounting wind and sea, little progress was made. Towing in tandem with *Wishart* was then attempted, the tug ahead, to assist the destroyer in holding her course. Every possible combination was tried – and, as Captain Bennehoff wrote, "all this required great coolness, patience, and a high order of seamanship." [32] The tow was completed successfully and *Thomas Stone* was brought to an anchor off Algiers at 1030 November 11. Rear Admiral Burrough sent Captain Bennehoff the following message: "My warmest congratulations on the splendid effort put up by U.S.S. *Thomas Stone*. The determination you have shown to take part in this operation, whatever the obstacles, is an example to us all."

[31] Sufficient boats and life rafts remained on board to accommodate all the crew and the remaining troops in case of need, and her two 50-foot tank lighters were lowered in order to serve as rescue craft if necessary. Landing boats were stationed on either side of the *Stone*, 100 yards distant, to serve to the best of their limited abilities as an anti-submarine screen.

[32] Report on Torpedoing and Salvage of *Thomas Stone*.

The passage of the 800 troops from the *Stone* in 24 landing craft commenced under cover of darkness. *Spey* led the boats away in three columns, at about 1900 November 7. Lieutenant (jg) R. C. Marler USNR commanded the boats; Major Oakes led the left column in the support boat. Ensign J. B. Wheeler took position at center rear with a boat repair crew. The landing craft were expected to make between eight and nine knots, but six knots soon proved to be their best speed, and, with mounting seas, this was later reduced to four. They had been gone only an hour when the first breakdown occurred. From that time on, what with broken oil-lines and overheated engines, there was never a period of over half an hour during which all boats were moving. When one broke down, all the others and the *Spey* had to wait either for repairs to be made, or for a line to be passed from the corvette.

At 0030 November 8, one boat had to be abandoned, leaking badly after a collision. By 0600 every boat was taking water, all gear and equipment were soaked, and the troops were miserable, wet and seasick. After a conference the commanding officers, all troops and equipment were taken on board the *Spey*. But Lieutenant Marler would not give up his boats. Radio reports had reached him of the high losses and serious shortage of small craft in the landings already taking place. Accordingly, he determined to bring in as many of his flotilla as the dwindling fuel supply would allow. Boats for which fuel could not be had were scuttled, and Lieutenant Marler followed the *Spey* with three ramped boats, two Higgins landing craft and two support boats.

By this time the *Spey* had had enough of this recalcitrant brood, and her other duties were pressing. She would no longer proceed at less than eleven knots, and the best the support boats could make was only nine-and-a-half knots. Their compasses were unreliable, the sky was overcast, and another night's dead-reckoning navigation might take them well off their course. The corvette commander agreed to tow the two support boats but no others. Accordingly, the other craft were scuttled shortly after noon and *Spey* proceeded at twelve knots with the support boats in tow. One of them broke away at about 1800 and the other at 1900; and then there were none.

At 2030 *Spey* reached the point where the *Stone's* troops should have debarked twenty hours earlier, and stood by for the rest of the night under orders. Next morning (9 November), resistance having ceased, she rounded Cape Matifou and landed the troops and equipment on the main passenger quay in Algiers. Thus Major Oakes's men after all were able to come ashore dry-shod and standing up, thanks to the gallant British corvette.

4. *Air Raids, 8–15 November*

Almost at the moment when French resistance around Algiers ceased, the Axis picked up the ball. Between 1650 and 1735 on D-day, 8 November, the ships of Group Charlie at anchor off the beaches east of Cape Matifou were subjected to a determined dive-bombing and torpedo attack by about 21 JU–88s and Heinkel 111s. The large transports were the main targets. Captain Edgar in the *Chase* kept his ships at anchor, partly because they were well disposed for mutual support, and partly because anti-aircraft fire was coolly maintained at a greater volume than had been expected from transports. Apparently they had no smoke-pots: certainly none were used. H. M. auxiliary anti-aircraft cruiser *Tynwald* and other escorts went promptly into action, but from their position to seaward they were unable to repel torpedo plane attacks, which came from the land side. One aërial torpedo hit U.S.S. *Leedstown* in the stern, destroying her steering gear and partially flooding her after section, leaving her dead in the water. H.M.S. *Cowdray* suffered a bomb hit in the fireroom, killing several men and wounding many. She was subsequently assisted to Algiers Bay by H.M.S. *Algerine* and was there beached to prevent foundering. Minor damage was caused S.S. *Exceller* from a near bomb miss astern, and the *Samuel Chase* had narrow escapes from two torpedoes.

During the night, Captain Edgar received orders to move into Algiers Bay in the morning, and all ships except the crippled *Leeds-*

town got under way between 0530 and 0630 November 9. One JU–88 made a shallow-dive attack on S.S. *Exceller* en route, making two near misses near her stern. H.M. corvette *Samphire* was ordered to stand by *Leedstown*. Again the commander of the *Samuel Chase*, wishing to use his Coast Guard training to assist a stricken vessel, made a salvage suggestion to Captain Edgar, and again was turned down. According to his plan, the *Chase* could tow the *Leedstown* to Algiers Roads and there come alongside and take her into the harbor.[33]

Leedstown, now helpless, at 1255 was attacked by two planes which scored three near misses, opening seams and increasing the damage previously inflicted. At 1310 she was struck amidships on the starboard side by two torpedoes from an unknown source and immediately listed to starboard. There now appeared no reasonable prospect of saving the vessel nor was there any chance of landing more cargo; and, with over 500 men on board, heavy loss of life was likely if abandonment were postponed till after dark. The ship was therefore abandoned at 1320. After another bombing at 1615, she sank in twenty fathoms southwest of Matifou. According to one of the *Leedstown's* medical officers, "Some of the boys who jumped overboard were washed back into the ship by the suction of water running into the two torpedo holes, and had to jump over again." [34] A beach party from *Samuel Chase*, aided by French and Arabs, saved many lives by assisting *Leedstown* survivors ashore, for the undertow on the beach was strong and almost all the lifeboats and rafts capsized in the surf as they came in.

Upon their arrival in Algiers Bay on the morning of 9 November, the cargo steamers *Macharda* and *Maron* were ordered into the harbor and the rest of the group, except *Samuel Chase* and *Dempo*, followed in that afternoon. While waiting their turn, the two last ships anchored about two miles southwest of Cape Matifou. There they were subjected to another air attack. Two

[33] *Samuel Chase* War Diary 8 Nov. 1942.
[34] Account of Lt. (jg) Asher Hollander in Baltimore *Sun* 17 Dec. 1942. Crew members killed numbered 2; 6 were missing, several wounded.

near misses caused slight damage to *Dempo*. Commander Heimer quickly got *Samuel Chase* under way, and his excellent handling caused her to escape damage when attacked simultaneously by two torpedo planes. *Almaack* and *Exceller* entered Algiers Harbor in the late afternoon of 9 November; *Chase* and *Dempo* steamed in next morning. Unloading by lighters had begun even while the ships lay in the roadstead.

The rest of Captain Edgar's transport division,[35] *Samuel Chase* with *Leedstown* survivors on board, *Almaack* and *Dempo*, departed Algiers at 1800 November 12. At Gibraltar they and three or four British transports were formed into a convoy under command of Captain Edgar, with H.M. escort carriers *Argus* and *Avenger* and five destroyers as escort. At 0314 November 15, at lat. 36°20′ N, long. 7°32′ W, this convoy was so unfortunate as to run into a concentration of U-boats. In rapid succession *Almaack*, *Ettrick* and *Avenger* were torpedoed. *Avenger*, one of the first escort carriers built in the United States for the Royal Navy, blew up with a tremendous flash and roar, and went down with almost all hands.[36] *Almaack* was towed to Gibraltar and salvaged, but *Ettrick* sank at the end of a towline. *Samuel Chase's* luck held out, and, with Captain Edgar still embarked, safely reached Greenock on 21 November, returning later to Algiers with reinforcements. The crippled *Thomas Stone* remained in Algiers Harbor, subsequently dragged aground in a heavy swell, and defied all efforts to haul her off. She was finally decommissioned in 1944 and sold as junk to the French.

5. *Politics Again*[37]

The first United States Naval unit to enter Algiers Harbor was Lieutenant Marler's detachment of landing craft crews from

---

[35] Except S.S. *Exceller*, not ready to sail, and *Thomas Stone*, disabled.

[36] Report of torpedoing of *Almaack* 18 Nov. 1942. The submarine appears to have been *U-380*.

[37] Authorities in 2nd footnote to Chapter I, esp. Demaree Bess in *Sat. Eve. Post* 10 July 1943, 87ff.

Thomas Stone. H.M.S. *Spey* set these men ashore on the principal quay early in the morning of 9 November. After a vain effort to make contact with Captain Edgar in *Samuel Chase*, Lieutenant Marler established a post on the end of the pier, divided his company into three watches, posted sentries, mounted machine guns for protection against aircraft strafing, and hoisted a flag on a tower at the pierhead. The Stars and Stripes had an effect more embarrassing than glorious; for, as Lieutenant Marler relates, "The local police assumed that the United States Navy had taken over the port, and came to me with requests of every nature. They wanted permission to join the American armed forces and be given arms to fight." [38] This was not the last contact of our young "jg" with the cockeyed political situation in Algiers, the thread of which we must pick up once again.

During D-day and the following, General Eisenhower remained at his temporary command post in Gibraltar, where he could keep a finger on Algiers, Oran and Casablanca, and readily communicate with Washington and London. On the ninth he decided to send Generals Giraud and Mark Clark to Algiers, the one to take over the command of French troops and civil affairs which he had been promised, and the other to implement and continue the negotiations with Admiral Darlan. General Clark arrived in the late afternoon, just as the Luftwaffe was finishing off the *Leedstown*, and proceeded at once to French naval headquarters. There he discovered that Darlan's cease-fire of 8 November had not been delivered, or at least obeyed, outside the Algiers sector. He also discovered that General Giraud was regarded as a rank outsider by the French higher command in Algeria, and as a personal enemy by Admiral Darlan. A pretty situation!

On the morning of 10 November General Clark arranged a conference with Admiral Darlan, General Giraud, Mr. Robert Murphy, and Commodore Roy Dick RN (Admiral Cunningham's chief of staff) at French naval headquarters. General Clark, apparently fearing lest Darlan walk out on him, used Lieutenant Marler's

[38] Lt. Marler's Report, enclosure to *Thomas Stone* War Diary.

naval detachment to surround the building. As the Lieutenant tells it: —

About 1000 Lieutenant Colonel Richard Clare Partridge of the U.S. Army told me that General Clark and the American authorities had Admiral Darlan at a hotel approximately two miles from my base. They intended to put pressure on him to have all North Africa cease resistance and allow the Allied forces to enter, and there were no armed guards available to make enough show of force to hold the French Admiral and his staff if he decided to walk out. I sent 50 men with 10 machine guns, side arms, sub-machine gun, and hand grenades to the hotel under the charge of Ensign Wheeler and Ensign Culbert. We were relieved of this duty at 1300 and the men returned to the base. Ensign Culbert, through his knowledge of French, learned that the American General made satisfactory agreements with Admiral Darlan.[39]

Ensign Culbert had the word correctly. At first Darlan hedged on sending the necessary orders to stop French resistance. Clark threatened to displace him by Giraud. Darlan reminded him that Giraud had no legal or personal authority in North Africa. Clark then declared that Darlan must either issue immediate orders to French troops to cease resistance throughout Africa, or be taken into protective custody. After a brief conference with his staff, Darlan sent his cease-fire order at 1120 November 10. It required all night to pass the word to Oran and Morocco; but, as we have seen, Admirals Hewitt and Michelier and Generals Patton and Noguès received it just in time to stop an all-out assault on Casablanca next morning.

General Giraud, who had made an heroic escape from prison in Germany and resisted all overtures of Vichy, now found himself almost a pariah in Algiers. His own countrymen — except his friend General Mast — avoided him; General Clark was forced by circumstances to set him aside. Perhaps that is why Lieutenant Marler had the honor that evening of receiving a call from General Giraud, "who expressed his pleasure at seeing American Navy

---

[39] Marler's Report, enclosure to *Thomas Stone* War Diary. Marler apparently mistook French naval headquarters for a hotel.

forces in Algiers." The detachment's unusual position representing the United States Navy ended on the morning of 11 November when Lieutenant Marler returned his command on board *Thomas Stone*.

If Generals Eisenhower and Clark now thought they had Darlan in the bag, they were deceived. Not long after he had issued the general order to cease firing, Darlan received a radiogram from Pétain vigorously denouncing his action, and indicating in no uncertain terms that his orders were to fight the Americans. The Germans had intercepted Darlan's cease-fire order and passed it to Laval, who confronted Pétain with it and frightened the old Marshal into sending this message. Admiral Esteva at Tunis received a similar word and complied, since no Allied force was there to pull him the other way. Darlan, too, tried to wriggle out of the bag, informing General Clark he must now revoke the nonresistance order. "Damned if you will," replied General Clark. "Then I must be taken prisoner," said the Admiral. He was, in a sense, for General Clark used United States infantry to surround the Fenard villa where Darlan and his sick son were staying.

Later that afternoon General Clark turned his diplomatic talents to bringing Generals Giraud and Juin together, with other French generals subordinate to Juin. While they were conversing, news came that the Germans were marching into unoccupied France. Giraud's comment was significant. "What an appalling situation! It is time for all Frenchmen to get together." It was indeed. Although they never got together while the war was on, Hitler's march into southern France helped to prevent a civil war in North Africa. General Giraud further displayed his magnanimity by agreeing to renounce the command promised to him, at least for the time being.

General Clark, much as he distrusted Darlan, could not afford to eliminate him from the picture. In the first place, Darlan was the only French official in North Africa likely to get his orders obeyed, even in part. Secondly, Darlan was the only man through whom Admiral Esteva in Tunis, Admiral Godefroy in Alexandria,

Admiral de Laborde in command of the powerful French fleet at Toulon, and Admiral Collinet at Dakar could possibly be induced to join hands with the liberators of France. Americans in general find it difficult to comprehend why we should have had to use diplomacy to persuade French admirals to help the liberators of their country. Military men, however, understood the cruel dilemma that these officers were in. To the French Navy, Marshal Pétain was the government of France, and Admiral Darlan its official representative in North Africa. They might deplore the situation France was in, but they must obey orders; their tradition and professional ethics demanded it.

During the afternoon of 11 November Darlan agreed to order the French fleet at Toulon to get up steam and proceed to Africa, and to order Admiral Esteva to resist the Germans. General Clark then agreed (with General Giraud's consent) to leave Darlan in control of French political affairs in North Africa, while Giraud took command of the French armed forces. During the night, however, Darlan's subordinates revoked or held up these orders, alleging that since Marshal Pétain had replaced Darlan by General Noguès, the Admiral had no right to issue them. Learning this early in the morning of 12 November, General Clark declared that if Darlan's orders were not reissued at once, he would arrest all French leaders in North Africa except Giraud, and establish an Anglo-American military government over French North Africa. He gave them twenty-four hours to make up their minds. In the meantime, General Eisenhower, Admiral Cunningham and General Noguès arrived in Algiers. On the morning of the thirteenth Noguès agreed to ignore his mandate from Pétain and act as Governor of Morocco under Darlan, who in turn agreed to do his best at this late date to save Tunis and the Toulon fleet, and to work in concert with Giraud; he to be the head of the civil government in North Africa and Giraud to be commander in chief of the French armed forces. General Eisenhower accepted this arrangement. Mr. Churchill and President Roosevelt agreed to it on the fifteenth, and a formal accord to that effect was signed by

In front row, left to right, are General Noguès, French Resident General in Morocco; Brigadier General Hobart Gay, Chief of Staff to General Patton; and General La Houlle, commander of French aviation in Morocco. General Lascroux, commander of French troops in Morocco, carries a brief case

U.S. Signal Corps Photo

Left to right, Admiral Darlan, Admiral Sir Andrew Cunningham RN, General Eisenhower, Captain Butcher, and General Giraud with back turned

Meetings of Allied Leaders, December 1942

On "Yorker" Beach, Les Andalouses

On "Zebra" Beach White, St. Leu

Oran Landings, 8–9 November

Admiral Darlan and General Clark at Algiers on 22 November.

This arrangement was announced to the people of North Africa by a series of proclamations on 15 November. Darlan opened with the statement that Marshal Pétain, owing to the German occupation of Vichy and all continental France, was no longer in a position *"de faire connaître sa pensée intime aux Français,"* to make known his real wishes to the French. Before being deprived of his liberty the Marshal had renewed the assurance of his complete confidence in the Admiral, who now announced that every officer and civil official who had taken the oath of allegiance to Pétain should consider that they were faithful to the Marshal in obeying the Admiral's orders.

This statement was correct. On learning of the landings, Marshal Pétain sent Darlan a message to the effect that he was pleased that the Admiral was on the spot, that he approved of his action, and that he had complete confidence in him. On 10 November, as we have seen, under Axis pressure and threats, Pétain was forced to disavow Darlan's arrangement with a stern, "I have given the order to defend us against aggressors. I maintain that order." At the same time the Marshal directed that it be made known secretly to Darlan that he approved his action; that the above dispatch was necessary because of negotiations then in progress with the German occupation forces. Darlan, appreciating the importance of this secret message, replied immediately in the same cypher: *"Reçu, et bien compris."* And, on 12 November, upon receipt at Vichy of telegrams reporting Darlan's agreement with the Americans, and requesting approval, the Marshal sent the Admiral a second clandestine message. It assured Darlan that Pétain was in *accord intime* with President Roosevelt, although the presence of Germans prevented him from openly admitting it.[40] But for these secret messages from the Marshal, which for him had the force of commands, Darlan would never have ordered the cease-fire, or coöperated with the invaders of North Africa.

[40] Admiral Auphan *Les grimaces de l'histoire* (1951) pp. 280–90. Auphan, then Ministère de la Marine at Vichy, had these messages encrypted in a special code held only by Darlan and his naval staff. He cites date-time groups and texts.

On 15 November, Admiral Darlan made a public proclamation that he had appointed Giraud his military chief. Giraud at the same time issued a moving proclamation that Germany was the one enemy of France; that "united in the love of France and of the Marshal we have only one passion — Victory." General Clark in the name of General Eisenhower reassured the French people that his troops were there for the one and only purpose of sweeping the Axis from the soil of Africa, and restoring the unity and independence of the French Empire.

6. *Bougie and Bône Secured*[41]

Although the original plan for initial landings in Tunisia had been abandoned, to Admiral Cunningham's lasting regret, one mission of the Eastern Task Force was to seize beachheads in eastern Algeria and western Tunisia at the earliest possible date.[42] These operations were conducted entirely by British troops and the Royal Navy, but they must be mentioned briefly as part of the means by which 600-odd miles of western Mediterranean littoral were occupied by the United Nations.

Algiers ceased firing at 1900 on 8 November, and the next day all allied shipping entered the harbor and the Bougie force was embarked. H.M.S. *Roberts*, *Sheffield*, and *Tynwald*, with "Senior Naval Officer Bougie" in *Karanja*, escorted about 28 vessels, including all available British LCTs.

The landing at Bougie at dawn 11 November was unopposed, but the plan for a simultaneous landing at Djidjelli, thirty miles to the eastward across the Gulf of Bougie, had to be abandoned owing to heavy surf. Paratroopers were dropped there instead, to capture the airfield. This delay deprived the force of most of its fighter plane protection, and it sustained a heavy bombing attack at dusk 11 November. Several ships were damaged and

41 Principal source of this subsection is Cincmed's "Narrative of Events 8–17 Nov.," enclosed in Admiral Hewitt's of 13 Mar. 1943.
42 Naval Orders for Operation Torch Eastern Task Force 5 Oct. 1942, in Comnaveu's 25 Nov. 1942.

H.M.S. *Tynwald* was sunk. *Strathnaver* brought up more troops on 12 November, but heavy and damaging Axis air attacks continued until the thirteenth, when sufficient gasoline was got into Djidjelli for Spitfires to use the field and break up further air raids.

The port of Bône was likewise occupied without opposition by a force composed of the 6th Commando and two companies of British infantry. This force was put ashore by H.M. destroyers *Lamerton* and *Wheatland* at 0300 November 12. As at Bougie, Axis aircraft were not idle.

With these ports successfully occupied, escorted coastal convoys were established and additional troops and materiel began to arrive from Algiers preparatory to the entry into Tunisia from the west. On 15 November the 78th Division British Army, sent from Algiers in *Queen Emma* and *Princess Beatrix*, landed at Bône. Two days later United States troops relieved the British in the Bougie area. Pressing farther eastward, a British First Army infantry battalion entered Tabarka by proceeding overland from Bône.

The drive for Tunisia was under way.

CHAPTER X

The Capture of Oran[1]

8–11 November 1942

1. Plans and Forces

WHILE this curious story of military action, diplomacy, and political intrigue was unrolling at Algiers, another operation was revolving about Oran, some two hundred miles to the westward, almost completely independent of events at the capital.

The principal mission of the Center Task Force was to capture seaports in western Algeria, of which Oran, second city of the Barbary Coast, was the most important. Oran Harbor, modern and well equipped, lay behind the protecting wall of a stone jetty extending parallel to the shore for the distance of about a mile and a half, with a narrow entrance facing northeasterly. Mers-el-Kebir, scene of the British bombardment of French warships on 3 July 1940, is three miles west of Oran, facing northeastward on the bay. At the foot of this small Arab town the French had constructed a military harbor. Situated only two hundred and thirty miles east of the Straits, and at a point where the Mediterranean was still fairly narrow,[2] these two harbors had to be secured. And with them it was logical to take Arzeu, a small snug harbor on the other side of Cape Ferrat, twenty-five miles to the eastward of Oran.

The Oran-Arzeu attack was entrusted to the Center Naval Task

---

[1] Commander N.O.B. Oran Area (Admiral Bennett) Report on Operations U.S. Naval Forces Center TF Operation Torch, 30 Nov. 1942.

[2] The distance from Cape de Gata, Spain, to Cape Falcon near Oran is 85 miles.

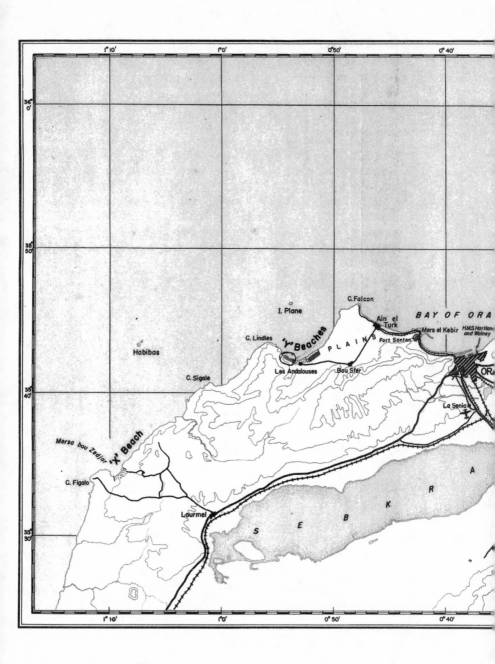

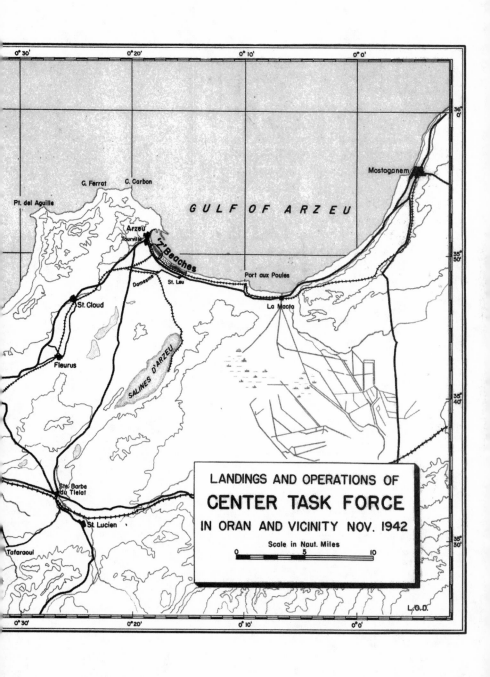

0° 30' 0° 20' 0° 10' 0° 0'

36° 0'

Mostaganem

G. Ferrat C. Carbon

Pt. del Aguille

GULF OF ARZEU

Arzeu
Tourville

"Z" Beaches

35° 50'

Damesme St. Leu

Port aux Poules

St. Cloud

La Macta

Fleurus

SALINES D'ARZEU

35° 40'

Ste. Barbe
du Tlelat

LANDINGS AND OPERATIONS OF

St. Lucien

CENTER TASK FORCE

Tafaraoui

IN ORAN AND VICINITY NOV. 1942

Scale in Naut. Miles

0   5   10

35° 30'

L.G.D.

0° 30' 0° 20' 0° 10' 0° 0'

Force commanded by Commodore Thomas Troubridge RN, with the Center Task Force commanded by Major General Lloyd R. Fredendall USA embarked. Troubridge's task force comprised an imposing array of British warships including the battleship *Rodney*, aircraft carrier *Furious*, escort carriers *Biter* and *Dasher*, headquarters ship *Largs*, anti-aircraft ship *Delhi*, thirteen destroyers, eight minesweepers, six corvettes, two former United States Coast Guard cutters, and numerous armed trawlers and motor transport ships. General Fredendall's attack force included three regimental combat teams of the 1st Infantry Division commanded by Major General Terry Allen,[3] half of the 1st Armored Division, a company of the 1st Ranger Battalion and various units whose numerical strength for the assault approximated 39,000 officers and men. These men had been training in Northern Ireland and Scotland since their arrival in the United Kingdom on 7 August. They took part in the practice landings in Scotland on 18–19 October. The United States Army was selected to land in this sector because it was thought that the French stationed near Oran, where their Fleet had been attacked by the Royal Navy, would be antipathetic to British forces.

According to the plan[4] two of General Allen's combat teams were to be landed in the Gulf of Arzeu ("Zebra" beaches) and the other, commanded by Brigadier General Theodore Roosevelt Jr. USA, in the Andalouses area ("Yorker" beaches), whence they were to converge on the city of Oran, capturing it by a double envelopment. After securing the beachheads two mobile columns from the 1st Armored Division, commanded by Brigadier General L. E. Oliver, were to be landed. One of these columns was to follow the 1st Infantry Division ashore near Arzeu and the other make an independent landing at Mersa Bou Zedjar ("X" beach), about fifteen miles west of Les Andalouses. The first task of these

[3] 1st Infantry Division G–1 Report, Enclosure 1.
[4] Commanding General II U.S. Army Corps Outline Plan Oran Task Force, 11 Sept. 1942.

mobile columns was to strike inland, capture the airfields at Tafaraoui and La Senia southeast of Oran, and the town and air-drome of Lourmel back of "X" beach. About five hundred para-troopers of the 2nd Battalion 509th United States Paratroop Infan-try were to be flown in from the United Kingdom by the 60th Transport group and dropped in the vicinity of the airfields to assist in their capture. As soon as practicable units of the XII Air Force, General J. H. Doolittle, were to be staged in to use the fields.

A Naval Advanced Base Unit designed to operate and patrol the ports of Oran, Arzeu and Mers-el-Kebir was created out of the Advance Group Amphibious Force United States Atlantic Fleet, stationed at Rosneath, Scotland. It comprised 94 officers (82 Navy, 9 Army, 3 Marine Corps) and 779 enlisted men (520 Navy, 209 Army, 50 Marine Corps). Special functions were assigned to designated sections of this unit and practised at Rosneath. Salvage and repair materiel was collected in the United Kingdom. An ex-perienced salvage officer and ten qualified divers were obtained from the United States, anticipating that the French would scuttle their ships and sabotage port facilities. The Army members of this Naval Advanced Base Unit were engineers especially trained in repair and upkeep of landing craft and also qualified to repair and operate floating cranes or other harbor equipment. A special anti-sabotage unit, trained to save ships that the French would probably try to destroy, was embarked in H.M.S. *Hartland* and *Walney*, whose mission was similar to that of *Broke* and *Malcolm* at Algiers.

A part of the Advanced Base Unit sailed from the Clyde with the assault convoy on 26 October, leaving the rest for the first follow-up convoy which departed 1 November. We shall describe the unfortunate adventures of the *Hartland* and *Walney* in their frontal attack on Oran before taking up the main landings on beaches on either side of the city.

2. HARTLAND *and* WALNEY

The former "Lake" Class United States Coast Guard cutters *Pontchartrain* and *Sebago*, rechristened *Hartland* and *Walney* when commissioned in the Royal Navy,[5] and two British motor launches, *ML–480* and *ML–483*, were designated to carry an anti-sabotage unit into Oran. The Royal Navy, in view of what it did to the French ships at Mers-el-Kebir in 1940, entertained no illusions about its popularity with the French in that region. The higher command granted *Hartland* and *Walney* permission "to wear the largest size American Ensigns they could carry," in addition to their own White Ensigns.[6]

The objects of this particular mission were (1) To capture the batteries at Saint-Grégoire and the battery on the heights above Môle Ravin Blanc at the east end of Oran Harbor; (2) to capture and hold the wharves; and (3) to board the merchant ships in Oran Harbor in order to prevent sabotage.

Captain F. T. Peters RN commanded this enterprise in *Walney*, but the British officers and men under him, other than ships' crews, numbered only 52. The Americans who participated embarked at Gibraltar. Lieutenant Commander G. D. Dickey commanded the small Naval contingent (5 officers, 22 bluejackets, 6 Marines) on board *Hartland*. Lieutenant Colonel George C. Marshall USA in *Walney* commanded a battalion of two specially organized companies of the United States 1st Armored Division, about 400 officers and men, distributed among both ships. *Hartland* was responsible for objective Number 3, the prevention of sabotage to ships in the harbor.

Although the inclusion of an anti-sabotage unit in the Oran operation was heartily approved by the United States Naval Command in Europe, the British plan for executing the project met with sharp dissent from Rear Admiral A. C. Bennett, Commander

[5] Two of ten 250-foot cutters transferred to Britain in May and June of 1941.
[6] British Operation Plan Center Task Force 14 Oct. 1942.

Advance Group Amphibious Force Atlantic Fleet. Admiral Stark supported his objections, which were based on the timing and scope of the operation. The plan was to enter the harbor at H plus 2 hour (0300 November 8). Admiral Bennett, in a letter to Lieutenant General Eisenhower of 17 October, gave his considered opinion as follows: —

An entry into the port by these cutters, with additional objective of seizing batteries fully manned, prior to the capitulation of the town by the military authorities, or at least before our Army is about to enter the town, is suicidal, and will probably result in defeating the purpose of the party. . . . If determined resistance is met from the French Navy, which seems to be the general opinion, it is believed that this small force will be wiped out before the Army can enter the city, if they go in at H plus two. If there is no resistance, the problem is a simple one, and much less number of personnel would suffice. If resistance is determined, then I am convinced that five times the number of troops would be insufficient.[7]

The Admiral noted that the operation order stated, "It is highly improbable that the order to immobilize the port will be given by the French Commander until it is clear that the port cannot be held," and declared his judgment to be that "this time, as closely as it can be determined, is the proper time for these ex-Coast Guard cutters to enter the port."

That hour, he believed, would strike considerably later than H plus 2; and its determination, on which the success or failure of the mission would depend, should be made on the spot rather than in an operation plan. Admiral Bennett also protested orally and in writing to Admiral Sir Andrew Cunningham. Unfortunately, all his protests were in vain.

Admiral Cunningham later admitted: "The moment chosen could hardly have been less fortunate, since the French alarm to arms was in its first full flush of Gallic fervour and they had not yet been intimidated by bombing or bombardment."[8]

At 0100 November 8, both cutters and both motor launches

[7] Bennett Report on Center TF, Enclosure B.
[8] Cincmed Report Operation Torch 30 Mar. 1943.

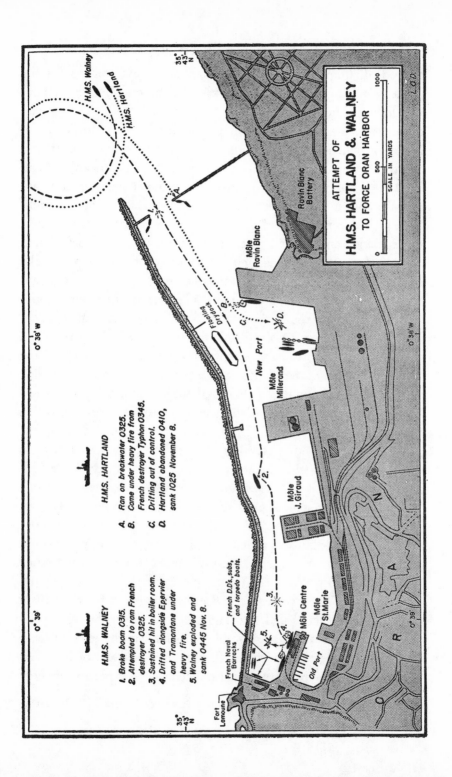

ATTEMPT OF
H.M.S. HARTLAND & WALNEY
TO FORCE ORAN HARBOR

SCALE IN YARDS

0   500   1000

L.O.D.

H.M.S. WALNEY

1. Broke boom 0315.
2. Attempted to ram French destroyer 0325.
3. Sustained hit in boiler room.
4. Drifted alongside Epervier and Tramontane under heavy fire.
5. Walney exploded and sank 0445 Nov. 8.

H.M.S. HARTLAND

A. Ran on breakwater 0325.
B. Came under heavy fire from French destroyer Typhon 0345.
C. Drifting out of control.
D. Hartland abandoned 0410, sank 1025 November 8.

Ravin Blanc Battery

Môle Ravin Blanc

Floating Drydock

New Port

Môle Millerand

Môle J. Giraud

Môle Centre

Môle St.Marie

Old Port

French Naval Barracks

French D.D.'s, subs, and torpedo boats.

Fort Lamoune

35° 43' N

0° 39'

0° 38' W

35° 43' N

0° 39'

0° 38' W

arrived off Oran.[9] For two hours they stood by, waiting for the predetermined hour. The town was blacked out, but lighthouses and lighted buoys continued to function. All hands except gun crews were stationed below in proper locations for orderly debarkation when the ships reached the dock. The approach began shortly before 0300, just as air-raid sirens were heard ashore. H.M.S. *Walney*, leading, missed the entrance on her first approach, and as she maneuvered for another try, a shore searchlight picked her up. The Ravin Blanc battery on the *môle* nearest the entrance and several machine guns immediately opened fire. Both cutters and motor launches commenced putting up a smoke screen, but the offshore wind blew it away. On the second approach, searchlights picked up the ships when they were about half a mile from the harbor boom, and they were immediately brought under heavy point-blank fire from 4.7-inch, 3-inch, and machine guns ashore. In the confusion *ML–483* crashed into the *Walney*, but the cutter gained on the turn for the second approach and broke the outer harbor boom about six hundred yards ahead of the *Hartland*. A moment later she broke the inner boom, which consisted of a row of coal barges, and boldly steamed right up the 300-yard-wide harbor past Môle Ravin Blanc, drawing fire from two submarines docked between it and the next quay, Môle Millerand. Having passed this *môle*, she was about to turn and ram a French destroyer standing out of the harbor when her bridge was shot away. The destroyer raked her decks in passing but she continued and had almost reached her objective, the Môle Centre at the head of the harbor, when she came under fire from the French torpedo boat *Tramontane* and destroyer *Épervier*, who were alongside the *môle*. Their point-blank fire was too much for the gallant cutter. Bodies were piled two and three feet deep on her decks. A few survivors managed to scramble ashore on the jetty in Basin Aucour, and the remainder swam; but three quarters of her crew and embarked troops were casualties. Rent by an explosion at about

[9] Naval Commander Center Task Force (Commo. Troubridge) Report of 13 Nov. 1942.

0445, *Walney* capsized and sank only a few yards from the head of the harbor.

H.M.S. *Hartland* fared no better. Baffled by the darkness, she ran her bow onto the sloping breakwater when attempting to enter, and searchlights caught her when backing off. Heavy shell and machine-gun fire from shore wiped out all gun crews after they had returned only three shots. Yet *Hartland* pluckily continued toward her objective, the inside berth of Môle Ravin Blanc. At about 0345, when preparing to round the end of this quay, she came under the fire of two 4.7-inch guns on the French destroyer *Typhon*, moored to the *môle* only one hundred feet from her. It was like shooting ducks on the water with buckshot. The submarines that had fired on *Walney* also joined in. *Hartland* caught fire in several places and lost all control and power. She drifted several hundred yards, absorbing merciless shelling from the *Typhon* until the destroyer had to check because her fire was endangering other French ships beyond. Flames raging below in the *Hartland* drove all hands topside, where they were mowed down by machine-gun fire from the destroyer, the two submarines, and guns ashore. Her superstructure burned fiercely, illuminating the surrounding water. All attempts to fight the fires proved futile and the ship was completely abandoned by 0410.[10]

Half the men on board *Hartland* were killed. About 200 officers and men of the United States Army, 2 Marines and 3 bluejackets lost their lives. Survivors were held as prisoners by the French until released by the arrival of American troops on the afternoon of 10 November. Medical aid, food, and cigarettes were furnished to them, and in other respects they received friendly and courteous treatment from the French.

Lieutenant Commander Dickey had the highest praise for the coolness and courage of the Marines and bluejackets under his command, every one a Casabianca. They had action stations in the

---

[10] Survivor's story by Lt. V. A. Hickson, *N.Y. Times* 10 Dec. 1942. An explosion occurred on board *Hartland* at 0525 but she did not sink until after another great explosion at about 1015.

captain's cabin in the afterpart of the ship. Fire and smoke from enemy hits made conditions almost unbearable, yet not one attempted to leave his station. "Upon abandoning ship officers and men again showed the highest kind of leadership and spirit in helping to save the lives of many United States soldiers who were unfamiliar with the ship and the use of the life jackets." And at the wharf, although physically exhausted, they continued to save lives by pulling men out of the water.[11]

It is difficult to see how this operation could possibly have succeeded unless, as Admiral Bennett observed, the French had elected not to fight; and in that event it would have been unnecessary. The *Hartland* and *Walney* had two strikes against them before they even started. The British, who had been successful in pulling off commando raids, inspired by the famous attack on Zeebrugge in 1918,[12] attempted the same tactics here, overlooking the basically different conditions in this operation. A commando raid is a hit-and-run affair — raise as much hell as possible and get the hell out; but at Oran the attack forces were supposed to hit and stay. For commando tactics, surprise is absolutely essential; here surprise was sacrificed by setting the attack two hours after the main landings near by had alerted the French. And there was too much fire power ashore and afloat in the harbor for a hit-and-run raid to succeed, without naval fire support on our side.[13]

Flushed with their success in disposing of the two cutters, four French warships sortied from Oran after bigger game. They were promptly taken under fire by the Royal Navy covering force, which sank destroyer *Tramontane* and minesweeper *La Surprise*, and drove the others back to port, where destroyer *Tornade* was beached.

[11] Admiral Bennett Report, Enclosure C.

[12] Similarity to Zeebrugge was denied by Admiral Cunningham, who stated that the "Direct assaults . . . were in no sense planned as imitations of Zeebrugge. . . ." Cincmed Report 30 Mar. 1943.

[13] It might also be argued, if the Safi affair (see above) succeeded, what was the matter with this? But the Safi objective was far easier; tactical surprise was obtained; no French warships were present; and our two destroyers had plenty of fire support from other ships, which the *Hartland* and *Walney* lacked.

3. *The Landings*

a. Arzeu

As at Algiers, there were three independent landings in addition to the frontal attack on Oran Harbor. But in the Oran region there was disparity in the size of the forces involved in each landing, although virtually all troops were American. Arzeu, upon the capture of which the "success of the whole project" hung,[14] was allotted the major strength.

The Arzeu mission was to be launched by an attack on the town and surrounding batteries by four companies of the 1st Ranger Battalion. As soon as the Rangers had the situation ashore in hand, the port was to be taken over by members of the United States Navy Advanced Base Unit. Somewhat later the main body of troops and equipment was to be debarked on the three Zebra beaches stretching about four miles southeastward on the Gulf of Arzeu from Tourville to St. Leu. These forces consisted of the 16th and 18th Regimental Combat Teams 1st Infantry Division, and once the beachheads had been secured they were to cover the landing of Combat Command B, whose flying column was immediately to strike southwest for the airfields.

At the appointed hour (2300 November 7), the assault transports stood into the Gulf of Arzeu and launched their landing craft. The four United States Ranger companies from the transport *Royal Scotsman*, together with a few British troops, landed shortly after midnight on D-day, 8 November, and established positions on the north side of the town without opposition. Meanwhile, the United States Naval Advance Party under Captain Walter C. Ansel, together with a British Advance Party under Commander H. Archdale RN, and a dozen United States Marines under Lieutenant Colonel I. C. Plain USMC, were embarked in an assault

[14] U.S. Center Naval Task Force Operation Plan, Annex H. See above, p. 191*n*.

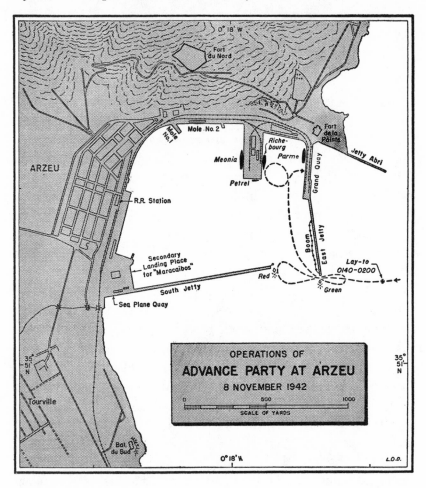

OPERATIONS OF
ADVANCE PARTY AT ARZEU
8 NOVEMBER 1942

SCALE OF YARDS

landing boat belonging to H.M.S. *Royal Ulsterman*.[15] Wearied of waiting for the appointed signal from the Rangers denoting that their landing had been successful, and observing that all was quiet in the harbor, the advance parties started in at 0200. They were delayed in identifying their position by confusing the lights on the jetties. The French had very slight inkling of the imminence

---

[15] *Royal Ulsterman* was a 340-foot Landing Ship Infantry (LSI) converted from a cross-channel passenger steamer and equipped to transport British-type Landing Craft Assault (LCA).

of the assault, for these navigational aids were functioning and the boom net had not been drawn across the harbor mouth. Proceeding to the inner harbor, this combined advance party seized three small steamers and a patrol boat lying in the port.[16] The French crews offered no resistance in the darkness. After daybreak machine guns, snipers, and one small fieldpiece opened up from the town but were speedily silenced by troops already ashore. By 0745 the Rangers had consolidated the area around Fort de la Pointe. All defenders had been taken prisoner by 0830.

The main landings on the Zebra beaches had in the meantime progressed satisfactorily despite bombardment from the coast batteries on Arzeu heights. Landing craft targets were well concealed by the Royal Navy's judicious use of smoke. The 18th Regimental Combat Team's initial assault wave, embarked in H.M.S. *Ettrick*, S.S. *Tegelberg* (Netherlands) and S.S. *Reina del Pacifico* (British), landed 1120 strong on Zebra Beach Green between 0120 and 0130. By H plus 2 hour (0300) 36 combat vehicles had been put ashore on two Zebra beaches. An hour later the division command post moved into a local kindergarten. Mopping-up operations in Arzeu were completed at 0840 and the situation was well in hand on the beaches, despite the fact that wind and sea were making unloading increasingly hazardous. But the 18th RCT met strong resistance on advancing northwest of Arzeu.

Shortly after H-hour the 16th Regimental Combat Team landed unopposed on Zebra Beach White in the vicinity of St. Leu. The 1st Battalion Landing Team of the 16th Infantry quickly took Damesme, St. Leu, and Port aux Poules — thus extending the eastern perimeter of the Arzeu beachhead. Apparently the defenders were taken completely by surprise. Initial opposition was slight and disorganized. The 1st Battalion Landing Team encountered resistance at La Macta which they overcome only with the aid of naval gunfire; they pushed on towards Mostaganem on the 9th.[17]

---

16 French S.S. *Richebourg* and *Parme*, Danish S.S. *Meonia*, and French patrol boat *Pétrel*. Bennett Report, Enclosure E.

17 Combat Team 16 Report in 1st Infantry Div. Report, Enclosure 5.

The flying column of Combat Command B also landed with slight opposition, on Zebra Beach Red at 0057, and soon set up its command post at St. Leu. Just before dawn the tank-laden "Maracaibos," H.M.S. *Misoa* and *Tasajera*, came up to the beaches. They were unloaded by 0759. These outwardly unprepossessing ships were prototypes of the now well-known LSTs. Shoal draft oilers, designed for navigating Lake Maracaibo, Venezuela, they possessed two features that made for easy conversion to tank carriers: like most oilers their machinery was located well aft and their mean draft was only 10 feet. The Maracaibos ranged between 365 and 385 feet in length, and were of about 60-foot beam. Their war cargo capacity was either twenty-two 25-ton tanks or forty 5-ton vehicles. In converting them to LSTs, the Maracaibos' bows had been slightly elongated and squared off, to house a bow landing ramp which was closed under way by a pair of massive doors. These were opened when the vessel drove head-on ashore, and from them a 60-foot bridge section could be pushed out to span the gap between ship and shoal water.

Their performance with the Center Task Force was cited as "highly satisfactory," [18] and the Eastern Task Force wished that it had been so equipped. Trimmed down by the stern, the Maracaibos drew only seven feet forward as they came up on the beaches, and the bridge sections were projected out of the bow doors and reached into shallow enough water for the tanks to run ashore under their own power.

By the afternoon of 8 November, resistance near Arzeu had been overcome, but tough fighting near St. Cloud held up the advance and Fleurus was only taken on the night of 9–10 November. On D-day two ships of the assault convoy had been brought inside Arzeu harbor and were unloading on the quays instead of over the beaches, while landing craft used the seaplane ramp and the shore to the east of the harbor. This was fortunate, since Beach Green had to be closed sixteen hours after the initial

[18] War Dept "Lessons Learned" 12 Feb. 1943, Annex F, section 6.

landing on account of rising surf, and the weather rendered Beach White inoperative an hour later, at 1800 November 8.[19]

b. West of Oran

The landings west of Oran, although delayed in starting, went off as smoothly as those on the Arzeu beaches. As planned, the transports made contact with the beacon submarines, H.M.S. *P-54* and *Ursula*, who guided them in but unfortunately were two-and-a-quarter miles off position. There were the usual delays in getting the boats away, but by 0135 on 8 November, only half an hour behind schedule, the first landing was effected by the 26th Regimental Combat Team of the 1st Infantry Division on the Yorker beaches at Baie des Andalouses, twelve miles west of Oran. The ships proceeded toward shore to complete discharge of men and materiel, covered by aircraft from the British carriers. The 26th Regimental Combat Team, commanded by Colonel A. N. Stark Jr. USA, was composed of the 26th Infantry (146 officers and 3086 men), the 33rd Field Artillery Battalion (29 officers and 576 men), the 2nd Battalion of the 531st Engineers Regiment (25 officers and 620 men), batteries C and D of the 105th Coast Artillery Battalion (13 officers and 326 men).[20]

At 0425 the situation was reported favorable and these forces deployed for their several objectives, which combined to make the western prong of the pincers. The 3rd Battalion Landing Team struck east for Bou Sfer, which it captured at 0740, but was pinned down by artillery from the fort on the heights above Mers-el-Kebir. Meanwhile the 2nd BLT had pushed northeast to clear Cape Falcon and capture Ain el Turk — a tough 36-hour job.

During the morning the battery of Fort Santon opened fire on the landing beaches. H.M.S. *Rodney's* and several cruisers' gunfire silenced it that afternoon.

[19] Cominch *Notes on Amphibious Warfare No. 1;* 1st Inf. Div. G-4 Report, Enclosure 4, 17 Nov. 1942.
[20] 26th R.C.T. Report 21 Nov. 1942.

Farther west at Mersa Bou Zedjar landing operations were carried out by the western or "Green" flying column of Combat Command B. First assault units landed unopposed at 0143 and at 0230; a third Maracaibo, H.M.S. *Bachaquero*, headed in to Beach X. By 0346 both headlands flanking the beach were reported clear, and twenty minutes later the LST grounded and began to thrust out her pontoon landing bridge. She had completed discharge by 0830. The flying column was on its way, and against severe opposition occupied Lourmel by 1125.[21]

From both directions the other mobile columns pushed overland towards the airfields of La Senia and Tafaraoui south of Oran. Unfortunately the paratroops' mission had been a failure; by miscalculation some had been dropped near Lourmel and others were immobilized over a wide area in the neighborhood of La Senia. But the eastern or "Red" flying column of Combat Command B captured Tafaraoui, fifteen miles inland from Oran, at 1215.[22] By 1630, twenty-six of the XII United States Army Air Force Spitfires, staged in from Gibraltar, were making use of Tafaraoui airdrome. The Green column, proceeding directly from Lourmel, captured La Senia at 0900 November 9, with up to 2000 prisoners. Apparently all planes fit to fly escaped. During the rest of that day the various columns had plenty of fighting. Those advancing westward from Arzeu captured St. Cloud and Fleurus, and by the morning of 10 November the pincer movement was beginning to exert strong pressure against the well-fortified French positions in Oran itself.

Next day, 9 November, debarkation continued, in the face of increased surf on the Yorker beaches and resultant loss of landing craft. Although in the main the Oran operations went off more smoothly than at Algiers, the same lack of training in boat handling was apparent, and available craft were not used to best advantage owing to divided control.[23] There were not enough British Landing Craft Mechanized (LCMs) for discharging stores; and,

[21] Combat Command B Report, Green column.
[22] Combat Command B Report, Red column.
[23] 1st Inf. Div. G-4 Report, Enclosure 4, para. 6.

Oran Harbor, view from Fort Santa Cruz in July 1943

Oran Harbor, salvage operations, 13 November 1942

since they lacked the capacity of their American counterparts, those available were overloaded. The same confusion and lack of forethought in bringing supplies ashore were evident. Two entire United States medical detachments were hamstrung by failure to land their equipment with the personnel, who were scattered over a three-mile stretch of beach. The equipment did not show up until four days later.[24] Intelligence was partly to blame; one of the beaches of Les Andalouses, reported "excellent" in the appreciation, was discovered to be bar-bound two hundred yards offshore, where landing craft grounded.[25]

As the day of 9 November advanced, the French destroyers *Épervier* and *Typhon*, still full of fight, having been ordered to get under way and to seek another refuge, sortied from Oran Harbor but were effectively engaged by H.M.S. *Aurora* and *Jamaica*. *Épervier*, on fire, beached herself, but *Typhon* returned to scuttle herself right across the narrow harbor entrance. Meanwhile the ground forces, as we have seen, were advancing, assisted by air support from the Royal Navy and Air Force. With three of the four important airfields in our hands and aircraft being staged in from Gibraltar, the final assault was planned for 10 November. Oran surrendered that morning after two columns of Combat Command B had broken through to the center of the city. Formal resistance in this area ended with the surrender of French forces to General Fredendall at 1230.

No sooner had Oran been occupied by United States forces than our naval salvage men went to work on the port. As *Hartland* and *Walney* had failed to save shipping from being scuttled, the harbor was cluttered up with sunken ships, including the two cutters and three French submarines. Luckily, damage to shore installations was slight,[26] and the *avant port* or outer harbor of Oran was avail-

[24] Lt. Col. C. J. Mellies's 48th Surgical Hospital Report, in Compilation of Torch Reports 23 Dec. 1942 p. 30.

[25] 1st Inf. Div. G–2 Report, Enclosure 2.

[26] Some security detachments, which entered Oran simultaneously with leading combat units, prevented any major sabotage ashore. (Report of Lt. Col. Alfred D. Starbird USA, Observer Center Task Force, quoted in Cominch *Notes on Amphibious Warfare* No. 1 p. 6.)

able for immediate use. At Mers-el-Kebir there was no damage whatsoever, except that a stray 16-in. shell from H.M.S. *Rodney*, fired at the fort in that vicinity, sank a 400-ton floating crane which was ultimately salvaged by our naval party.

The Center Task Force encountered more severe opposition ashore than either the Eastern or the Western, and proved to be composed of excellent fighters. The 1st Infantry Division suffered casualties of 23 officers and 343 men, and captured 1364 prisoners. And the Royal Navy landing craft performed well under not very favorable conditions.

According to Major General Terry Allen usa, "The one single factor which contributed most to the success of this operation was the joint planning in London where the Army staffs and Navy staffs worked side by side through the whole planning stage." [27]

There were, to be sure, many incidents which showed a lack of understanding by one service of the needs and limitations of the other. But, as Admiral Cunningham stated, the operation was carried out with accepted inadequacies in training and equipment. All manner of ships from passenger liners down to Venezuelan tankers had to be pressed into service and refitted. Landing craft of adequate size and power had not yet come off the production lines. Improvements and refinements in amphibious warfare could and did come later. But in November 1942 the time was ripe and the United Nations did well to seize the occasion. The success of Operation "Torch" proved that the decision to undertake this great adventure, which at one time seemed almost a desperate adventure to the overall military commanders, was fundamentally sound and wise.

[27] Hq. 1st Inf. Div. 1st U.S. Army Report 25 Dec. 1942, enclosed in Compilation of Reports Section V p. 22.

CHAPTER XI

The Navy in the Tunisian Campaign

November 1942 – May 1943

About 1 December 1942 the Royal and United States Navies commenced using Zone "Able" time (Greenwich minus one hour) in Algerian and Tunisian waters.

1. *The Race for Tunisia, November–December 1942* [1]

WHEN Admiral Darlan came to terms with General Eisenhower shortly after our landings in North Africa, he promised to do his best to bring the entire French Navy and all French armed forces in North Africa into an active partnership with the United Nations. There is no doubt that Darlan did his best, or that he accomplished a great deal; but his efforts were most effective where the armed forces of the United States and Britain were present in considerable strength. Thus, his orders to cease fire were obeyed fairly promptly throughout Algeria and Morocco. Admiral Godefroy at Alexandria and Admiral Robert at Martinique paid no attention to him, but their ships had been neutralized for many months, and the logic of events finally forced them into line. The failure of the important French fleet at Toulon, including as it did the new battleship *Strasbourg* and other capital ships,

---

[1] This brief account of the opening phase of the Tunisian campaign is compiled largely from numbers of the O.N.I. *Weekly* from 11 Nov. 1942; U.S. Military Academy *The War in North Africa* Part 1 "Operations in Egypt and Libya" (1944); *North African Campaign* (State Department Information Series No. 94A for November) 12 Dec. 1942; Alexander G. Clifford *The Conquest of North Africa, 1940–1943* (1943).

to steam across the Mediterranean was a disappointment.

The difficulty here seems to have been the fact that Admiral de Laborde, fleet commander, waited in vain for such orders from Pétain and that the special emissary whom Darlan dispatched thither to try to arrange a sortie was picked up by the Germans and never got through. Having delayed until unoccupied France was occupied, it is questionable whether the capital ships could have got out in the face of overwhelming German air power. The harbor exits had been reported mined and the Axis would undoubtedly have been alerted by any attempt to sweep a channel. A courageous dash might have succeeded.[2] In the end, as the first Germans entered the city on 27 November, the frustrated Toulon fleet was sabotaged and scuttled, according to plan. Only a few short-handed ships failed to execute the signal. So the enemy was able to make use of only two of the *Provence's* turrets when the Allies entered Southern France in 1944. Five submarines elected to risk the mine field. Three joined the Allies; one was interned in Spain and one was scuttled.[3]

On 23 November, Dakar fell to the United Nations without a shot, and our right flank was secure. Governor Pierre Boisson satisfied himself that Darlan's order to cease resistance did indeed express the real will of Marshal Pétain, and decided to place his province under the Admiral's orders. Soon after, Vice Admiral William A. Glassford was sent to Dakar to implement this agreement.[4] Dakar was a second triumph for the Roosevelt-Eisen-

---

[2] Testimony of Rear Admiral Louis Blehaut in *N.Y. Times* 9 Dec. 1945. The British Covering Force steamed for several days off shore in order to support the French fleet if it came out.

[3] Information from Service Historique de la Marine, 28 Aug. 1952.

[4] Memo. from Lt. Col. Bradley J. Gaylord USA of Gen. Eisenhower's Staff, 25 Apr. 1943; information obtained by the writer from Admiral Glassford, who found the situation at Dakar very delicate. The French Navy had a powerful force there, whose officers were completely loyal to Pétain and refused to take orders from Governor Boisson, who was a far from willing adherent to the Darlan policy. By the time all North Africa was reconquered by the United Nations, the logic of events brought this French force into line. The battleship *Richelieu*, cruisers *Gloire*, *Montcalm*, and *Georges Leygues*, and other ships were sent to United States Navy Yards for reconditioning. The last three lent a hand in the invasion of Southern France in 1944.

hower diplomacy; Tunis a conspicuous but probably unavoidable failure.

Although the French protectorate of Tunisia [5] had been earmarked by Mussolini as his booty, Hitler had not interfered with the French régime. The Axis had never occupied Tunisia because their armed forces were engaged in Tripolitania and Libya, and their main supply lines ran direct to Tripoli and Benghazi. The Resident General of Tunisia, corresponding to General Noguès in Morocco, was the five-star French Admiral Jean-Pierre Esteva. Vice Admiral Edmond-Louis Derrien at Bizerta commanded the French naval forces in Tunisian waters, and General Georges Barré was head of the French Army there.

Our "fifth-column" activities in Tunisia were, in part at least, in charge of Mr. Hooker A. Doolittle, the American Consul at Tunis. After the liberation of France Admiral Esteva was cashiered and condemned to life imprisonment for "national unworthiness," but there is now no doubt that he was merely the victim of what Mr. Churchill calls "the cataract of events." Mr. Doolittle did not regard him as any more pro-Axis than Darlan or Noguès, and believed that if we had snapped into Bizerta as Admiral Cunningham wanted, or if we had sent an armored regiment racing into Tunisia to join forces with General Barré, who was only too willing to welcome it, the Admiral would have coöperated. In that case, the United Nations would have saved thousands of lives and months of time. Unfortunately the difficulties of doing either thing were insuperable. The Axis beat us to the draw, but Tunisia proved to be a trap for thousands of their troops flown in to reinforce it.

We have already seen how Darlan tried to bring Esteva promptly into line. The dispatch was held up by subordinates, but it got through by 10 November. The United Nations had nothing to implement these orders. British forces did not even enter Bône, near the Algeria-Tunisia border, until 12 November. In the mean-

---

[5] Tunisia, like Morocco, was still legally a French protectorate, ruled by a native Bey, with a dual régime.

time, on the ninth, the Germans began flying in planes to the Tunisia airfields, whose French staffs had been instructed to expect them. Forty bombers landed at El Aouina airdrome that day. A week later one brought Admiral Platon, Pétain's colonial minister, from Vichy. His mission was to convince Esteva that the Axis would still win. Esteva hewed to that line. Admiral Cunningham never doubted he did so under duress, and Robert Murphy also testified in 1948 to Esteva's eagerness to coöperate with Allied landings in Tunisia.[6]

On 13 November the first German troops arrived in Tunisia by ferry planes. By nightfall, Mr. Doolittle believed there were between three and four thousand Germans in the country, mostly air ground force personnel; and he got out. During the following week Axis troops flowed into Tunisia by air in unprecedented numbers. Frenzied efforts were made by the Germans to convert Tunisia into an African bastion, for the British Eighth Army (General Montgomery), after winning the Battle of El Alamein on 3 November, was pursuing Rommel westward. All Egypt was again in British hands by 12 November. Derna was occupied on the 16th. Tunisia, from the Axis point of view, must be saved as a Rommel rallying point, since its topography offered means of defense that were denied by the Libyan desert.

Thus, while the British and American ground forces in Algeria, faced with difficult logistic problems, were forming for an eastward advance, the Axis consolidated its position in Tunisia, with the active collaboration of the authorities at Vichy. By the time the Allied eastward drive began, almost every French element (except General Barré's troops) which might have joined them had been disarmed or was actively on the Axis side. The German troops, with admirable strategic sense, concentrated on occupying the eastward-facing ports of Sousse, Sfax and Gabès, in order to keep their front door open to sea routes from Italy, and prepare

6 Information from Mr. Doolittle and letters from Cunningham and Murphy, Oct. 1948, cited by Service Historique de la Marine.

a back door where Rommel might enter and barricade himself — the Mareth Line.

The British First Army sent paratroops into Tunisia from Bône as early as 14 November, but it is believed that they were captured. The slowness of General K. A. N. Anderson, Commander Eastern Task Force, in coming to grips with the Germans, was inevitable. Bougie, his harbor of debarkation, well to the westward of Tunisia, was in part blocked by sunken French ships and could not be worked to full capacity. Supply lines feeding the First Army were long and thin [7] and subject to increasingly heavy Axis air attacks from Sardinia, Sicily, and from newly developed all-weather airfields in the neighborhood of Tunis and Bizerta. Nevertheless, the Allies made good progress for a time. They captured Medjez el Bab, thirty miles southwest of Tunis, and on 29 November occupied Djedeida, a rail center only twelve miles from the capital, which they began to shell. Motorized troops cut the railroad between Tunis and Bizerta and threatened the coastal highway. This afforded a prospect for a speedy wind-up of the Tunisian campaign that was to prove illusory. By 4 December the Allies were forced to give ground in western Tunisia, and on 13 December they abandoned the Djedeida area.

In the meantime winter rains had set in and both sides were literally and figuratively bogged down, with the advantage to the Axis — who were in possession of all-weather flying fields.

These initial setbacks cost the United Nations another group of ships that might have been useful. Admiral Derrien, commanding the French Navy in Tunisian waters, refused to allow the Germans the use of his force. In consequence General Ganse, acting for General von Arnim, the Axis commander in Tunisia, ordered him on 8 December to surrender all his ships, installations and men at Bizerta, and gave him thirty minutes to decide, the alternative being death for him and his men. The Admiral, helpless without Allied support, surrendered. His force of four destroyers, half a

[7] Lt. Col. J. H. Myers USA "Military Railway Service in World War II" *Military Review* Feb. 1945, pp. 35-36.

dozen submarines and several small minelayers and gunboats was taken over and more than 1600 French officers and men of their crews were insolently shipped back to Toulon via Italy for demobilization.

Untoward events in Tunisia did not affect the relentless westward drive of the British Eighth Army in Libya. Montgomery was supported by the Royal Navy Inshore Squadron and Mobile Beach Party, who leap-frogged along the coast in support of each advance.[8] The Germans announced that their forces were "advancing *westward* without any opposition," and they certainly advanced fast. The British took Benghazi on 20 November, and on the 24th were near El Agheila, the high-water mark of General Wavell's offensive in 1941. Rommel began his withdrawal from El Agheila towards Tripoli on 13 December and, a week later, his weakened forces were being relentlessly pursued 140 miles to the westward of that city.

The year 1942 ended with the situation in Tunisia static. The First Army was bogged down in Algerian mud; the Eighth Army, delayed by sandstorms, was gathering itself to push the Afrika Korps into Tunisia. The Royal Navy, respecting the powerful air forces that the enemy had deployed, was not yet ready to challenge Axis control of the Straits of Sicily, the short air and sea route between Italian territory and Tunis. Malta stood firm. But the Germans and Italians had won the race into Tunisia.

2. *The United Nations Build-up*[9]

a. Morocco

Despite the alleged tardiness of the United Nations in entering Tunisia, the speed and effectiveness with which they set about

---

[8] British Admiralty publication *The Mediterranean Fleet: Greece to Tripoli* pp. 91–94.
[9] Principal sources are War Diary Sea Frontier Forces W.T.F. (later called "Moroccan Sea Frontier Forces") 19 Nov. 1942 and subsequent dates; Cdr. Melvin F. Talbot "The Logistics of the Eighth Fleet and Comnavnaw" 1946.

converting sleepy little African ports into bustling terminals and training centers was cited by Admiral Hewitt as one of the remarkable achievements of the war. "Vigorous and rapid exploitation" of "lodgements in North Africa" had been stated by the Combined Chiefs of Staff as strategical purpose number two in the concept of Operation "Torch." The United States Navy undertook to operate the Moroccan ports and Oran, while the British accepted responsibility for Algiers and ports to the eastward.

Personnel for the operation of the Moroccan ports sailed with the Western Naval Task Force, and the first contingent of Rear Admiral Hall's Advance Base Unit — including a quarter of a battalion of Seabees — landed on the beaches at Fedhala, Safi and Port Lyautey on 8 November. Naval Section Bases were set up at Safi and Fedhala as fast as French opposition was overcome, and the important task of clearing the harbors to accommodate ships of the assault convoy began immediately. On 12 November the first contingent of the Casablanca Base Unit, consisting of 33 officers and 188 men, was transported thither from Fedhala. The limited quarters ashore had already been snapped up by the Army, and for some time naval personnel had to make the best of tents and camel barns.

Naval Air Station Port Lyautey was activated on 13 November with Navy Patrol Squadron 73 which flew down from England, and was served by tender *Barnegat*. Squadron 92 of Navy Catalinas flew up from Bathurst the same day, encountering en route a French submarine near Villa Cisneros that they sank by depth charges. This was *Conquérant*, one of the three that escaped from Casablanca and went missing. U.S.S. *Biscayne* steamed up from Freetown to Casablanca on 18 November to take care of Squadron 92; daily patrols by air and surface craft were immediately instituted; the U-boats could no longer safely operate close to the Moroccan shore.

About half of the dozen vessels sunk near Port Lyautey had been salvaged by mid-December. Work continued on the rest, which obstructed the Wadi Sebou, until that river was clear throughout its navigable sector.[10]

On 19 November, the day before *Augusta* returned to Hampton Roads, Admiral Hall was detached from duty as Admiral Hewitt's acting chief of staff and established headquarters at 10 Place de France, Casablanca. His command received the official title of Sea Frontier Forces, Western Task Force.[11] The follow-up convoy (UGF–2) brought over 400 officers and men to operate this new sea frontier.[12] His task organization was broken down into three main divisions: (1) Commander A. G. Cook Jr.'s Escort Unit, consisting of eight minesweepers; (2) Commander J. A. Briggs's Patrol Wing, comprising Naval Air Station Port Lyautey, the two patrol squadrons and their tenders; (3) the Base Unit, comprising the Naval Operating Base Casablanca (Captain H. G. Sickel commanding) and section bases at Fedhala and Safi. These units were augmented by the arrival on 25 November of the "Spitkit" Convoy of submarine chasers, patrol craft and motor minesweepers escorted from Bermuda by United States tanker *Maumee*.

The torpedoings off Fedhala on 11 and 12 November marked the last depredations of Axis U-boats close inshore at Morocco for some time. Three or four surfaced submarines were sighted within a hundred miles of the coast and ineffectually bombed on 21, 22 and 25 November by planes of the patrol squadrons, but on 17 December the French trawler *Poitou* was torpedoed 16 miles north of Mazagan.

Fortunately the Moroccan ports were at the maximum range of Axis bombers; no further defensive air operations were required to protect Allied positions and no air attacks developed for almost seven weeks. On the last day of 1942 an estimated half-dozen Axis planes came over blacked-out Casablanca and dropped several bombs without doing any material damage to ships or harbor in-

---

[10] Report and Estimate of Salvage Operations as of 18 Dec. 1942 (Enclosure to War Diary Sea Frontier W.T.F.).

[11] Name changed to Moroccan Sea Frontier 17 Feb. 1943.

[12] Almost 200 additional personnel, survivors of U.S.S. *Almaack* and *Leedstown*, were added to N.O.B. Casablanca on 26 Nov. 1942.

stallations. The attack was at least well-timed, since about half the ships of Convoy UGS-3 had entered port the evening before. Although Army shore batteries and ships in the harbor put up heavy anti-aircraft fire, it was ineffective.

Once order had been established in unloading at Casablanca and the Army began to get its belongings away from the docks, the Base Unit began to function smoothly with good French coöperation. Subsequent arrivals and departures of merchant vessels were handled on schedule and with dispatch. Coastwise convoys were established with escorts furnished by the Frontier Forces. Admiral Hall's "Spitkits" patrolled and escorted vessels through the protective mine fields that ringed the harbors and ultimately stretched for 22 miles from Casablanca northeastward. This field consisted of three rows of moored Mark-6 mines planted by ships of Mine Division 50.

Admiral Giffen's Covering Group and Admiral McWhorter's carrier planes had sunk so many French and neutral merchant ships that Casablanca harbor was sadly cluttered up with hulks. Three of them had been hit or sunk by 16-inch shells intended for *Jean Bart*, wringing from Admiral Hall the observation that he "earnestly wished the *Massachusetts* had stayed home!" Salvage operations were immediately begun by the advance base unit, with whatever apparatus and labor the French could furnish. In response to an urgent call to Washington for experts, Captain William A. Sullivan then in New York salvaging U.S.S. *Lafayette* (ex-*Normandie*), was flown to Casablanca on 23 November with a crew of divers and other salvage artists. Shortly afterwards the first tangible results were achieved when minesweeper *Abbé Desgranges* was floated and returned to the French Navy.

The second homeward-bound convoy (GUF-2), consisting of 19 merchant ships and oilers escorted by *Arkansas* and 9 destroyers, departed Casablanca 29 November. Two days later arrived UGS-2 of 25 ships with an ample contribution to the United Nations build-up.

In Casablanca salvage operations continued unremittingly. The sunk French steamship *Île d'Ouessant*, occupying important pier space, was patched, pumped out and towed out of the way across the harbor on 3 December. By the middle of the month the large French floating dry dock was raised. It had over a hundred holes in walls and pontoon deck, where an unexploded 16-inch shell was lying. Holes plugged and pumps in order, this dry dock was pronounced ready on 18 December for its first customer, destroyer *Hambleton*. Subsequent work performed by it lightened the load on the already overtaxed facilities at Gibraltar.

The French in the meantime worked on their own naval vessels, salvaged destroyer *Albatros* and floated *Jean Bart*, whose guns were removed and sent to the United States for installation on the

KEY TO CHART OPPOSITE

Positions of major damaged and sunken ships in Casablanca Harbor compiled from photographs by Commander A. C. Brown USNR and checked by Commodore W. A. Sullivan USNR.

1. French Corvette, capsized.
2. Trawler, capsized.
3. Floating dry dock, holed and scuttled.
4. Battleship *Jean Bart*, holed and stern resting on bottom.
5. Submarines *Amphitrite*, *Psyché*, and *Oréade*, sunk.
6. French S.S. *Porthos*, capsized at dock.
7. Wreck of French minelayer sunk in 1939.
8. French S.S. *Lipari*, burned and sunk.
9. French S.S. *Savoie*, sunk by two 16-inch hits and one 100-lb bomb.
10. French S.S. *Île d'Ouessant*, sunk by two 16-inch hits.
11. French S.S. *Schiaffino*, bomb damage and barely afloat.
12. Italian S.S. *San Pietro*, sunk.
13. French prison ship *St. Blaise*, sunk.
14. Destroyer *Frondeur*, capsized and sunk.
15. Submarine lifting craft, holed and scuttled.
16. Destroyer *Brestois*, sunk.
17. Cruiser *Primauguet*, beached.
18. Destroyer Leader *Albatros*, beached.
19. Destroyer Leader *Milan*, beached.
20. French S.S. *Fauzon*, damaged by two 16-inch hits.
21. Destroyer Leader *Le Malin*, afloat, holed by 16-inch hit and bombed.

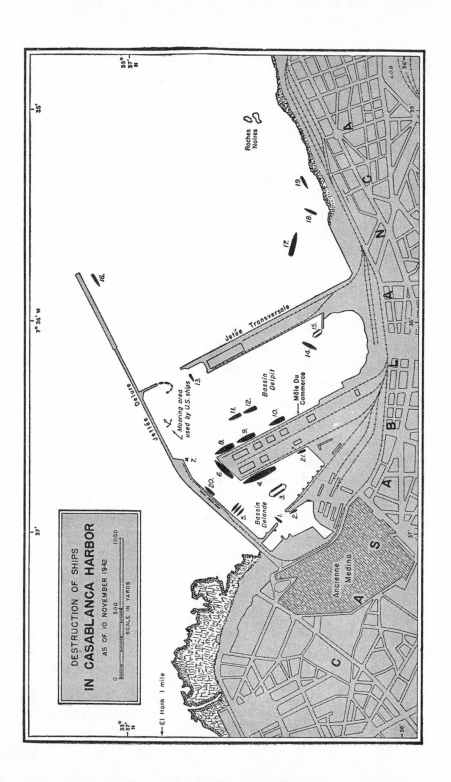

DESTRUCTION OF SHIPS
IN CASABLANCA HARBOR
AS OF 10 NOVEMBER 1942

SCALE IN YARDS
0   500   1000

El Hank 1 mile

33°
37'
N

37'

7° 36' W

35'

33°
37'
N

Jetée Delure

Jetée Transversale

Mooring area
used by U.S. ships

Bassin
Delande

Bassin
Delpit

Môle Du
Commerce

Roches
Noires

Ancienne
Medina

C   A   S   A   B   L   A   N   C   A

Richelieu. After V–E day in 1945, *Jean Bart* proceeded under her own power to Cherbourg. Five or six French and Italian merchant vessels were raised and salvaged by Captain Sullivan's crew. By the end of 1942 they had the harbor almost completely cleared, with more berths available than before the war. This practice stood Captain Sullivan in excellent stead when he was later called upon for the colossal tasks of clearing the harbors of Palermo, Naples, Marseilles, Cherbourg, Le Havre and Manila.

Cessation of hostilities with the French happily placed Morocco at a considerable distance from the fighting, and made it possible to use Casablanca as a port of entry, exactly as General Eisenhower and Admiral Hewitt had intended. The transatlantic crossing with its U-boat hazards was hereafter shortened by routing convoys from the United States to Casablanca, where rail and army trucks picked up troops and materiel for transport eastward. The railroad from Casablanca to Algiers via Port Lyautey, the Taza Gap in the Middle Atlas, Oujda and Oran, afforded a far from de luxe service; troops had to be content with the old *"40 hommes, 8 chevaux"* boxcars of 1917 vintage. But it carried immense quantities of freight to the fighting front in Tunisia.

As the war pushed eastward and the Royal Navy got the western Mediterranean under control, the importance of Casablanca as a troop-transport terminus diminished. It became a great reserve depôt of fuel and ammunition, feeding the United Nations in North Africa; and, in connection with the Port Lyautey airdrome, it was soon the center of anti-submarine warfare in the east Atlantic.

b. Algeria [13]

United States naval port parties for the operation of Oran and Arzeu were landed with the assault troops of the Center Task Force. Rear Admiral A. C. Bennett, Flag Officer in Charge Oran

[13] Principal sources: Commander U.S. Naval Operating Bases Oran Area (Rear Admiral Bennett) Operations of U.S. Naval Forces Center Task Force 30 Nov. 1942; War Diary N.O.B. Oran 1 Dec. 1942 and ff.

Area,[14] was Rear Admiral Hall's opposite number in the Mediterranean. Once established on the beach, these port parties set up three United States naval stations at Oran, Mers-el-Kebir and Arzeu. The minor ports of Mostaganem and Nemours were immediately surveyed and held in readiness for shoal draft vessels.

The condition of Oran Harbor when the fighting stopped was even worse than that of Casablanca, and there had been wholesale sabotage as well. Twenty-five scuttled ships, including *Hartland*, *Walney*, and three "floating" dry docks that no longer floated, about filled up the harbor. Admiral Bennett's port parties entered Oran during the afternoon of 10 November and forthwith began to clear a 20-foot channel to the inner harbor. The French fully cooperated, placing their pilots, tugs, salvage equipment, lighters and port facilities at the Admiral's disposal. A British salvage ship called *King Salvor*, which had been sent up from Gibraltar, also assisted. On 8 December Captain Edward Ellsberg USNR, on loan to the Army, was appointed Chief Salvage Officer "Torch" Area by General Eisenhower.

The first major task of this salvage force was to raise the 2400-ton dry dock, and this was effected in an incredibly short period. Before the end of November it was used to dock the French destroyer *Épervier*. Another dry dock and six steamers were salvaged by 9 December. All obstructions to the inner harbor of Oran were finally removed and the port was opened to normal traffic on 7 January 1943. Shortly after, Oran became the most important United States Navy operating and supply base in North Africa.

Anti-submarine measures were placed in effect in the Algerian harbors, the British supplying the nets and booms. A large volume of traffic was handled under Royal Navy escort between Gibraltar and Algerian ports. Force H made Mers-el-Kebir a port of replenishment and Admiral Bennett's staff acted as liaison in delicate negotiations between United States armed forces and the British and French Navies.

[14] The name of his command was changed to Amphibious Forces Mediterranean on 8 Dec. 1942.

As the port of Algiers was a responsibility of the Royal Navy, few United States Naval personnel were stationed there initially. But Rear Admiral B. H. Bieri, deputy chief of staff Atlantic Fleet, Captain Jerauld Wright, and a few other naval officers were attached to General Eisenhower's Allied Force Headquarters.

Algiers Harbor, left in better shape than the others at the close of hostilities, took care of an enormous volume of shipping. The Bougie assault forces were mounted there as early as 10 November, and many troopships sailed thence for the eastern ports. German submarines were increasingly active in the western Mediterranean. The Luftwaffe, leaving Casablanca largely alone because of the extreme range, concentrated on Algeria. But its strikes were not uniformly successful: during the week following the invasion (8–15 November) naval anti-aircraft fire claimed to have destroyed 23 Axis planes, with 10 "probables." [15] The city and harbor of Algiers suffered numerous air raids, but the principal targets of Axis bombers were the eastern ports, in an attempt to frustrate the Allied drive into Tunisia. Aircraft were over Bône almost every night; and Bougie, Djidjelli, Philippeville and Tabarka were pounded heavily.

[15] A.F.H.Q. G–3 Report 20 Nov. 1942.

KEY TO CHART OPPOSITE

1. *Chêne*	16. "*Petit*" Dock
2. *Ajaccienne*	17. *Lorraine* (oiler)
3. Barges	18. H.M.S. *Hartland*
4. H.M.S. *Walney*	19. Large Floating Dry Dock
5. *Tourterelle*	20. *Château Pavie*
6. *Toulonnaise*	21. *St. Martin*
7. *Jean Auguste*	22. *Pigeon*
8. *Sidi-Bel-Abbes*	23. *Mitijda*
9. *Cassaigne*	24. *Boudjmel*
10. *Forfait*	25. *Spahi*
11. *Tijditt*	26. *La Ferrier*
12. *Menhir-Braz*	27. *Diana*
13. *Cérès* (scuttled submarine)	28. *Bonaise*
14. *Pallas* (scuttled submarine)	29. *Typhon* (destroyer)
15. "*Moyen*" Dock (submarine *Danaë* spilled out when dock was scuttled)	

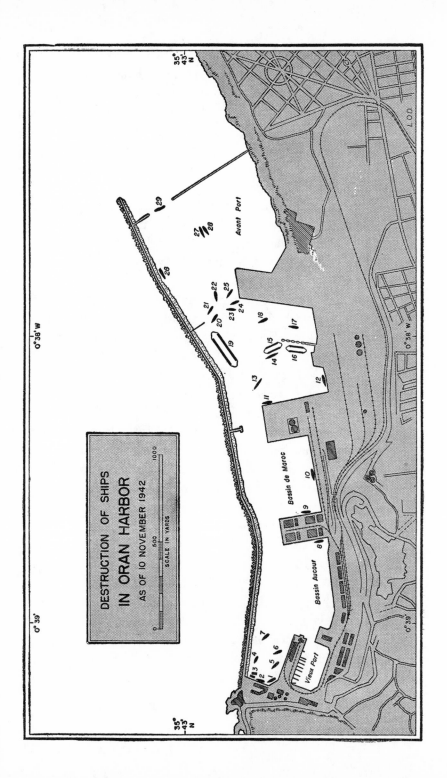

DESTRUCTION OF SHIPS
IN ORAN HARBOR
AS OF 10 NOVEMBER 1942

SCALE IN YARDS
0   500   1000

Avant Port

Bassin de Maroc

Bassin Aucour

Vieux Port

0° 39'   0° 38' W

35°
43'
N

Air attack claimed a British destroyer badly holed at Bône on 29 November and a corvette sunk in Algiers on 8 December.

On 12 December, a flock of Italian one-man submarines sneaked into the outer anchorage at Algiers and fastened limpet mines on four ships. One sank and the other three were damaged, two of them joining *Thomas Stone* on the beach. The fourth was brought into the harbor.[16]

Another sinking in which heavy loss of life was barely averted occurred on 21 December when the British troopship *Strathallen*, in Convoy KMF–5, was torpedoed eighty-five miles northeast of Oran. H.M. destroyers *Panther* and *Verity* landed 2,470 survivors at Oran and Mers-el-Kebir.[17]

For some time after the African landings, there were no United States Naval vessels in the Mediterranean, except transports. Admiral Bennett had the anomalous assignment of running a United States naval operating base without ships.

There were good reasons for this situation. The British have a paramount interest in the Mediterranean because of the Suez Canal, as the United States has in the Caribbean because of the Panama Canal. In addition, they had the preponderance of naval power in the classic sea, and a long tradition of dominance. Since the days of Nelson, only Mussolini with his *Mare Nostrum* slogan, and Hitler, had seriously challenged British sea power in the Mediterranean. The Royal Navy had held, in the western half of the sea, during the lean years 1940–1942; even tiny Malta had not flinched — and the British Army survived defeat. Now that our great ally was beginning to get her own back — with Rommel on the run, the U-boats on the defensive, and the Italian Navy reduced to a fleet in being — she naturally wished to resume her preponderant rôle. President Roosevelt understood this situation very well and when General Eisenhower was set up as Allied Commander in Chief, British commanders were appointed over the three allied services, Army, Navy, and Air. They exercised the dominant and active con-

[16] A.F.H.Q. G–3 Report 12 Dec. 1942.
[17] War Diary N.O.B. Oran.

trol over each arm in the Mediterranean although the major strength in each was American and not British.

The Royal Navy had so many commitments in other waters that it could not restore the prestige of the White Ensign along the Barbary Coast and in the Levant, or make further advances, without considerably more aid from United States sea, air and man power. This meant that there had to be an American seagoing command in the Mediterranean even if it was subordinate to Commander in Chief Mediterranean, "Cincmed" (Admiral Sir Andrew Cunningham RN). On 3 February 1943, Admiral King set up the United States Naval Forces Northwest African Waters command ("Comnavnaw") to be effective 1 March; and when Admiral Hewitt came over to exercise this command, on 16 March 1943, he also became Commander Eighth Fleet, including all United States naval forces in the Mediterranean. Although this command was still under Cincmed, the United States Navy assumed an increasing share of the planning, logistics, and combat. It provided most of the ships, ammunition, and fuel; and Admiral Hewitt's staff was charged with a heavy share of the naval planning in important amphibious operations in the Mediterranean — Sicily, Salerno, Anzio and Southern France. Admiral Hewitt respected the Royal Navy point of view and kept his own command in line. His innate modesty, combined with his determination to get the job done, enabled him to carry the burden of a task for which he received too little public credit. Admiral Cunningham highly appreciated Admiral Hewitt's character and ability, and exercised the overall command with restraint and consideration.

The United States and Royal Navies can always settle their own differences. But with the French, whose pride rose as their power fell, it was not so easy to reach an agreement. The joustings and maneuvers of irreconcilable French factions in Algeria continued to bedevil the common cause, and on 24 December Admiral Darlan was assassinated. General Eisenhower, making one of his numerous switches from the military rôle to that of diplomatist, persuaded the French leaders to accept General Giraud as High Commissioner

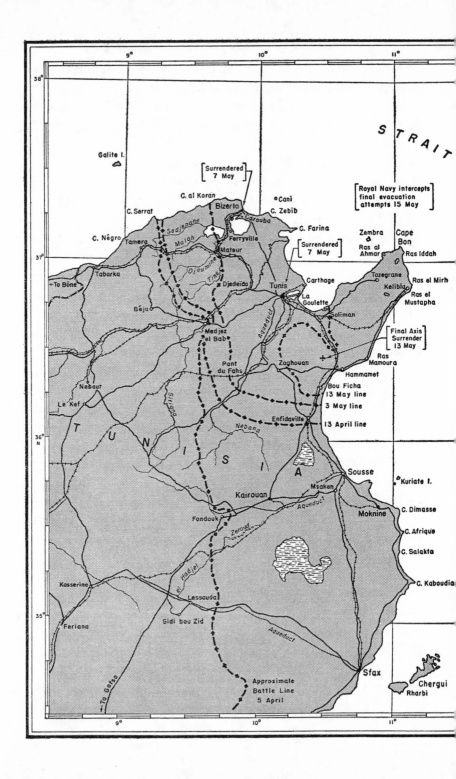

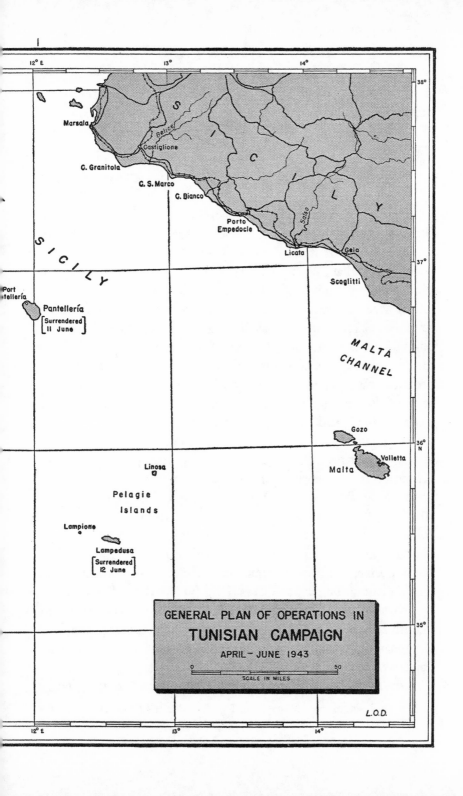

GENERAL PLAN OF OPERATIONS IN
TUNISIAN CAMPAIGN
APRIL – JUNE 1943

0   50
SCALE IN MILES

L.O.D.

of French Africa on 27 December 1942. Thus the New Year dawned with brighter hopes for French unity in the face of the common foe; but, as it turned out, General de Gaulle acquiesced in the appointment of Giraud only as a *modus vivendi*.

3. *North Africa Cleared of the Axis*[18]

Across the deserts in Libya, General Rommel had been granted little respite since General Alexander's breach of El Alamein on 3 November. The strategy of his westward regression was to fall back faster than Montgomery's Eighth Army could outflank him. At Buerat, midway between El Agheila and Tripoli, on a short line between the sea and a series of almost impassable *wadis* to the south, he again turned at bay. Montgomery paused to let supply build up for another and final surge forward. On 15 January 1943 the dry river courses were crossed by the "desert rats" and flanking pressure was applied in conjunction with a frontal attack that squeezed Rommel's forces out of the bottleneck and again sent them rolling to their rendezvous with doom.

On 23 January, while General Anderson's First Army was sustaining further reverses in western Tunisia, the Eighth took Tripoli. Rommel's forces scurried on to the westward and by the 29th were into southern Tunisia. By 7 February the Allies had occupied all Libya, and Mussolini's vaunted African Empire was no more. Joined at last with General von Arnim, the German commander in Tunisia, Rommel's forces dug in behind the sanctuary of the Mareth Line, a series of strategic fortifications in southeastern Tunisia below the city of Gabès, built by the French in 1939. By 17 February the Eighth Army had arrived in position before the Mareth Line and for a month thereafter both sides were occupied in preparations for the struggle for possession of this important objective.

In the meantime the static condition in north and central Tunisia

[18] Principal sources are Military Intelligence Division *To Bizerte with the II Corps* (1943) and *The Mediterranean Fleet, Greece to Tripoli*.

gave way to a series of violent Axis offensives before which the British, French, and American forces were obliged to give hard-earned ground. These attacks, launched from Pont du Fahs on 20 January 1943, pushed out the defense arc all along the line as a stream of Axis supplies and reinforcements (estimated at a thousand men daily) poured across the Sicilian Straits in "flying boxcars." Rommel's forces, now well within central Tunisia, launched an offensive through the Kasserine Pass on 20 February. The pass was retaken five days later by American forces. In the extreme north, the Axis launched another offensive designed to give them elbow room. On 3 March they occupied Sedjenane on the Mateur–Tabarka coastal road. The British counterattacked south of Tamera on 14 March and the battle line continued in its fluid state, with the British abandoning Tamera on 18 March. In three weeks, the Axis forces had advanced thirty miles in that sector.

Further south the fortunes of war favored the United Nations. On 17 March General Patton's 1st Infantry Division and 1st Armored Division occupied Gafsa, driving eastward toward the sea. Two days later the British Eighth Army began to attack the Mareth Line. On the 30th it crumbled and Montgomery broke through. He took Gabès that day, Sfax on 10 April, Sousse on the 12th, and Enfidaville on the 20th. In the north the Allies seized the initiative, reoccupying Sedjenane and pushing eastward towards Mateur. When this railroad junction fell to the Allied forces on 3 May, communication lines between Bizerta and Tunis were severed. This practically decided the contest for Tunisia, and the enemy began to concern himself with evacuation. Rommel was recalled to Germany. Cornered in the northeastern part of Tunisia, Axis forces fought with their backs to the sea and the Royal Navy, with a heavy score to settle, took particular and effective steps to see to it that a wholesale evacuation such as at Dunkirk would not take place.[19]

[19] The plans for this operation, appropriately named "Retribution," were promulgated on 13 April and provided for an immediate concentration of light naval forces of the Levant fleet. It did not prove necessary to put the complete plan into effect, however, and in summation the British Vice Admiral, Malta,

On 7 May Bizerta fell to the American II Corps, commanded by Major General Omar N. Bradley USA. On the same day the British took Tunis, and the French, Pont du Fahs. Two days later, General Krause surrendered 25,000 Germans southeast of Bizerta. In a swift drive to the southward on 11 May, British forces knifed through to Hammamet from Tunis, thus cutting off the Cape Bon peninsula and the remaining organized forces. From then until noon 13 May, when all enemy resistance ceased, the campaign consisted of mopping-up operations on the final pockets of resistance.

General von Arnim, commander of all Axis forces in North Africa, Marshal Messe, commander of the Italian First Army, and some 275,000 other prisoners were taken. Only a small number of the enemy attempted to escape by sea, and owing to the vigilance with which the Royal Navy carried out its patrols, only a handful succeeded in crossing the Sicilian Straits. Almost 900 soldiers attempting to escape in small boats to Pantelleria were intercepted and taken prisoner by 15 May.

After the fall of Tunisia, Allied air and sea power were supreme throughout the southern Mediterranean and a convoy route was opened right through to the Suez Canal. As Admiral Hewitt expressed it, "the severed life line of the Empire was spliced." [20] According to German Lieutenant General Walter Warlimont, deputy chief of Armed Forces Operations Staff and chief of the Joint Planning Staff, "The loss of Tunisia was considered by the entire German Army to be a catastrophe second only in magnitude to that of Stalingrad." [21]

Vice Adm. A. J. Power RN, said, almost with a touch of pique: "Two features of the operation are prominent. Firstly, the complete absence of any Axis men of war or shipping, which was very disappointing, and, secondly, the manner in which the Axis Air Forces deserted the theatre of operations and left our destroyer patrols to operate without inconvenience." Cincmed Report 13 Nov. 1943, Enclosure 1.

[20] Admiral Hewitt "The Influence of Sea Power on the Victory in Europe" prepared in May 1945.

[21] Seventh U.S. Army Interrogation Center, Bulletin of 24 July 1945.

4. *Motor Torpedo Boat Operations*

a. PT Background [22]

Between the completion of the landings in North Africa in mid-November 1942, and the beginning of the Sicilian operation in July 1943, Motor Torpedo Boat Squadron 15 was the only United States naval unit engaged in hostilities against enemy-held littoral in the Mediterranean.[23] Routine escort-of-convoy work went on, and almost daily Axis bombing attacks of North African ports kept ships and shore anti-aircraft batteries busy. But this plucky squadron was sole representative of the United States Navy in offensive action in all the Mediterranean Sea.

Since this is the first occasion in this history where United States Navy motor torpedo boats are mentioned, a few words as to how they came to be are in order.

The small, fast, hit-and-run motor torpedo boat was first developed by the Italian Navy, which used it with considerable success against the Austrians in World War I. During that war the Electric Boat Company of Bayonne, New Jersey, built several hundred 80-footers known as MLs for the Royal Navy, but the United States Navy ordered none for another twenty years. The reasons for this tardiness, other than the prevailing naval apathy to small craft, were (1) the conception that motor torpedo boats were chiefly defensive instruments, on which the Navy hated to spend money, as it was long since committed to the doctrine that offensive operations overseas were the best defense; and (2) the belief that torpedo bombing planes would be more efficient. But the torpedo bomber could not compete with the motor torpedo boat in stealth or (until aircraft radar was developed) in night attack.

[22] Compiled from "Data for the History of Motor Torpedo Boats U.S. Navy," corrected by G. Adamson and D. Van Patten's art. in *U.S. Naval Inst. Proc.* July 1940.
   [23] A point acknowledged by Admiral Hewitt in a letter filed in Lt. Cdr. Barnes's "jacket" at the Bureau of Personnel: "First of the Eighth Fleet forces to be in combat with the enemy when he was engaged in operations against the withdrawal from Tunis."

President Roosevelt, who as Assistant Secretary of the Navy in the last war had been convinced of the value of these craft, now sponsored a congressional appropriation of $15,000,000 for the development of a suitable boat. American speedboat designers had learned a thing or two during the prohibition era: PTs and rum-runners have much in common. As a result of the appropriation, eight experimental motor torpedo boats, designated PT (Patrol Craft Torpedo) were built by the Navy, and by three private builders. Two 58-footers (*PT–3, PT–4*) were accepted, and a 70-footer, designed by Hubert Scott-Paine and powered with Rolls-Royce engines, was purchased from the British government. This last, *PT–9*, became the "ancestor" of United States Navy MTB Squadrons. Elco was awarded a contract in 1940 for ten similar boats, powered with 1200-horsepower Packard engines.

In 1941 exhaustive trials, shakedowns and experiments were made with these two types, but neither was considered satisfactory, and it was decided to lend-lease all the Elcos but one to the Royal Navy, which expended them in the Mediterranean.

Elco now designed a new 77-foot boat for the United States Navy, *PT–20*, and was awarded a contract for 29 of them. Higgins Industries of New Orleans, in the meantime, had designed a so-called "Dream Boat" 76 feet long, with three 1200-horsepower Packard engines. And as other builders, too, wished to compete, Admiral H. R. Stark, then Chief of Naval Operations, ordered trials in the summer of 1941. At this so-called "Plywood Derby" over a 160-mile course from New London around Block Island, *PT–20* won the first race in smooth water by turning up an average of 38 knots, and *PT–21* of the same model won the second, in rough water, with an average speed of 25 knots. While Elco demonstrated its superiority and was given an order to build more 77-footers, the Higgins entries did very well and that firm was awarded a contract for 78-footers. The first Higgins squadron, No. 13, was commissioned in September 1942. Squadron 14 was lend-leased to Russia; Squadron 15, that came out to Bône, was the third.

In the fall of 1940 the Packard Company established a training

PT–117, an early Elco type Motor Torpedo Boat, on trial run

PT-211, Higgins type, tied up at Bastia, Corsica, early 1944. The rocket racks and radar were installed subsequent to the operations described in this volume

school for engineer personnel at their plant in Detroit; the other officers and men, almost without exception naval reservists, had their basic training in the Torpedo School at Newport, Rhode Island. Squadron 3 of six Elcos was shipped to the Philippines in time to take part in the campaign of 1941–1942; and six more, although still in their cradles on shipboard or ashore at Pearl Harbor, opened fire on the attacking Japanese planes on 7 December. The operations of Squadron 3, which are related in another volume, brought the type into the public as well as the naval eye, and resulted in many modifications in doctrine, training and equipment — of which the most immediate was the establishment of a training center at Melville, Rhode Island. This began functioning in March 1942. The first compilation of MTB doctrine, *Motor Torpedo Boats, Tactical Orders and Doctrine*, came out in July.

The Higgins 78-footer, of which Squadron 15 was composed, was less fast but more maneuverable than the Elco 77-footer. It was powered by three Packard engines, capable of 1350 horsepower at 2500 revolutions per minute,[24] all with direct drive. It carried four Mark-8 torpedoes fired from tubes by compressed air, and four .50-caliber twin-mounted machine guns. But complete fitting of all Squadron 15 boats for combat to include SO radar was not completed until July 1943.

Motor Torpedo Boat Squadron 15, whose skipper was Lieutenant Commander Stanley M. Barnes, consisted initially of twelve PTs (Numbers *201–212*) divided into two sections. Commissioned in New Orleans early in 1943, the squadron proceeded under its own power to Norfolk, where Numbers *201–204* were loaded on Navy oiler *Enoree* and *205–208* on *Housatonic*, for shipment to the Mediterranean.[25] These two groups debarked at Gibraltar early in April, proceeded to Bône, and were there attached to the British Inshore

---

[24] This engine was last of a series developed by Packard for aircraft in the 1920's.
[25] PTs *201–204* were in charge of Lt. Comdr. Barnes. Lt. E. A. Du Bose usNR, squadron engineer, took over PTs *205–208*. Of the original group, PTs *209–212* had remained behind in charge of the squadron exec., Lt. J. B. Mutty usN. These and six more boats (PTs *213–218*) were later attached to the Mediterranean squadron, but did not arrive in Tunisian waters until late May 1943.

Forces for temporary duty, beginning a congenial association which was to last for the next eighteen months.[26] Since Squadron 15 had no battle experience, Commander Barnes welcomed the assistance afforded him by Lieutenant Commander R. A. Allen RNVR, whose men had fought in the English Channel and were already wise to the ways of Axis E-boats.[27]

b. Operations of Squadron 15 [28]

On 27 April, the whole squadron sailed on its first mission. First blood was drawn on the night of 8 May. *PT–206*, in charge of Lieutenant Commander Barnes, set out in company with British MTBs *316* and *265* on a patrol mission in the coastal area between Cape Bon and Ras el Mirh to the southward. At 2245 they entered a bay south of Ras Iddah and sighted a small Axis merchant ship 400 yards from the shore. Stealing up on their quarry, *PT– 206* fired one torpedo at 350 yards' range, and, before skedaddling off to Sousse, had the satisfaction of observing the ship explode. This was not the only excitement that night. *PT–203*, commanded by Lieutenant (jg) Robert B. Reade USNR, in company with British MTBs *61* and *77*, was patrolling in the vicinity of Ras el Mirh when one of the British boats ran aground 300 yards off the beach under the guns of an Axis fort at Kelibia. The men set their boat on fire so that it would not fall into enemy hands. Lieutenant Reade, in the light of the burning boat, under the machine-gun fire from shore and with a Heinkel 111 overhead, brought his boat in, picked up the crew, and pulled out safely while the bewildered fort was still blinking challenges at him.

Two nights later, 10 May, the PTs had a successful action against

[26] Joint patrols were instituted with units of the British 10th MTB Flotilla based at Bône and the 7th MTB Flotilla at Sousse. As anticipated, there were a few difficulties encountered during the first few weeks of these combined operations with the British: the old bugbear of varying communication procedure and equipment as well as disparities in doctrine. Heterogeneous task units of British and American boats were unavoidable, however, until the American Squadron was built up to strength.
[27] Axis equivalent of Royal Navy MTBs and United States PTs.
[28] Squadron 15 War Diary (PTs *201–208*) 4–25 May 1943.

Axis E-boats. It is best told in the words of the Squadron's unofficial narrative:—

Returning from an eventful patrol off Cape Bon, the *202*, *204*, and *205* were skirting the shore to give wide berth to Allied destroyers stationed in the bay of Tunis and be back along friendly coastline before daylight and possible plane attack. Suddenly they found themselves in the middle of an argument between a British destroyer [29] which had wandered south out of its designated area, and German E-boats. The destroyer, having heard German voices over the E-boat's radio planning an attack on her, opened up with four star shells and 40-mm fire in the direction where the American PTs also found themselves at the time. With all this disturbance, the *202* and the *205* lay smoke to clear out, but Ensign E. S. A. Clifford, who was last in the PT formation on the *204*, seeing an excited E-boat reply to the destroyer by opening fire, turned and strafed it going away, leaving it burning. Out of the confusion, another destroyer [30] followed the *205* for an hour, firing star shells. Figuring that he couldn't make it all the way back, Lieutenant (jg) R. H. O'Brien decided to take the *205* into Bizerta, which was supposed to have been evacuated by the Germans on the 7th. Shore batteries doubted his identity as Allied, however, and there were a few tense moments while they shelled him briefly. Still it appeared safer inside than out, so he proceeded in without being hit and picked his way into the shambles of Bizerta harbor where he tied up and rested easy. Two hours later he was disgusted when British landing craft came in and asked him to move out of the way so that photographers could take pictures of them as the first Allied craft to enter the harbor.[31]

It was not until they had returned to base that the British destroyers realized that not all the vessels engaged that night had been enemy. The report of the 6th Destroyer Flotilla stated that: "A full

[29] H.M.S. *Lamerton* and *Wilton*, both *Hunt* class destroyers equivalent to United States DEs, were in on this fracas and Capt. J. W. Eaton RN, commander of the 6th Destroyer Flotilla, stated that "whatever they were engaging, they were themselves obviously having a riotous time." Cincmed's Report of 13 Nov. 1943, Enclosure 1c.

[30] Possibly this was H.M.S. *Lamerton* whose report stated that she had chased a suspected E-boat but that it finally got away after being subjected to "further heavy gunfire." Report of Commanding Officer 12 May 1943 in same document.

[31] "Arabian Nights in the Mediterranean, a PT Odyssey — MTBron 15, 1943," a 62-page typed manuscript, property of Lt. Cdr. Barnes.

discussion between destroyer and coastal craft officers on return to Bône made it clear that both enemy E-boats and American coastal craft were encountered at the same time. The *Hunts* were engaging the E-boats on one side and did not see the friendly recognition signals on the other." [32]

As soon as practicable after the Axis surrender, the American boats were brought up from Bône and based at Karoubia Bay, Bizerta, where they enjoyed a comparatively quiet maintenance and training period lasting from 13 to 27 May. At this time, SO radar was installed on all the old boats, and ten new ones that came over shortly had it already. Before the end of May the boats were operating along the coast of Sicily and as far north as Sardinia in search of enemy intelligence, and they constituted the only United States naval forces in the capture of Pantelleria.

5. *Arrival of the New Landing Ships*

a. LST, LCT, and LCI [33]

An important event in the first half of 1943 was the arrival in Northwest African waters of the first seagoing American landing ships and large landing craft. This is an appropriate place to describe the origin of the LST (Landing Ship Tank), LCT (Landing Craft Tank), and LCI (Landing Craft Infantry).

The fall of France and the British evacuation of Dunkirk showed that any war by the United States against Germany would have to be carried out on entirely different lines from those of World War I, when we were able to use the excellent terminal facilities of French harbors. The implications of this, tremendous and far reaching, were not immediately realized. The United States Army em-

---

[32] C.O. 12th Cruiser Squadron, 18 May 1943, in same document, Enclosure 1c. The PTs were accused of being off station, but actually the destroyer skippers admitted that they had gone farther south in search of excitement and were themselves off station. The recognition signals of two star cartridges were mistaken for 20-mm fire.

[33] O.N.I. publication *Allied Landing Craft and Ships* 7 Apr. 1944; Earl Burton *By Sea and by Land, the Story of Our Amphibious Forces* (1944).

barked on a large field gun and tank building program without considering how these and other vehicles necessary in modern war were to be landed on coasts held by the enemy. Even President Roosevelt, so quick to apprehend needed changes in naval warfare, remarked to his Naval Aide, early in 1942, that he considered special tank landing craft to be a mistake. "Freighters are much easier to build." [34]

Admiral Joseph M. Reeves, the former Commander in Chief of the United States Fleet who had conducted the landing exercises at Culebra in 1934, was largely responsible for bringing this important problem to the attention of the high command. In a memorandum to the Chief of Naval Operations dated 24 February 1942 he declared:—

There are building in this country a great number of tanks without adequate means of transporting them to the theater of war. This task is more complicated than is at first apparent. It involves more than the mere transportation of the tanks overseas. It includes the more difficult problem of landing them on a hostile shore. In such an offensive campaign it is unlikely that there will be available open ports and harbors with docking and hoisting facilities. Large numbers of tanks, especially in the first stages of the campaign, will have to be landed against opposition on hostile beaches. *A special type of landing craft is required for this operation.*

It was for want of these big landing craft that Safi had to be taken on D-day, in order to put tanks ashore from *Lakehurst* and deploy them for the prompt capture of Casablanca.

The Royal Navy had ordered the construction of about 200 Landing Ships Tank in the United States, under their "1799 Programme," in January 1942. But none of these were ready in time for Operation "Torch." Three makeshift tank landing ships, shoal draft oilers from the Maracaibo, were converted to LSTs by the addition of bow doors and ramps, and used, as we have seen, in the invasion of Algeria, where they proved their value. Some experimental British LCTs of early unstandardized designs, not yet in

---

[34] Memorandum from Capt. John L. McCrea to Admiral Stark, 20 Feb. 1942.

mass production, were also used. But the assembly lines in the United States were already turning out LSTs, LCTs, LCIs, and the smaller ramped landing craft, in vast quantities.

Landing ships and craft were given Number One priority over destroyer escorts, aircraft carriers, and everything else in May 1942, when the next big operation was expected to be a cross-channel invasion of France. All available shipbuilding resources were turned to building them. Contracts were let in every section of the country, and the fine accomplishments of newly created "cornfield" ship-yards was a revelation to long established shipbuilders on the East and West Coasts.

The first standardized United States Navy LSTs were floated out of a building dock at Newport News, Virginia, in October 1942.[35] Such high priority had been assigned to them that the keel of an aircraft carrier, already laid in the dock, was hastily yanked out to make room for several tank ships to be built in her place. These diesel twin-screw vessels measured 328 feet in length by 50-foot beam and were capable of transporting a deadweight load of 2100 tons. The apparently irreconcilable demands of sufficient draft for seaworthiness on the high seas and shoal draft for coming up on a beach were achieved by employing the principle of diving-tanks, as on a submarine. The loaded seagoing draft of an LST was 8 feet forward and 14 feet 4 inches aft. After blowing ballast on landing this was reduced to 3 feet 1 inch forward and 9½ feet aft. If the beach gradient was right (and that was the catch), the LST could be beached close enough to shore to discharge tanks or vehicles by her bow ramp into shoal water. Another characteristic of the LST was its ability to transport as part of the deckload a fully found Landing Craft Tank (LCT),[36] next smaller tank carrier in the family of seagoing landing vessels.

[35] The British built three experimental LSTs, H.M.S. *Boxer, Bruiser,* and *Thruster,* 390 feet in length and powered by steam turbines, but the standardized LST for both Royal and U.S. Navies was the American design with diesel engines.
[36] Initially designated LCT(5) because the British had experimented with four earlier types of LCT, all over 150 feet in length, some of which took part in the 8 November landings near Oran.

The United States Navy LCT was not designed for ocean crossing, but it was a substantial triple-screw vessel about 120 feet long,
capable of carrying either four 40-ton tanks, three 50-ton tanks, or
150 tons of cargo. It had a cruising radius of almost a thousand
miles at 10 knots. The LCT could be transported to the theater of
operations in three watertight sections to be assembled and welded
on arrival at an Allied controlled port; but the normal method of
getting it across was on the deck of an LST. Powerful cranes
loaded it aboard, where it was secured on top of a system of rollers.
When the LST reached her destination she was given sufficient list
by manipulating ballast tanks so that the LCT launched itself over
the side without any other assistance. In transporting them across
the Atlantic it was not uncommon for the LST's deck-loaded LCT
to have one or two smaller personnel landing craft stowed aboard,
like Chinese nested boxes.

The first LCTs, completed in October 1942 before any LSTs
were available, crossed the ocean on freighters that reached the
Mediterranean in January 1943. One of them, deckloaded on the
Liberty ship *Arthur Middleton,* was lost when that freighter exploded off Cape Falcon near Oran.[37]

The third type of large landing ship initially developed was the
diesel-powered Landing Craft Infantry, Large — designed LCI
or LCI(L).[38] Its dimensions were: length, 158½ feet; beam, 23
feet; draft, 3 feet forward and 5 feet aft; to which a full load of 205
men and 32 tons cargo (in addition to crew and stores) would add
8 inches. Although lacking sufficient quarters and mess facilities to
take care of this number of troops for more than 48 hours, the LCI
was a seaworthy twin-screw vessel with cruising radius of 8,000
miles at 12 knots. Not designed to carry vehicles, she had a sharp

[37] War Diary Naval Operating Base Oran 1 Jan. 1943. There were only 3 survivors of the *Middleton*. This was the first LCT(5) casualty of the war.
[38] The (L) stood for "Large," and was used in combined operations to dif-
ferentiate the 158-foot American LCI from the 105-foot British LCI, the latter
being designated LCI(S) for "Small." In this work, it will be understood that
plain LCI means LCI(L). It is an anomaly to designate these 158-foot vessels C
("Craft") instead of S ("Ship"); but originally it was planned to ship them across
in sections and assemble them at the theatre of operations.

bow without landing ramp. On hitting the beach, troops were disembarked by means of gangways hinged to fixed platforms on the bows, something like the "brows" of ancient triremes.

In May 1942 the Joint Chiefs of Staff directed that a substantial fleet of LST, LCT, and LCI as well as smaller landing craft be completed in time to take part in the cross-channel invasion of France then scheduled for February 1943. Although that operation was postponed in favor of "Torch," landing ships and craft fortunately did not lose top priority in construction. They were badly needed, both in the Mediterranean and in the United Kingdom, and the sooner they came out, the earlier we could begin training sailors to operate them and soldiers to use them.

In order to train crews to handle these hitherto untried types of vessel, as well as the smaller boats, Landing Craft Group AFAF was commissioned at Norfolk and placed under the command of Captain William P. O. Clarke of Admiral Hewitt's staff. He wrestled with the problem of training officers and men to handle vessels of radical design that existed only on paper so successfully that crews were ready to man the landing ships when they were delivered in the fall of 1942.

These big additions to the family of beaching ships made it possible to revive an ancient technique in landing operations, the shore-to-shore. Operations such as those that we have described in Morocco and Algeria were known as "ship-to-shore assaults." Seagoing attack transports were escorted to pre-assigned release positions a few miles off the invasion coast, and lay to or anchored. Personnel landing craft were then swung out, lowered and moored alongside the mother ship, while troops crawled down into them by means of cargo nets slung over the side — guns and light tanks being lowered into other waiting craft by the ship's booms. We have seen how precarious the ship-to-shore method was, especially at night, or in rough weather. Engines stalled and boats drifted off in the darkness, blocks on the ships' davits jammed, and tackle fouled. Although ship-to-shore methods could not be abandoned for long ocean passages, or even for short ones that required a very large number of troops, the shore-to-shore method based on the use of the LCI, LST and LCT proved to be a most valuable revival. In shore-to-shore technique the landing ships load troops, vehicles, and supplies at a port of embarkation and steam directly to the target area, where they beach themselves as planned, and the troops and vehicles walk, roll, or splash directly ashore. This was the most ancient method of amphibious warfare as practised by ancient Greeks, by Norse Vikings, and by pirates generally. It was first employed by the Royal Navy in the attack on Pantellería on 11 June 1943, and by the United States Seventh Fleet in the Pacific for landing on the Trobriand Islands on 30 June. By that time Admiral Hewitt's staff had worked out a doctrine for shore-to-shore that was brilliantly vindicated in the landing of the 3rd Infantry Division at Licata in Sicily on 10 July 1943.

b. "Spitkit" Convoys [39]

As new landing ships were delivered to the Navy by East Coast builders they were manned and organized into flotillas at the amphibious training bases at Little Creek, Virginia, or Solomons Island, Maryland. Those built on fresh water were sent down the Mississippi and organized at New Orleans or other Gulf ports.[40]

The first landing ship group to be commissioned in the United States Navy, "LCI Flotilla One," was organized at Little Creek in mid-December 1942, and had its designation changed to Flotilla 2 on 1 January 1943. This was also the first group of United States Landing Craft Infantry to steam across the Atlantic.[41]

[39] War Diary LCI Flotilla Two 12 Dec. 1942; E. Burton *By Sea and by Land,* pp. 94–96.
[40] On 4 Feb 1943, 31 LCI(L)s were escorted from Galveston to the Canal Zone for transfer across the Pacific under Cincpac. Three days later 18 LCI(L)s left Hampton Roads for the Canal for ultimate assignment under Comsopac. (War Diary, Cinclant.)
[41] These landing craft were not, however, the first LCI(L)s to cross the Atlantic. On 21 Jan. 1943, 12 British LCI(L)s built in the United States left Hampton Roads for Bermuda escorted by a U.S. oiler, tug and 2 DDs. Ten of them reached Gibraltar unescorted on 9 Feb., proceeding to Oran and Mers el Kebir later in the same month. The first standard LSTs to cross the Western Ocean were ten American-built ones for the Royal Navy, which departed New

Commander L. S. Sabin Jr. had this flotilla of 24 infantry landing craft ready for sea on 14 February 1943. They rendezvoused
off Little Creek with their escort: destroyer *Cole*, two minelayers,
one fleet tug, and one SC; and took their departure from the Virginia Capes on the morning of 15 February. The temperature stood
at thirteen degrees above zero, and a twenty-knot breeze kicked
up a choppy sea which shot icy spray across the "Elsies" as a fore-
taste of what was to come. The flotilla kept good station through
the day, but after dark the weather worsened and there blew up a
heavy snowstorm from the NE which later turned into sleet. This
was followed by dense fog which shut in so quickly that radio
silence had to be broken to advise the fleet to reduce to two-thirds
speed. Commander Sabin was not sanguine in expecting his order to
be followed, for his report of the voyage contains the succinct statement: "I was fairly certain that only a few ships would get the
message, especially because by this time about 80 per cent of the
officers and men were seasick." [42] And each little ship had a total
complement of only 24.

When the fog lifted next morning, only eight of the LCIs were
in sight from the flagship. The escort vessels were dispatched to
round up stragglers, and after a five-hour delay the convoy was
reformed. It had been under way for only half an hour when
another heavy snowstorm set in, the wind increased to seventy
knots, and the sea made up accordingly. Commander Sabin reported
that on board his flagship the topside was untenable except in the
pilothouse and on the conning station, but he described the ships as
tough and sturdy, and warmly praised the spirit and resourcefulness
of their crews, who twelve months ago had been "lawyers, ac-
countants, advertising men, grocery clerks, soda jerkers and garage
mechanics. Not so now. They're sailormen. They stick to it." [43]

The battered convoy safely stood into St. George's Bay, Bermuda,

---

York 27 Jan. 1943, escorted by *Cole, Bernadou*, and *Dallas* for Gibraltar. War
Diary Cinclant, Jan.–Feb. 1943; War Diary N.O.B. Oran, 16 and 21 Feb. 1943.
  [42] "Report of Passage of LCI(L) Flot. Two" Report of C.O. to Com. AFAF,
21 Feb. 1943, Enclosure A.
  [43] Letter of Cdr. Sabin 13 Mar. 1943.

Convoy of LCI(L)s en route to Mediterranean, 1 April 1943

An LST launching an LCT from her deck

Rangers practising a landing from LCTs near Arzeu, December 1942

on 18 February. Almost all the LCIs had incurred engine trouble or acquired topside leaks, and a fortnight was spent in Bermuda reconditioning the flotilla for the remainder of the passage. Then they were formed into a new convoy, together with ten LSTs for the Royal Navy, a tanker, four destroyers and other ships. This was a bad month in the North Atlantic for submarine attacks, but on 23 March 1943 the convoy arrived safely at Gibraltar without even having had a sound contact. The six United States LSTs and half of the LCI Flotilla were routed to Arzeu; the remaining LCIs proceeded to Mostaganem where they entered on a sustained training period in conjunction with the 3rd Infantry Division United States Army.

One member of the second lot of landing craft to cross the Atlantic,[44] *LCT–33*, lost no time in distinguishing herself. On 20 April while making a routine passage from Ténès to Arzeu, she was attacked by a German JU–88, whose contempt for the little target caused its destruction. As the big bomber came in for a second run to rectify a near miss on the first, the LCT gunners found their mark and the Junker crashed in flames against a near-by mountain. The skipper, Ensign Jesse A. Anderson USNR, and his gunners received the warm congratulations of Admiral Hewitt.[45]

Admiral Conolly now had a sizable fleet of landing ships distributed among various harbors, small and large, along the Barbary Coast. Commander Sabin, in charge of Eastern Bases and Training Group, was located at Ténès. Commander J. H. Leppert took over the Western Bases and Training Group with headquarters at Beni Saf.

By 26 May when the fifth landing ship convoy [46] arrived in the

[44] Convoy UGS–6A, which sailed from Bermuda 27 Mar. 1943, included 21 LSTs with LCTs loaded on deck, 30 LCIs, and various minesweepers, patrol craft, and freighters that brought the total number to 92.

[45] Comnaveu's 10 June 1943. 105 rounds of 20-mm were fired by *LCT–33*.

[46] The others were as follows, omitting escort vessels: —

3rd Convoy: UGL–2, 37 LCI, 32 LST carrying 29 LCT, dep. Bermuda 13 Apr., arr. Gib. 30 April.

4th Convoy: UGL–3 (part of Convoy UGS–7A) 14 LST, dep. Bermuda 20 Apr., arr. Gib. 6 May.

5th Convoy: UGL–4, 19 LST carrying LCT, dep. Bermuda 9 May, arr. Gib. 24 May.

Mediterranean, practically all the large beaching vessels to be used against Sicily had been assembled. Training them for that invasion went into high gear, with practice landings both day and night in over a dozen stretches of the southwestern Mediterranean coast.

Within 48 hours after the fall of Tunis and Bizerta the first wave of landing craft had departed from Arzeu to establish advanced amphibious bases and training group under Captain R. M. Zimmerli, who had made an overland dash by truck convoy, arriving Bizerta 9 May. They found the Tunisian ports full of sunken hulks and many of their facilities destroyed, but Captain Sullivan's salvage and repair crews cleared things up with their usual energy, and as more berths became available more landing craft were staged eastward. By the end of May, Admiral Conolly had established his headquarters at Bizerta, Captain K. S. Reed remaining in charge of headquarters at Arzeu.

Although there was considerable congestion and overlap in the sharing of captured ports in Tunisia, in accordance with agreement all were operated by the Royal Navy; the British Flag Officer, Tunisia, had headquarters at Bizerta. The United States Navy, however, had the use of a small dry dock at La Goulette in Tunis Bay, and used the French submarine and seaplane base in the inner harbor of Bizerta as an advanced amphibious base.

CHAPTER XII

Pantelleria[1]

All times are Zone "Baker" or Greenwich minus
two hours (Z-2).

1. *The Anchored Carrier*

GENERAL EISENHOWER was reluctant to exploit the Tunisian victory prematurely by moving up the Sicilian D-day
from 10 July. He decided to use the time at his disposal to capture
the Italian island of Pantelleria, although his air force advisers regarded it as not worth the effort, alleging that it could easily be
neutralized by air bombing. But the General wished to deny to the
enemy the excellent radio direction stations on the island, use of
which would have prevented tactical surprise in the forthcoming
Sicilian operation; and he wanted the island as an advanced base
for Allied fighter planes. The Combined Chiefs of Staff signaled
permission on 13 May 1943 for Operation "Corkscrew," which
did indeed draw the cork from the Sicilian bottle.

Pantelleria was the ideal fixed airplane carrier. It might well have
suggested to Virgil his description of the floating Delos, which
Phoebus Apollo anchored, "gave immobility, and contempt for
winds." [2] Its 42½ square miles of rocky land lies ESE from Cape
Bon, Tunisia, not quite halfway across the Sicilian Strait. Enemy
strength on Pantelleria was correctly estimated by Intelligence to
be about 10,000 men, with 100 gun emplacements and an inde-

[1] Cincmed (Admiral Sir Andrew Cunningham RN), "The Occupation of
Pantellería and the Subsequent Capture of Lampedusa, Lampione and Linosa"
30 Nov. 1943. Eisenhower's Dispatch on Operation "Corkscrew," June 1943;
Army Air Forces Historical Studies No. 2 "Reduction of Pantellería and Adjacent Islands" (May 1947). This Chapter has been completely revised with the
kind assistance of Dr. Albert F. Simpson, Air Historian.

[2] *Aeneid* iii 77, "*immotamque coli dedit et contemnere ventos.*"

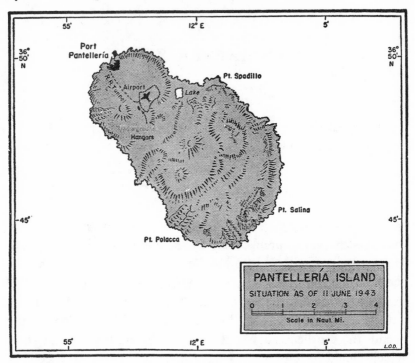

terminate number of aircraft. The Margana airport was large
enough to support a hundred fighter planes, most of which could
be accommodated in a hangar roofed with concrete and dirt covering 30 feet thick, cut into the side of a hill. Port Pantellería on
the northwest end of the island had been equipped as a seaplane
and torpedo boat base.

The southwest coast facing Tunisia was almost a sheer cliff,
ringed with coastal batteries; the only suitable landing beaches lay
inside the harbor. Occupation of the island in the face of determined defense would have been a formidable undertaking. But
Pantelleria had become more of a liability than an asset to the
enemy since his collapse in Tunisia, a change appreciated by the
unfortunate garrison left there.

General Eisenhower, wishing to conserve manpower for the
Sicilian operation, decided to try shattering the garrison's morale

by air bombing and naval bombardment, in the hope of inducing surrender before assault. But, since Italian reaction to this treatment could not certainly be predicted, the British 1st Infantry Division, Major General W. E. Clutterbuck, was prepared to make an amphibious assault if necessary. The important air phase was assigned to the Northwest African Air Force, Lieutenant General Carl Spaatz USA; the naval phase to Rear Admiral R. R. McGrigor RN. The only United States Naval forces participating were the motor torpedo boats of Squadron 15.

Beginning with heavy bombing raids on 8 May by United States B–25s and light British bombers of the Western Desert Air Force, air attacks on Pantelleria were progressively stepped up. The Royal Navy began throwing in 6-inch shells on the night of 30 May and again bombarded on 1, 5, 8 and 11 June. General Eisenhower and Admiral Cunningham watched the 8 June bombardment from H.M.S. *Aurora*, which was assisted by four other light cruisers and eight destroyers.

On the night of 5 June, units of Commander Barnes's Motor Torpedo Boat Squadron 15 were given the task of sweeping around the island, keeping a watch for Axis attempts either to reinforce or to evacuate the garrison. *PT–209, –210, –212,* and *–218,* commanded by Lieutenant E. C. Arbuckle USNR, cruised close aboard the north shore at eight knots with motors throttled down and mufflers cut in. They observed pillars of smoke and flame ascending skyward as our bombers were at work overhead.[3] During 6–9 June, Allied planes dropped an average of almost 600 tons of bombs daily on Pantelleria, and on 10 June, D-day minus 1, 1571 tons of bombs were released in one of the heaviest and most concentrated air attacks of the war up to that time. Radio Rome petulantly described it as "another example of plutocratic exhibitionism." Some 3647 sorties were flown by the Northwest African Air Forces in ten days; 5285 sorties during the entire operation; and only 14 planes were lost. In the ten days' blitz only 250 Axis aircraft were sighted, and 57 of them were shot down.

[3] Squadron 15 War Diary, Mission Report No. 4, 5 June 1943.

There were two planned interruptions to the bombing program. On 8 and 10 June Pantelleria was given a six-hour respite during which propaganda pamphlets were substituted for explosives. But as these invitations to surrender were not acted upon, the assault force — the British 1st Infantry Division — was embarked at Sousse and Sfax, and sailed in three convoys, two fast and one slow, escorted by destroyers and minesweepers of the Royal Navy, on the night of 10–11 June. These convoys comprised three transports, one "Maracaibo," numerous landing craft infantry and landing craft tanks. Rear Admiral McGrigor flew his flag in headquarters ship *Largs*.

By 0545 on D-day, 11 June, the two fast convoys and escorts, having made rendezvous, steamed to the waiting position nine miles distant from Port Pantelleria. As yet no enemy aircraft had been sighted. At 0955 the transports received the signal to lower landing craft.

In the meantime, the 15th Cruiser Squadron Royal Navy was approaching from the westward to take up positions for bombardment; and United States Motor Torpedo Boat Squadron 15 was out in force, patrolling a line between Pantelleria and Porto Empedocle, Sicily, to prevent enemy E-boats from interfering with the operation, and to halt any attempt at last-minute evacuation. Five British motor torpedo boats and motor gunboats were attached to the squadron. Few E-boats showed up, and very few Italians tried to evacuate in small boats. The PTs were heavily bombed at 2130 by Junkers 88s with the loss of one man, but Axis aircraft failed in their efforts to harass the landing operations.

Conditions on D-day were perfect for a landing. Visibility was poor and air clammy, with intermittent drizzles. Allied fighter planes drove off waves of enemy Focke-Wulf 190s and the British silenced shore batteries which opened up and revealed the fact that they were still functioning after ten days' "precision bombing." At 1032 the assault landing craft, accompanied by minesweepers, stood toward Port Pantelleria. At about 1100 some Allied aircraft spotted a white cross on the airfield through the pall of smoke and dust and wheeled for home with bomb bay doors unopened. And at 1155 H.M.S. *Laforey* signaled that she had sighted a white flag flying from the semaphore tower.[4]

At that very moment the first assault wave hit the beach, meeting small-arms fire which was quickly silenced. As soon as the commander of the landing force was able to contact the Governor of the island, Admiral Gino Pavesi, the latter offered to surrender both island and garrison, consisting of 78 Germans and 11,121 Italians.

There was only one casualty among the British assault troops, and that from the bite of a jackass.[5] His was the final resistance offered on Pantelleria.

Why did Pantelleria surrender? That question has been the subject of an acrimonious "whodunit" controversy between Army, Navy and Air Forces — the R.A.F. and A.A.F. teaming up against the Royal Navy, the United States Navy, and both Armies. If, as Admiral Pavesi told the British at the time, it had been a water shortage that compelled him to surrender, the answer would have been simple; but the British found ample water supplies on the island. Later, the Admiral admitted he had radioed Rome for permission to surrender on 10 June, the eve of assault; but he never sent a surrender signal to Malta until 1100 June 11, which was just 28 minutes after the British landing craft had commenced standing toward shore, in full view of the Italian garrison. According to General Eisenhower's chief of staff, Admiral Pavesi declared that he was unaware of the impending assault, and estimated the assembly of warships as mere indication of a more intense naval bombardment.[6] Admiral McGrigor observed, with some acerbity, that the Italian Admiral could hardly have been so unnerved by air bombing that he failed to comprehend what was meant by

---

[4] Eisenhower Dispatch, p. 11. According to a cable message Algiers HQ to War Dept., 15 June 1943, the flag had been raised at 1137.

[5] Admiralty *Naval Bulletin* No. 51, 2 July 1943.

[6] "Lessons from Operations against Pantellería," Cincmed Report on Pantellería, Enclosure 10.

landing craft full of soldiers converging on his island.[7] Unquestionably the isolated garrison had been pounded into a deplorably unheroic state of mind (according to their Duce's standards) by the prolonged air bombing; but hardly to a point where they were ready to surrender, as a facetious Air Force officer remarked, "to the Vassar College Daisy Chain coming ashore in canoes." The victors ascertained that air bombing and naval bombardment combined had destroyed only half the island's guns and that casualties were only 150 to 200 killed and a like number wounded. One ponders over what would have happened at Pantelleria if the garrison had been Japanese, or even German.

In any event, Operation "Corkscrew" provided a useful dress rehearsal for the full-scale invasions which were to follow; and the capture of it cleared the Straits for the invasion of Sicily.

2. *The Pelagies*

As soon as the surrender of Pantelleria was confirmed, the XII United States Army Air Force turned the aërial offensive against Lampedusa, a smaller Italian island eighty-five miles to the southward. Lampedusa, lying between Malta and the east coast of Tunis, is seven miles long by two miles wide and 436 feet in elevation at the highest point, the largest of the Pelagie group. Northeast of it is situated Linosa Island and, to the west, the lighthouse islet of Lampione. On the south coast of Lampedusa, near the only village, is a harbor suitable for and previously used by German and Italian E-boats in the earlier stages of the Tunisian campaign. Allied air attacks continued through 11 June, and before midnight were sup-

[7] Rear Admiral R. R. McGrigor RN remarked, "It is a matter of some interest that the island did not surrender to the Air Force when given the opportunity on D minus 3 and D minus 1 days, in spite of the heavy, accurate, systematic bombing which was increased in intensity every day and night. It was not until the garrison saw the traditional sight of the Army coming ashore in the boats of the Navy, under cover of the guns of the Fleet, that the white flags started to appear; and it was noteworthy that this was at a time when there was a complete lull in the bombing program." Rear Admiral Force "P" No. 724, 7 July 1943; Cincmed Report on Pantellería, Enclosure 1, para 18.

ported by naval gunfire from four light cruisers and six destroyers of the British force relieved from the Pantelleria operation.

Shortly after 1730 on the 12th, white flags were seen flying on Lampedusa and about 1900 a British naval officer went ashore to negotiate the surrender. One company of the Coldstream Guards occupied the island and took charge of over four thousand prisoners.

Lampedusa was barely in Allied hands before a large force of Axis aircraft retaliated. H.M.S. *Lookout* was heavily bombed by JU–88s, but no damage was done and anti-aircraft fire from the British warships soon dispelled the attack.

Early in the morning of 13 June, H.M. destroyer *Nubian* and two cruisers steamed off to Linosa Island, 28 miles to the northeastward, and took possession without firing a shot. The garrison of 240 hoisted the white flag on her approach and surrendered to two men and a boy in a whaleboat. In the meantime foul weather had set in, but on the 14th tiny Lampione Island, within sight of Lampedusa, was investigated by H.M.S. *Newfoundland* and *Troubridge* and found to be deserted. The lighthouse keeper, complete with proverbial daughter, had already departed in a small boat. Thus the last outpost of Mussolini's "Empire" on the south shore of the Mediterranean was disposed of. British tars celebrated their triumph in the barrooms of Malta, where the ribald strains of "Lampedusie Floozie" mingled with those of "Dirty Gertie from Bizerte."

The entire south Mediterranean littoral, and all the islands of the Sicilian Strait, were now in the possession of the United Nations.[8] Every objective of Operation "Torch" was secured; and the armed forces of the United States, Great Britain and France were in their last, intensive stage of preparations for the assault on Sicily that was scheduled for 10 July 1943.

[8] Tiny Gallite Island, 20 miles northwest of Cape Serrat, was taken over without opposition by U.S.S. *PT–203* on 19 May. The Axis garrison had been evacuated several days before.

APPENDIX I

Allied Ships Sunk in Operation "Torch"[1]

7–16 November 1942

TYPE	NAME	PLACE	AGENCY
		8 November	
DD	H.M.S. *Broke*	Algiers Harbor	Gunfire, sank on 10 Nov. under tow.
Cutter	H.M.S. *Hartland*	Oran Harbor	Gunfire, ships and shore batteries.
Cutter	H.M.S. *Walney*	Oran Harbor	Gunfire, ships and shore batteries.
AP-73	U.S.S. *Leedstown*	Off Algiers	Bombed and torpedoed by plane. Sank 9 Nov.
		9 November	
Corvette	H.M.S. *Gardenia*	Off Oran	Collision with H.M.S. *Fluellen*
		10 November	
Collier	S.S. *Garling*	37°00′ N, 02°00′ E	Torpedoed by U-boat.
Sloop	H.M.S. *Ibis*	10 miles N of Algiers	Torpedoed by plane.
DD	H.M.S. *Martin*	37°48′ N, 03°50′ E	Torpedoed by U-boat.
		11 November	
Transport	S.S. *Awatea* (Br.)	Off Bougie	Bombed.
Ammunition Ship	S.S. *Browning* (Br.)	35°52′ N, 08°45′ W	Torpedoed by U-boat.
Transport	S.S. *Cathay* (Br.)	Off Bougie	Bombed.
AP-50	U.S.S. *Joseph Hewes*	Off Fedhala	Torpedoed by U-boat.
Transport	S.S. *Nieuw Zeeland* (Neth.)	35°59′ N, 08°45′ W	Torpedoed by U-boat.
Transport	S.S. *Viceroy of India* (Br.)	36°26′ N, 00°24′ W	Torpedoed by U-boat.

[1] Principal sources: Cincmed's Report of Operation Torch 30 March 1943, Appendix 1, "Narrative of Events," O.N.I. *Weekly* 9 Dec. 1942 p. 20 "Report of Losses in Torch Announced by First Lord of Admiralty, A. V. Alexander." (Total loss of naval vessels only.)

TYPE	NAME	PLACE	AGENCY
		12 November	
AP–57	U.S.S. *Edw. Rut-ledge*	Off Fedhala	Torpedoed by U-boat.
Depot Ship	H.M.S. *Hecla*	35°42′ N, 09°54′ W	Torpedoed by U-boat.
AP–43	U.S.S. *Hugh L. Scott*	Off Fedhala	Torpedoed by U-boat.
LSI	H.M.S. *Karanja*	Off Bougie	Bombed.
AP–42	U.S.S. *Tasker H. Bliss*	Off Fedhala	Torpedoed by U-boat.
A.A. Cruiser	H.M.S. *Tynwald*	Off Bougie	Bombed.
		13 November	
Freighter	S.S. *Glenfinlas* (Br.)	Bougie Harbor	Bombed.
DD	H.N.M.S. *Isaac Sweers*	37°23′ N, 02°12′ E	Torpedoed by U-boat.
Freighter	S.S. *Manon* (Br.)	36°27′ N, 00°55′ W	Torpedoed in convoy by U-boat.
		14 November	
Transport	S.S. *Narkunda* (Br.)	Off Bougie	Bombed.
Transport	S.S. *Warwick Castle* (Br.)	38°44′ N, 13°00′ W	Torpedoed by U-boat in convoy MKF–1.
		15 November	
Minesweeper	H.M.S. *Algerine*	Off Bougie	Torpedoed by U-boat.
Escort Carrier	H.M.S. *Avenger*	36°15′ N, 07°45′ W	Torpedoed in convoy by U-boat.
Transport	H.M.S. *Ettrick*	36°12′ N, 08°02′ W	Torpedoed in convoy by U-boat; sank later under tow.
		16 November	
Freighter	S.S. *Clan MacTag-gart* (Br.)	36°08′ N, 07°23′ W	Torpedoed by U-boat.

Western Naval Task Force: Expenditure of Ammunition

8–11 November 1942 [1]

(Machine-gun ammunition and aircraft bombs not included)

Battleships					5″	Depth Charges
	16″	14″	5″			
Massachusetts	786	—	? [2]	Bristol [4]	450	17
New York	—	60	19	Dallas [5]	25	—
Texas	—	218	6	Doran	14	—
				Eberle	80	5
Heavy Cruisers				Edison	350	1
		8″	5″	Ericsson	724	—
Augusta		832	—	Jenkins	110	5
Tuscaloosa		1074	22	Kearny	999	—
Wichita		1263	350	Knight	70	—
				Livermore	12	15
Light Cruisers				Ludlow	1248	3
		6″	5″	Mayrant	670	1
Brooklyn		2761	326	Mervine [6]	221	—
Philadelphia		109	—	Murphy	486	—
Savannah		1196	406	Rhind	144	1
				Roe [7]	658	48
Destroyers				Rowan	79	13
		5″	Depth Charges	Swanson	797	15
				Tillman	245	12
Beatty		260	—	Wainwright [8]	710	10
Bernadou [3]		57	—	Wilkes	1087	10
Boyle		45	13	Woolsey	—	18

[1] Compiled primarily from information received from Lt. Henry G. Puppa USNR 27 Nov. 1945. Figures for aircraft carriers not available.

[2] *Massachusetts* expended 2¼ per cent of her 5-inch ammunition, number rounds unknown.

[3] 3-inch.

[4] Comdesron 13 letter to Com. AFAF 10 Dec. 1942.

[5] 3-inch.

[6] There is an unexplained discrepancy in the ammunition expenditure of Desron 15 which Lt. Puppa estimates from Capt. Hartman's Report 22 Jan. 1943 to Comamphorlant at 724 rounds of 5-inch for *Mervine*, *Knight* and *Beatty*. *Mervine's* Action Report of 15 Nov. 1942 gives herself 221 rounds, *Beatty* 260 rounds, and *Knight* 70 rounds, totalling 551.

[7] Comdesron 17, letter to Com. AFAF 1 Jan. 1943, reporting on Desron 11.

[8] Comdesron 8, letter to Com. AFAF 9 Dec. 1942.

An interesting basis of comparison is this table, furnished by the Bureau of Ordnance: —

ROUNDS OF AMMUNITION EXPENDED IN BATTLES OF SANTIAGO AND MANILA BAY, 1898 [9]

	13″	12″	8″	6″	5″	4″	6-Pdr.
SANTIAGO: —							
Indiana	13		61	33			1744
Oregon	34		123	41			1564
Texas		8		97			400
Brooklyn			100		473		1200
Iowa		31	35			251	1056
Gloucester							589
Vixen							27
Total	47	39	319	171	473	251	6580
MANILA BAY: —							
Olympia			36		281		1000
Concord				182			220
Petrel				116			
Raleigh				53	341		
Boston			48	162			220
Baltimore			73	123			547
Total			157	636	622		1987

[9] 3-pounder and 1-pounder ammunition omitted.

APPENDIX III

Western Naval Task Force: Summary of Beginning Action

8 November 1942

	Northern	Center	Southern	Covering Group
First troops landed	0515	0515	0430 [1]	——
First enemy resistance	0545	0604	0428	0651
"Batter Up!"	0615	0607	0428	0651
First Naval Gunfire	0604	0610	0428	0702
"Play Ball!"	0710	0620	0439	0704

[1] Time *Bernadou* grounded; first troops ashore a few minutes later.

Index

Names of Combat Ships in SMALL CAPITALS.
Names of Merchant Ships in *Italics*.

---

[1] *See also* names of plane types; French Air Force; Luftwaffe; Royal Air Force.